50 YEARS OF DUTY

50 YEARS OF DUTY

ONE POLICE OFFICER'S COMPELLING JOURNEY FROM STATE TROOPER TO COUNTY SHERIFF

GENE L. WRIGGELSWORTH, SHERIFF (ret.)
with SANDY WRIGGELSWORTH

Publishing support provided by
Ignite Press
55 Shaw Ave. Suite 204
Clovis, CA 93612
www.IgnitePress.us

ISBN: 979-8-9933958-0-7
ISBN: 979-8-9933958-1-4 (Hardcover)
ISBN: 979-8-9933958-2-1 (E-book)

For bulk purchases and for booking, contact:

Gene Wriggelsworth
genewrigg50@comcast.net

Library of Congress Control Number: 2025918499

Co-written by Cindy Dawn Tschosik
Photography by Mary Jo Wriggelsworth
Cover design by Olga Vynnychenko
Edited by Elizabeth Arterberry
Interior design by Jetlaunch

FIRST EDITION

I dedicate this book to all past, current, and future people who dedicate their lives to protecting and serving our brothers and sisters. Many of you share the same experiences and lessons shared in this book. Thank you, sincerely, for your service.

With tremendous sorrow and gratitude, I extend a deep thank you to each law enforcement officer who paid the ultimate price to protect and serve our neighborhoods, towns, counties, states, and country.

I salute each of you for your decision to answer the calling and to fulfill your duty of the Oath for the people of the United States of America.

Acknowledgments

Living a life with a career in law enforcement is tremendously gratifying, humbling, and rewarding. Each person involved in our country's law enforcement and military makes an oath to protect and serve, and takes it very seriously.

Each day, when we wake up, we are grateful to still be alive. Our thoughts turn immediately to our faith or higher power, our family, our duty, and our lives, because we know there is a chance we may not come home. Our careers demand that we dedicate extensive hours and sacrifice the security and safety of our lives to them, and our work takes a spiritual, psychological, emotional, and physical toll upon us.

We see tremendous events that seem miraculous, and we see the most traumatic and tragic outcomes citizens could never imagine. For some, it becomes too much, and finding relief from the pain can result in addiction, self-harm, and, unfortunately, suicide.

Collectively, we are all family; one for all, all for one. If one of us gets hurt or dies, we all hurt.

And we are not alone. We share each sacrifice and burden with those we love and care about the most: our spouses, significant others, children, parents, siblings, professional partners, colleagues, extended families, friends, and our communities. Living with and loving someone while pursuing our careers inflicts upon them the underlying worries and fears for our safety, security, and the nagging question whether we are coming home at the end of the day. Those who love us and support us suffer the most and give the most of themselves, and if we didn't receive that support, we could not honor our oath to protect and serve.

"Thank you" does not even begin to express my deepest gratitude for the love, dedication, and loyalty shown by those who brought me to this exact moment in time. You are why I am here today. You stand behind me to hold me up. You stand ahead of me to cheer me on. And you stand beside me to walk this life and career along with me, and I with you.

I humbly express my gratitude to every person who has ever entered my life and made me a son, husband, dad, grandpa, brother, nephew, cousin, neighbor, trooper, undercover officer, sheriff, mentor, community member, and volunteer. You have cared about me and for me, helped me grow, taught me important lessons, encouraged my resilience, picked me up at the low points, celebrated the high points, and believed in me. I thank you, immensely.

To my wife, Sandy Wriggelsworth, my bride, who made me a dad and stuck with me through countless stressful and exhilarating situations both in life and work. You still take my breath away.

To my sons, Mike, Scott, and Mark, you made me a dad three times over, and I am so proud of each of you for the men, husbands, and fathers you have become. Thank you for putting up with an absentee dad for many years, but never forget—I used to change your diapers. Always remember, Mom and I could never be prouder of you three boys than we are right now!

To our daughters-in-law, Kelli, Maryjo, and Kelly, thank you for being such important and endearing parts of our family, and for bringing our grandchildren into the world. We appreciate you very much!

To all our grandchildren, both your grandma and I are so proud of each of you great kids!

Andrew, Hayden, and Jacob, with his wife, Hannah.
Hannah, Jake, Hailey, Makenna, and Charlotte.
Rorie, with his wife, Kaili, and our first great-grandson, Kai; Reece, and Ryan.

To my father, Gerald (1915-1994), and mother, Ellen (1918-1988), for raising me, molding me into the person I became, teaching me to treat people kindly, and modeling how to respect *all* people.

To my grandmother, Winnie Wriggelsworth (1879-1973), for her unwavering mentorship, respect, support, and gratitude for a good life. "Gene, I lived long enough to travel with a horse and buggy and watch a man land on the moon. I've had a good life." Her husband, my grandpa Leroy Wriggelsworth (1881-1930), passed away when my dad (Gerald) was 16.

To my grandmother, Edna Sutton, and grandfather, Oro Sutton.

To the man who has been my friend since we were high school freshmen, Bill Pike, I can't imagine a life without you. We have done it all together, and I am forever grateful for your lifelong friendship.

To Captain George Craft (1926-1988), fellow Michigan State Trooper, the man who planted a little seed into my mind at 19 years old and consistently encouraged me to be a state trooper.

To the men and women I worked beside in the good times and the bad, your loyalty, passion, and commitment to protect and serve our communities inspired and motivated me to continuously reach new heights in my roles. It was an absolute honor to protect and serve with you:

Undersheriff Rick Boyd (1948–2019)
Undersheriff Matt Myers
Undersheriff Allan Spyke
Major Michael Carpenter (1944–2022)
Chief Deputy Greg Harless
Major Joel Maatman
Major Sam Davis
Chief Deputy Darwin Shaver
Lieutenant Gordon Smith, MSP
Major Richard Ghinelli (1943–2016)

To my administrative assistants over the years. Without you, the work still wouldn't be done. Thank you for being my first line of defense and offense:

Mrs. Jill Pierce
Mrs. Kathy Cole Brown
Mrs. Lori Newberg

To the people and communities I served who still continuously greet me and thank me, you are why I served. Thank you for allowing me to be a part of your lives and communities for 50 years.

To my readers, thank you for picking up this book. I hope you walk away with a new perspective and understanding of the work we do each day.

This book would never have happened without the team who diligently worked with me. Thank you to my team who generously and cheerfully supported me throughout this journey:

➢ My son, Scott, and our colleague, Traci Ruiz, for your inspiration.
➢ My daughter-in-law, Mary Jo, for sharing your talent as a photographer.
➢ My wife, Sandy, a.k.a. Precious, and my family—Mike, Kelli, Mark, and Kelly—for your reviews, input, and support.
➢ My grandkids, friends, and neighbors, for cheering me on.
➢ My co-writer, Cindy Dawn Tschosik, for your humor, compassion, vision, and talents in connecting the puzzle pieces of a 50-year law enforcement career

into this book, which will leave a legacy for my family and, hopefully, be an inspiration and educational piece for current and future law enforcement personnel and organizations.

➤ My publisher, Everett O'Keefe of Ignite Press, for bringing the entire book to the finish line. Your team is a well-oiled machine.

To our future law enforcement officers and all those who protect and serve, your role is one of the most important callings in the world. You did not make the decision to join lightly. There is a reason for you to be in this with us. Have pride when you wear your uniform, respect humanity in all people, hold true to your values, do your job to the best of your ability, always continue to learn, and always protect and serve.

With immense gratitude,
Gene

OATH OF OFFICE
MICHIGAN STATE POLICE

I do solemnly swear that I will support the Constitution of the United States and the constitution of this state, and that I will faithfully discharge the duties of an officer of the Michigan State Police and enforce the laws of this state to the best of my ability.

I will preserve, protect, and defend the public's safety as well as obey all rules, regulations, and carry out all orders lawfully given to me.

Gene L. Wrigglesworth

OATH OF OFFICE
INGHAM COUNTY SHERIFF'S OFFICE

I do solemnly swear or affirm that I will support the Constitution of the United States and the constitution of this state, and that I will faithfully discharge the Office of Ingham County Sheriff in and for the County of Ingham, State of Michigan to the best of my ability.

Gene L. Wrigglesworth

In Memoriam

My Fallen Friends

Throughout the United States, each day, law enforcement officers report for duty to protect and serve, knowing that our careers come with tremendous sacrifices. The gravest news we receive in our communities is that of losing one of our own.

According to the Officer Down Memorial Page[1], in 2024 alone, 164 people made the ultimate sacrifice, losing their lives in the line of duty. In the State of Michigan, we sadly lost five of our own in 2024. As an example, if five is an average for the state, that means that during my 50 years in law enforcement, 250 lives were tragically taken while they were performing their job to protect and serve.

In any career, losing one person is one too many. During my career in Ingham County and surrounding areas, I personally lost twelve men and women I called my friends and colleagues in uniform. Twelve too many. To lose one suddenly and tragically is the worst experience one can ever imagine. I hold each of them and their loved ones in my heart to this day.

In memoriam, I thank them and their families for their service and their sacrifice. May their souls rest peacefully, and may their families be comforted by the knowledge that our state and nation are grateful for their brave and unsparing contribution.

*****

Sergeant Paul Lawrence Cole, Ingham County Sheriff's Office

At 40 years old, Sgt. Cole died in the line of duty. He served in the Ingham County Sheriff's Office for 19 years.

As he responded to the scene of a domestic disturbance call involving a weapon, a herd of deer ran into the roadway in front of him. As he swerved to avoid the deer, his vehicle left the roadway and struck a tree.[2]

His watch to protect and serve sadly ended on Sunday, October 6, 1996. He is survived by his wife, Kathy, daughter, and two sons. Kathy worked for me as my administrative assistant in the sheriff's office for many years to support her family.

*****

TROOPER JAMES R. DELOACH, MICHIGAN STATE POLICE
TROOPER STEVEN NIEWIEK, MICHIGAN STATE POLICE

At 26 years old, Trooper DeLoach died in the line of duty. He served in the Michigan State Police for three years. I personally knew him from growing up in Holt, Michigan, and both our families were close. Responding to a call to assist a fellow trooper who was struggling with a suspect at a nearby tavern, he, along with Trooper Steven Niewiek, 24 years old, were struck by a train.[3]

Trooper DeLoach died on impact, and his watch to protect and serve tragically ended on February 1, 1992. He is survived by his wife.

Trooper Niewiek, who served in the Michigan State Police for two years, died later at the hospital during surgery. His watch to protect and serve sadly ended on Sunday, February 2, 1992.[4]

*****

POLICE OFFICER JULIE ENGELHARDT, LANSING POLICE DEPARTMENT

At 34 years old, Police Officer Engelhardt died in the line of duty. She served in the Lansing Police Department for 14 years and previously served the Ingham County Sheriff's Office. Two boys reported a man had taken their sled away, and as she responded to that call, the man shot her as she approached. Officer Engelhardt returned fire, critically wounding the suspect.[5]

Officer Engelhardt's watch to protect and serve tragically ended on Friday, February 12, 1988. She is survived by her two sisters.

*****

TROOPER LARRY LEE FORREIDER, MICHIGAN STATE POLICE

At 33 years old, Trooper Forreider died in the line of duty. He served in the Michigan State Police for seven years and was a United States Air Force Veteran. He was my partner at the Flat Rock State Police Post prior to his transfer to Alpena, where he pulled a car over for a defective taillight at 2:30 a.m. He was shot and struck twice by the driver, who had three passengers in the car. He bravely returned fire as the subjects were fleeing and struck one of the subjects, who was apprehended at the scene.[6]

For any person in law enforcement, losing one of our own is more than difficult. Losing a partner or former partner is even harder. We work so closely with any partner that a special bond develops because we must work together in synchrony on every call.

What makes this even sadder is that Trooper Forreider was killed before body armor was issued for protection. His wife had already purchased a vest for him, wrapped it, and put it under the Christmas tree.

On Thursday, December 5, 1974, Trooper Forreider's watch to protect and serve tragically ended. He is survived by his wife, two children, parents, two brothers, and three sisters.

*****

POLICE OFFICER JAMES SPENCER JOHNSON, EAST LANSING POLICE DEPARTMENT

At 44 years old, Officer Johnson died in the line of duty. He served in the East Lansing Police Department for 11 years and was a United States Army Veteran. Jim worked for me in the Tri-County Metro Narcotic Squad. Attempting to arrest a resistant woman for auto theft, he was shot by her male companion who emerged from the bathroom.[7]

Officer Johnson's watch to protect and serve ended on Thursday, October 25, 1984. He is survived by his wife and six children. As a result of his death, The 100 Club of Greater Lansing was formed to support families during their time of crisis.

*****

SERGEANT TODD LAWRENCE LEVEILLE, MICHIGAN STATE POLICE

Sergeant Todd Leveille died at 53 years old as a result of contracting COVID-19 while serving at the Lapeer Post. Todd worked for me from February 1993 until January 1995, after which he moved to join the Michigan State Police, where he served for 27 years.[8]

Beginning in early 2020, thousands of law enforcement officers, other first responders, and corrections agency personnel suffered tremendous illness and death due to COVID-related illnesses and other complications. Since March 2020, ODMP verified that over nine hundred law enforcement officers experienced a COVID-related death.[9]

Sergeant Leveille's watch to protect and serve sadly ended on Thursday, December 9, 2021. He is survived by his daughter.

*****

POLICE OFFICER MAC J. DONNELLY, JR., LANSING POLICE DEPARTMENT

At 35 years old, Officer Donnelly served in the Lansing Police Department for nine years and was a United States Coast Guard Veteran. During a bank robbery, Officer Donnelly attempted to rescue four hostages and was shot and killed by the bank robbery suspect. He was able to return fire and wounded the suspect. All the hostages were freed.[10]

Officer Donnelly's watch to protect and serve sadly ended on Thursday, June 16, 1977. He is survived by his five children.

*****

TROOPER GARY T. RAMPY, MICHIGAN STATE POLICE
TROOPER CHARLES B. STARK, MICHIGAN STATE POLICE

Trooper Rampy, age 27, died in the line of duty, having served the Michigan State Police for five years and seven months.[11]

Trooper Stark, age 32, died in the line of duty, having served the Michigan State Police for seven years and six months.[12]

Trooper Rampy and Trooper Stark pulled a drunk driver over at approximately 2:50 a.m. When the driver was unable to produce a license, Trooper Rampy walked him back to the patrol car, and the suspect ordered him to call Trooper Stark back to the cruiser. Brandishing a weapon he concealed in his pants prior to being pulled over, the suspect shot and killed both officers. The suspect attempted to flee but crashed the vehicle and was shot and killed by the officers when he opened fire on them.

Trooper Rampy's watch to protect and serve tragically ended on December 31, 1971. He is survived by his wife and son.

Trooper Stark's watch to protect and serve also tragically ended on December 31, 1971. He is survived by his wife, two children, parents, three brothers, and five sisters.

*****

POLICE OFFICER DEAN A. WHITEHEAD, LANSING POLICE DEPARTMENT

At 30 years old, Officer Whitehead died in the line of duty. He served in the Lansing Police Department for nine years. He was on air patrol with his partner when they spotted a burning motor home. They began to ascend after fire units arrived on the scene, but the helicopter struck electrical lines, then descended rapidly and struck the ground. Both officers fled the aircraft, and Officer Whitehead was killed instantly when struck by the rotor blades.[13]

Officer Whitehead's watch to protect and serve tragically ended on May 9, 1985. He is survived by his wife, parents, and three brothers.

*****

DEPUTY SHERIFF GRANT WILLIAM WHITAKER, INGHAM COUNTY SHERIFF'S OFFICE

Deputy Sheriff Whitaker, age 25, served in the Ingham County Sheriff's Office for one year and six months. Previously, he served in the Stockbridge Police Department and Waterloo Township Police Department. During a high-speed police chase, Deputy Whitaker's patrol car left the roadway and struck a tree, causing him to suffer fatal injuries.[14]

Deputy Sheriff Whitaker's watch to protect and serve tragically ended on Sunday, December 7, 2014. He is survived by his parents, Mary and Clyde, and two brothers.

*****

A Humble Dedication and a Lifetime of Enormous Gratitude

Sandy Lea Wriggelsworth, a.k.a. "Precious," has been my bride and the love of my life for more than 60 years. She stood by me during the good, bad, ugly, and extraordinary moments in my personal and professional life.

Sandy made countless sacrifices so I could pursue my career in law enforcement: moving away from all she knew to Flat Rock, Michigan, where I was assigned my first post as a state trooper; fretting over my safety during the civil riots in Detroit; forgoing her teaching career to raise our family; being the primary caregiver for our children while I worked long hours; maneuvering through hardships with media, political happenings, and countless other events. 60 years later, here we are, both retired, spending the most time together we have ever had, enjoying our volunteer work, and treasuring our three sons, their spouses, our grandchildren, and our lifelong and new friends.

In law enforcement, a 50-year career doesn't happen often. A 60-year marriage is also rare because of the inherent demands of the profession, such as working long hours, stress, various cases that are or are becoming dangerous, health risks, and incessant worry about a spouse's safety and their absence.

We often heard compliments that my Sandy was the "perfect partner" for a politician. Her smile, laugh, kindness, genuine care, endless community involvement, and support for Ingham County are the crux of what it means to build a village and a community, to stand for what is right for the people, and to make the county, town, state, country, and world a better place.

Sandy is the sole reason I was able to fully engage and serve in my various roles, continuously grow, improve, and be promoted. Together, we built a strong foundation for our family, and fortunately, it has stood the test of time. We are blessed.

There are not enough words in the world to express my wonder, my gratitude, and my love for you, Sandy. You continue to stand by my side without wavering through the good, bad, ugly, and extraordinary, in sickness and in health, and for richer or for poorer over all these years. You are more incredible than any wife I could ever have imagined.

It is because of you, my dear Sandy, that I am the man I am today, that I held a successful 50-year career, and that we are surrounded by a beautiful family of four generations and a bountiful group of wonderful friends. Your desire to join me to make the world a better place is why Ingham County has grown, evolved, and served our community members.

My love for you grows every day, and my gratitude is infinite.

I am humbled to be your husband. I am humbled to have such a beautiful family. I am humbled to have served for 50 years in law enforcement, and so many years in nonprofit organizations and volunteer roles. I am a better man because of you.

I am humbled to dedicate the success of my 50-year career to you, Sandy Lea Wriggelsworth, my precious bride.

With love and gratitude,

Gene

Gene

TABLE OF CONTENTS

Part 4: 28 Years as the Sheriff of Ingham County, Michigan: 1988–2016

Part 5: 50 Years of Legacy, Learning, Lessons, and Leadership, 1966–2016

FOREWORD

When Gene told me he was going to author a book about his police career as a Michigan State Trooper and the Ingham County Sheriff, I was elated to hear he would tell his story through such an impressive endeavor. This book is not a "shoot 'em up" or "get the bad guy" story, but rather a unique and relatable collection of human-interest stories from a man who always treats every human being with respect and dignity as a family man and man of the law.

Gene Wriggelsworth has been a treasured friend of mine for more than 65 years. My greatest memories with him include growing up together on the farm, playing football in high school, hearing his stories, raising our families together, and witnessing the journey of his notable 50-year career. We shared an unforgettable lifetime together, whether it was baling hay for his dad before football practice or swinging on ropes to jump into the pond for a swim. In our adult lives, we married, had children, and embarked upon different career paths, and now, we enjoy each other in retirement. I am confident, as you read this wonderful book, that you will find it intriguing, fun, enlightening, and inspiring.

In my more than eighty years of life, I have not met a more admirable man than Gene Wriggelsworth. His dedication to his faith, family, health, career, and community is unwavering. In all areas of his life, he earned a prestigious reputation built upon highly regarded credibility and esteemed integrity, inclusive of honesty, trustworthiness, reliability, strong work ethic, objectivity, transparency, and incorruptibility. Gene is a very serious man, and in his line of work, he must be. However, he has a very good sense of humor and laughs a lot, which is good, because it helps balance the doom and gloom.

I know for a fact that Gene's parents instilled these traits in him at an early age. I learned a few life lessons myself from Gene's dad on the farm during the hay baling season, and I also remember having the honor of experiencing his mom's delicious cooking.

Gene's storied life is not one everyone can say they have shared, but many can relate to or do share some of his experiences. Not everyone grows up on a farm, or serves an astounding 50 years in law enforcement. However, we all grow up somewhere, and millions of people are in law enforcement. Everyone's lives and stories are different, and at the same time, similar.

When you finish reading this book, I think you'll feel as if you really know Gene, his family, and his life's accomplishments made while serving the communities and people he swore the oath to protect and serve. When it comes to family, Gene and Sandy's marriage is one of faith, strength, and loyalty. They are genuinely good people. Of all the people you'll ever meet, you won't find three good boys like the three Wriggelsworth boys. Even now, after we both retired, I'm continually impressed by Gene's dedication to serving his communities with his wife, Sandy, in all their volunteer roles.

Whether you know Gene Wriggelsworth personally or are reading about him for the first time in this book, I know you will come to admire him, and learn and take away at least one thing that will help you better yourself.

Frank William "Bill" Pike,
Lifelong friend & retired Consumers Energy Co., West Metro Area Manager

"Joy is the simplest form of gratitude.
Gratitude unlocks the fullness of life.
It turns what we have into enough and more."
– Melody Beattie

PART 1

THE BEGINNING

CHAPTER 1

I DIDN'T KNOW
WHAT I DIDN'T KNOW

"YOU'RE GOING TO be a state trooper."

With a puzzled look on my face, I replied, "What the hell's a state trooper?"

"You're going to be a state trooper."

I didn't aspire to be a state trooper, and the notion I would become a sheriff 25 years later wasn't even on my radar. It was my senior year of high school. Sandy, who would become my wife, and I were dating. Her family had moved to Lansing and lived next door to state trooper Sergeant George Craft. At 6'1" and 220 pounds, he was a man both friendly and foreboding. As the first state police trooper I ever met, he was a bit intimidating, but I was more in awe of him than anything.

I didn't have any training or education in law enforcement. Was I fit enough? I was tougher than nails, so that wasn't an issue. Could I do it? I had no idea if I had what it took, or how or if this was going to happen. I started examining my past to see if I had relevant skills. As I had worked four years at manufacturing jobs, I supposed those skills enhanced my hand-eye coordination; that would be good when driving at fast paces and aiming a gun. Back in 1963, I was a state champion wrestler for Owosso High School. That was nice, a little helpful, but frankly, during 50 years in the force, I never wrestled anyone. Fortunately.

Henderson, Michigan was my childhood home, and for three years after high school, I worked construction, manufacturing, and warehousing jobs. My first job was working as a mason tender for a construction company which was idle during the winter. So, I stayed in Owosso, close to home, and found a job with manufacturer Midland Ross, a maker of semitruck brakes for Ford. All new hires had a 90-day probationary period, and they laid me off after 89 days. That didn't deter me from applying to Toledo Commutator down the street, where they made electric motor rotors to generate electrical power for products of all sizes, ranging from electric toothbrushes to diesel locomotives.

I enjoyed working at Toledo Commutator; they often called me to come in for the Sunday night shift, around 11:00 p.m., to make a bunch of commutators. I operated a high-pressure heated mold that compressed a tiny piece of plastic that held the little copper pieces together. At 18 or 19 years old, I worked in the factory on this big press machine all by myself at night. If my hand were to get caught in the press, I would bleed out and die, because temperatures reached eight hundred degrees or more. There was no one else in the plant. I was solo; caution, precision, and excellent eye-hand coordination were key. It took both hands and eyes to operate. At the same time, with each hand, I pressed the two buttons to close the heavy press machine. Once closed, it pressed the molding material on the commutators.

After there was a strike and Toledo Commutator closed for a long time, I found that the General Motors Warehouse in Swartz Creek, Michigan was hiring. On hiring day, I walked with my application in hand to the end of the line. It was so long that I walked a couple blocks down the street, near the local tavern. That gave me time to check out my fellow competitors. Most were in disheveled clothing and in tennis shoes that were untied, and they had unkempt hair. I was glad to be dressed up in a suit. Nervous and shaking, I finally reached the window, handed my completed application to the guy, and waited. He looked at me, looked down at the paperwork, he looked at me again, looked down again, and wrote in big letters, "Clean cut, clean, and eager." He called me the next day and I started work. The pay was double, and I loved working at that place. My boss, Pete Harrington, was a great guy. I will never forget him.

The huge storage warehouse was big enough that trains drove into the building to unload rail cars filled with car parts. I was a grunt, or what they called a "stock picker." They gave me a list of parts to collect, box, and ship to GM dealers all over the world. It was a peaceful environment compared to previous loud manufacturing warehouses. The only noises I heard were made by other workers and the occasional truck lift from time to time. The quiet was nice, and those 14 months were a valuable experience.

When Sergeant Craft planted the seed in my mind to be a state trooper, I wasn't sure what my future held other than building the famous American Dream: hopefully marry my then-girlfriend, Sandy, have kids, get a house with a white picket fence and a dog. At 20 years old, law enforcement was never on my radar. I didn't know much about the state police, but he kept mentioning it and encouraging me. The right time came along when I started thinking, *You know, I don't like this factory thing.* Doing the same thing every day was boring, but I was making a lot of money.

To be a state trooper, the application process was interesting. The minimum age was 21, and I was 20. The civil service test required a grade of 70% or higher. The first time, I didn't meet the 70%, but I didn't fail. I called the Civil Service Department and asked, "So, what? Am I done?"

He assured me I could retake it in 30 days. With confidence, I replied, "I'll be back."

The next time through, I received the study guide, studied more, and attended a prep session. The test was just a bunch of silly questions. For example, one of the questions I'll never forget is, "What's the difference between flammable and inflammable?" That's a question for a state police trooper? That's not something you learn in high school. It was those types of things that, if you didn't have any reference for it before, why would you know it now? Right?

All the studying made a substantial difference—I passed! But there was still more to go before acceptance to recruit school. I recalled talking with my parents about leaving GM. Dad was a farmer; it was all he knew, and he never stepped out of that comfort zone. He replied with angst, "What if you don't make it?"

I would like to think he was simply afraid I wouldn't have an excellent job like the one I had at GM if I didn't become an officer. His response fueled my determination to make it through recruit school, and I knew at that moment that I would never quit no matter what was asked of me. They would need to carry me out of school in a casket before I quit.

Next was the oral board meeting with four uniformed state police: one lieutenant, one sergeant, and two state troopers. Four decorated men versus me was very intimidating. The questions were designed to evaluate how I would handle certain situations, and some were impossible for me to answer without any experience. For instance:

"You stop a car for speeding.

"The driver says, 'I wasn't speeding.'

"Your reply is, 'In my opinion, you were speeding because I was following you at a higher speed.'

"The driver insists again they were not speeding. What do you do?"

I knew I didn't have the information to answer correctly, so I said, "Respectfully, I've never been a police officer in my life. I assume once accepted for the position, you will give me some training."

Apparently, they liked all my answers, including this one, because a week later, a letter in the mail read, "Congratulations, you've been accepted into recruit school!"

September 19, 1966 was my first day of recruit school, and I was one of the youngest recruits in my class. About half had law enforcement experience, and the other half had no experience, like me. Recruit school was an intense 12 weeks of boot camp and study. 110 guys were jammed into a gym at the old police headquarters, slept in double-stacked twin bunks, and shared three showers and three toilets. It was a trying experience with many men in too small of a space. It wasn't surprising some got sick, which tested the availability of toilets, and some left in the middle of the night. Boot camp was a never-ending endurance test of physical, emotional, intellectual, and mental stability. Each day, we performed calisthenics and ran; there was a lot of running. The PT (physical training) instructors harassed us and called us names while teaching us to march in cadence and stand at attention. Classroom work was led by lots of different instructors who were all integral in our education, even the one named "Sandman" who put us to sleep.

Graduation was a momentous event! That day, we sat and waited for our assignment as a new trooper to be called. Eventually, the speaker announced, "Gene Wriggelsworth, Flat Rock, Michigan."

I wondered, *Where the hell is Flat Rock?* It happened to be thirty miles south of Detroit: two hours from my home in Henderson, two hours from Sandy's home in Lansing, and two hours from everything and everyone we knew. Remember, it was the 1960s; staying in touch with family was expensive, and two-hour-long road trips were not easy. Cars were slow, they spread exhaust fumes everywhere, and fuel prices were high. Unlike the unlimited talking and texting today, each call that reached beyond a certain number of miles was a long-distance phone call, with fees charged by the minute. It was expensive! No, we didn't have text or social media back then, nor the internet! How did we survive?

As a new adult in the world, I didn't know what I didn't know. I did know that the life of a trooper would not be easy; in fact, for any law enforcement employee, it is not easy. The first two years in Flat Rock were tough. Even tougher was when I was transferred in my second year to East Lansing. Sandy stayed in Flat Rock with Baby Mike until I could find us a place to live. We were ninety minutes away from each other for about three months; talk about hell, guilt, sweat, and tears. An official state trooper post wasn't yet constructed in East Lansing, so the state rented an old schoolhouse that was going to be torn down. It was freaking miserable, with an entire open floor plan, the beds and bathrooms in plain sight. People were coming and going all the time for day shifts and night shifts. There was no privacy, and it was impossible to find quiet and sleep. I was relieved when the three months ended.

However, time brings progress. Progress is good. Today, recruits live in brand new academy housing with nice rooms and accommodations. They sleep in double beds, no bunks, and there are more than three bathrooms. We have cars that must pass emissions tests for pollution control, paved roads, higher speed limits, interstates, highways, tollways, unlimited phone minutes, social media, and the internet. The year after my graduation, the first Black men joined recruit school, and three years later, the first females joined. Today, females and males have separate housing, as they should. And my wife and I have lived together ever since that dreadful third year. We raised our three sons, who are now grown and raising their own families while flourishing in their own careers.

Yes, progress is good. From growing up on a farm and working in construction, manufacturing, and warehousing to listening to words from a good man, I took a step forward into the unknown, which provided me with gifts beyond the American Dream of a strong marriage, a good family, and a nice home, even without pets and the picket fence. I hope my family and the people I served for over 50 years will agree with me that my roles in our community have made a difference in our towns, Ingham County, Michigan, and the USA. I can't imagine a better life.

CHAPTER 1 LESSONS

1. **Open Yourself to Possibilities.** Oftentimes, other people see more in us than we do. Listen carefully and be open to the seeds they plant in your brain and heart.

2. **Never Stop Learning.** Study, pay attention, and don't take education for granted, especially exams. Those "silly questions" on the entrance exam were critical to my work through all 50 years, and even apply today. And yes, I learned the importance of the difference between "inflammable" and "flammable."

CHAPTER 2

FAMILY IS EVERYTHING

I CERTAINLY HOLD my family dear to me. My wife, Sandy, is the best wife for a husband in law enforcement. Today, after 60 years of marriage, she continues to be the glue that holds our family together. If I didn't have Sandy, I wouldn't have achieved a 50-year career in law enforcement, and I wouldn't have had three great sons, who have given us three wonderful daughters-in-law, eleven grandchildren, and one great-grandchild. . . so far. We would not have celebrated my 80th birthday, Sandy's 80th birthday, and our 60th wedding anniversary. When we married, we decided that I would work and Sandy would be a stay-at-home mom.

Anyone in law enforcement will tell you that the job is hard on relationships, whether it's dating, partnership, or marriage. Divorce is prevalent throughout all areas, and I do think my career was hard on her. The sheriff's job alone had its downsides, with being in the newspapers and on TV so often. Some of the news was not accurate, so she became a champion at navigating both accurate and inaccurate reporting.

> **Scott**
>
> "I tell everybody that Mom was the perfect politician's wife," explained Scott, the Wriggelsworth's middle son and the current Ingham County Sheriff. "She is incredibly gregarious. You find a person who does not like my mom and I'll call you a liar, because I don't think there is one out there."

My wife and sons have been incredibly supportive of me in my career, even as hard as it was on them. With all my shift work as a state trooper, an undercover officer, and a sheriff, Sandy and I did the best we could to raise our sons and model the importance of family and serving others. I describe Sandy as one of the most supportive wives around. She certainly could have complained about my shift work and job demands, but she never did.

At home, Sandy took on both a father's and mother's role in raising our boys. I tried to be involved as much as I could, even though most days of the year, I was only able to peek in on the boys when they were sleeping. To check in, I called her from the pay phone, since we didn't have cell phones back then, and she'd say, "Well, I have a school meeting today; I have to do this; or I have to do that."

When I was able to attend parent-teacher conferences, teachers called her by her first name. When I walked in, I'm sure they wondered, *Who the hell is this guy? Oh, these boys* do *have a father.*

Of course, I'm not there to help, and anyone in a job like mine feels bad about not being there. I'd come home from work at four in the morning, and I missed the kids. I missed going to meet the teachers and see them play sports. Before I went to bed, I went to their rooms and saw them sleeping there. I covered them up and tucked them in a little bit because I felt bad for my absence.

Mike

"Growing up was pretty normal, other than when Dad started working with the Tri-County Metro Narcotic Squad," shared Mike, the oldest son, who is now a senior sales representative selling mobile communications products for a channel partner of Motorola. "Undercover required more of his time, and sometimes he would be gone for days. But despite Dad being busy, he always had time for his kids. He was the dad that would teach or coach baseball or softball. He was a good role model and good father. He still is."

Sandy was a tough woman, always willing to take up the slack and do what she had to do to make the family work. She never let the grass grow under her feet from the minute Mike, our oldest, was born, and she was always on the move with the boys from when they were newborns until adulthood. Her mothering was a strong part of what made our boys who they are today, because they are strong family people, too.

Scott

"I admire my parents for their tag team approach to everything they needed to do," shared Scott. "They complemented each other very well then, and they continue to do so to this day."

When the boys were in school, Sandy made our house a home and cared for our boys in all the ways I admired, from teaching them how to do chores and homework to having time to play.

Mark

"We lived in a really nice place to grow up," reminisced Mark, the youngest son, who has retired after 25 years of serving as a captain at Eaton County Sheriff's Office and as the Chief of Police in Mason. Mark now works as a family division officer of the Ingham County Circuit Court. "We lived on a dead-end street near a park, and it was fun. I was an outdoorsy kid, and to live by a sledding hill, a pond, and a park was cool. We had a lot of friends, and we walked to school with them. I have lots of fond memories and lifelong friends I still talk with today."

Sandy dove into various community activities, always taking time to make our home, town, county, and state better. Additionally, Sandy's unwavering support for our family, my career roles, and her genuine care for the people in our community filled both of our lives with more blessings than we ever thought possible.

GROWING UP

Gene Wrigglesworth, four years old, in Henderson, Michigan. Circa 1948.

Careers, marriages, and parenting are parts of our lives where both good and bad things happen. No one said life was meant to be easy, so we all have our challenges in between the good times. I was born in Owosso, Michigan on November 7, 1944, which was an election day and FDR's (former President Franklin Delano Roosevelt) fourth election. My mother always said, "I can remember what I was doing that day." She wasn't voting. Some people say that I was imprinted that day to serve my state and country, especially since FDR died the following April.

Wriggelsworth Farm in Henderson, Michigan. Circa 1960.

Gene's parents, Gerald and Ellen. Circa 1980.

Gene's grandmother, Winnie Wriggelsworth, age 92. Circa 1970s.

When I was about four years old, my parents bought a farm near Henderson, Michigan. My parents and my grandparents represented the model for family closeness, hard work, honesty, and commitment. My dad was a farmer, and for the better part of her life, my mom worked in a factory, manufacturing little rotors for electric motors. She worked nights quite often, and I never held it against her, because it was what she had to do to help take care of our family of six. My siblings and I attended school in a one-room schoolhouse. It was great because, by the time you reached fifth grade, you had already heard the classes five times!

Gene's photo from the one-room schoolhouse he attended with his siblings.

Gene, 8th grade graduation picture from Washington School in Owosso, Michigan.

Gene, freshman year of high school.

Gene dons his Owosso High School letter sweater. Fits like a glove. 2025.

After my paternal grandfather had a stroke and passed away, my grandmother moved in with us. She helped with the cooking, sewing, and whatever needed to be done. When I moved out at 21, Grandma continued to live there for several more years. My sister, Fay, was two years older than me. My sister, Lois, was three years younger than me and later worked for me in the sheriff's office as a corrections officer, and my brother, Wayne, is eight years younger than I am. Unfortunately, both sisters have already passed away.

Gene Wriggelsworth and his three siblings.
From left to right: Fay, Lois, Gene, and Wayne. Circa 1957.

The Ora Sutton Family
Circa 1951
back row
Lester Sutton, Marion Sutton, Marion Sutton Clyde Sutton

seated row
Wilber Huff, OJean Sutton Huff, Edna Sutton, Ora Sutton, Ellen Sutton Wriggelsworth, Lois Wriggelsworth, Gerald Wriggelsworth

seated on ground
Bill Sutton, Fay Wriggelsworth, Beverly Sutton, David Sutton, Gene Wriggelsworth, Lester Sutton Jr., Ron Huff,
Sandy Huff, Nancy Sutton

The Sutton family photo (Gene's maternal family side)
Gene, six years old, sitting third from right in the second row from the ground with Gene's Mom,
Ellen Sutton, sitting directly above Gene. Circa 1950.

When it came to leadership and work ethic, I would suggest that my dad instilled such values in me. He was very demanding. If we were going to bale hay on Tuesday, we baled hay on Tuesday, and it didn't matter whether we had football practice. The farmwork still needed to be done, and on those days, we had to finish whatever was needed before we left for practice.

We had a lot of fun, too. I remember playing on the hay mound with the neighbor boys, taking the rope to jump in the water of our gravel pit, and swimming from one side of the sandbar to the other. We wouldn't let our kids do that today, but it was fun. At about 14, I was old enough to drive a tractor. It seemed like a rite of passage of sorts because then, I worked the fields. I was good enough at baling hay, which is a laborious job, but I was strong.

With that type of upbringing, I demanded it from my kids, too. For better or worse. I believe growing up in a rural environment requires a lot of attention to detail, which was part of what made me the way I am. I don't like unfinished products or projects. If things get started, I expect them to be done in a timely manner. My people at the sheriff's office figured me out quickly. I had to chuckle at Captain Rick Miller. Great guy. I had some issues one day and told him what I wanted. He passed it off to a lieutenant while he said, "And just so you know, the old man wants this done. I would suggest you get it done. Hurry."

When he mentioned it to me, I replied, "Why is that?"

"Because I figured you out, sir. You tell me you want something, you want it done? I will get it done."

So, I guess my dad's way works.

My mom was a loving person. She was the dearest person you would ever want to meet. She doted on us kids, and she worked full time herself. She lost her thumb while on a stamping press. As she pushed the stuff through, it punched three holes right through her thumb. That had to hurt.

At the time, we had 4-H ball games and other activities. Because of her night shift, she needed to sleep during those hours. With four kids in so many activities, as kids, we just expected our parents to be there and drive us around whenever we needed. When I look back on it as an adult, I appreciate how she was a strong woman and always incredibly supportive of us. We lived seven miles from town. When I was in the eighth grade, they had dances at the YMCA. After dinner, Mother would drive me to the Y and wait for a couple of hours to bring me home. She was mother, father, everything, all rolled together.

My dad was frugal and beyond cheap. It was likely a behavior instilled by the wars, and from when he was sixteen, as he became the head of the household when his dad died. After he married my mom, he saved all their money for years. If something needed to be fixed in the barn or for the dairy processing, he fixed it, but the house, by his priorities, could fall apart.

I can understand, because when we were first married, Sandy and I saved and avoided borrowing money. We ate a lot of noodles. Always, though, as a kid, and with my kids, too, it was most important that we had food on the table, clothes on our backs, and remained in good health. Everything else was a bonus.

My mother considered central heat a necessity. While we were grateful for the warmth from the wood-burning stove for years, she told my father that if they were going to have another child, she did not want another baby to live without warmth throughout the whole house. She was already pregnant when she declared that, and the next thing we knew, the whole house was warm. Once they had a taste of a more comfortable home, she convinced Dad to redo the kitchen with new cupboards. Over time, he became a little more comfortable spending his hard-earned wages.

Then, more comfort came when they struck gravel on our farm while digging a ditch for the drain tile. Gravel was a hot commodity then, as the state was buying it to build I-75 through Flint, Michigan. Life was a little less strenuous, but both my parents and grandmother continued to work hard. For respite, my Uncle Weston, my dad's brother, took my grandmother once a week on Saturdays to his sister's house.

Grandma was a great lady: tough as nails, which seems to be a theme with the women in my life. One day, she and my dad were harvesting crops. While Dad had to tend to another issue, he said, "If the water pump belt comes off, do not put it back on."

Well, it fell off, Dad was not around, and as the motor ran, she tried to put it back on. Her arm twisted at the elbow, and it was gone. He was not too happy, but she didn't let losing an arm slow her down. She darned her socks and anything else needing stitching, and she became a second mother to us. Sadly, at 94 years young, she fell off my aunt's steps and broke her hip. It did her in, and I visited her in the hospital.

"Grandma, how are you doing?" I greeted her.

She was lucid though confused, and replied, "Gene, I lived through riding in a horse and buggy and saw a man land on the moon. I have had a good life."

The next day, unfortunately, she passed away. She must have been in excruciating pain. Behind her, she left quite a legacy.

I think with the combination of my loving mother, my demanding dad, and my unstoppable grandmother, you get Gene. For better or for worse.

FROM PROM TO GRADUATION, TO A WEDDING, AND OUR FIRST SON

Gene and Sandy. Senior prom at Owosso High School. 1963.

Gene and Sandy's high school graduation from Owosso High School. Owosso, MI. 1963.

On our wall, I have a picture of Sandy and myself from my graduation. We attended the same school, and I did not even know her until my junior year. My good friend,

Brad, and I played football together, and he was dating a good friend of hers. She found out Brad and I were friends, and asked, "Do you know Brad? Let's double date with him."

She wanted to spy on Brad to see if he was serious with his girlfriend. But the tables turned.

Sandy

"I did use Gene to spy on Brad," Sandy chuckled. "I'm very matter-of-fact about that. But there was something about Gene I liked, and one of the things was his work ethic. I also liked that he had a big family since I was an only child. 60 years later, we have three kids, a bunch of grandkids, and one great-grandchild. Sorry, Brad."

"After high school, a woman's choices were to go to college or get married, or both. Then, you had your family, and that was just how life was. In the 1960s, the only options for women were to become secretaries, nurses, or schoolteachers. That's what we did."

"During college, I lived in a dorm with other girls and had that whole experience. Gene and I dated throughout those years, and I spent time on the farm to see his family. Going to his grandma's house on Sundays was a big deal. I witnessed how hard it was to work on a farm, and I realized his family never left the farm for trips. I asked Gene if farming was something he wanted to get into, and thankfully, he said 'no,' because I knew I couldn't live the secluded life of a farmer's wife."

In July 1965, at 21 years old, I married my bride, Sandy. It was a big wedding at a local Episcopal cathedral. The reception was in the Jack Tar Hotel Ballroom. My mother-in-law planned it, and the venue was across from Michigan's Capitol Building. The room known today as the current governor's office is where I danced with my new bride and where I told her she was going to be my wife forever.

Gene and Sandy Wriggelsworth's wedding. This photo was taken in the
Jack Tar Ballroom, which is now Michigan's Governor's Office. 1965.

It was a busy first year of marriage. I worked for the General Motors Warehouse, shipping parts all over the country, and Sandy was still in school, getting her education to become a schoolteacher. A year later, in 1966, she became pregnant with our first son, Mike. It was a momentous occasion for both of us!

Sandy

"I was supposed to be a student teacher at MSU, but they wouldn't let me since I was pregnant. Shocked, I asked, 'Are you kidding? You don't think that by the age of 17 or 18 people know how this happens?' The administration explained they didn't want my students to see that I was pregnant. So, I finished my few classes, put my student teaching on hold, and prepared for the birth of our first child."

Then, I received my acceptance letter for recruit school! We lived in University Village, right behind the police barracks, which meant that even though I was living in the barracks for school, Sandy wasn't far from me.

Sandy

"It was funny because we lived right behind where Gene trained for recruit school. If I wanted to get up at 5:30 a.m., which I rarely did, I could see him running."

Our family was growing. Four years later, Scott was born in 1970, and Mark was born in 1975. Our family was complete and our whole lives were ahead of us. Neither one of us alone, nor just us working together, could have managed it by ourselves. For it takes a village, and we were blessed to be surrounded and supported by incredible people in all the counties we traversed who shared in our life.

CHAPTER 2 LESSONS

1. **Family Is Everything.** Stress, lack of sleep, and night shifts are just three factors that contribute to the disruption of families. The key to avoiding or reducing stress is to spend as much free time as you can with each other to balance the bad and the good.

2. **Be Flexible in Your Journey.** Life is not always linear for a lot of us.

3. **Identify Your Individual and Family Values.** Hold strong to them, for they are your foundation for how to live, learn, and grow as one and together. Here are the ones we covered in this chapter:

Sandy

- Communication
- Church/Faith

Gene

- Work Ethic
- Honesty
- Faith

Mike

- Work/Life Balance
- Unconditional Support
- Encouragement

Scott

- Collaboration
- Integrity
- Respect/Dignity

Mark

- Strong Marriage and Family
- Work Hard
- Arrive Early

CHAPTER 3

LIFE IS NOT LINEAR

AT 18 YEARS old, it's not easy to know what you want to be when you grow up. After high school, each of us is fortunate to choose whether we live our lives working a job we need or like, we go to college, or we join the trades, the military, or law enforcement. Some may choose to get married, find a partner, and raise a family. And still, some may choose not to work, or don't need to work. I'm sure there are other options, but these are the ones I think of.

The greatest lesson I've learned in my life from working with the people I know is that "life is not linear." There is no cookie-cutter roadmap, blueprint, or textbook on how to live your life, plan every step of your vocation, live with a partner, and raise your children. Life has a funny way of unveiling itself to each of us, and I appreciate that I've enjoyed the path that was laid before me. I've worked hard, yet I know many people work extremely hard and their lives are filled with many challenges.

I never saw myself in any law enforcement role. After growing up on a farm, I supposed that it may have been a logical direction, or manufacturing, since I did well in it. However, every day was the same. I can't put a widget on top of a widget all day long.

When I started listening to Sergeant Craft's advice, I found police work intriguing because every single day was different. There was a lot of diversity in work, people, opportunities, and challenges. Some days, it's just pure boredom; the next day, it's sheer dark terror. I think that's what most of us enjoy, along with all the people we meet. As sheriff, I met Presidents Clinton and Obama and many governors because of what I did for a living. That's kind of neat.

The people who worked for me and with me also made my work enjoyable and interesting. Otherwise, I'm fairly sure I wouldn't have had a 50-year career. It's been interesting to see how people join the force. Some people join because "it's all in the family," or they dreamed of being a police officer since they were four years old, or, like me, someone saw something in them that made them a good fit for such a career. However, most of the people I know decided for other reasons. One gentleman became a police officer to "get girls." Another, Sam Davis, I knew was the right person for the job even though his background in education was vastly different from law enforcement. I saw something in him that made him right for the job as jail administrator. If you asked any number of people in law enforcement, I don't think you'll get the same answer.

Another reason I loved my career was because of the depths of the devotion, loyalty, and passion that everyone has for their careers in law enforcement. The continuous opportunities to learn more, grow, and develop your skills to get promoted is also an encouraging reason to join.

GREGORY HARLESS, Chief Deputy (ret.), Ingham County Sheriff's Office

I started working for Gene at the sheriff's office in 1989. My journey into law enforcement was a bit unconventional because I graduated from paramedic school in 1984 with my paramedic license. At the time, the sheriff's office had a paramedic division, and I saw that as a direction to get into law enforcement. After getting my license, I completed the police academy in 1985. I was hired in June of 1985 as the paramedic deputy for the Ingham County Jail until 1986.

At the time, EMTs were staffed on ambulances, and it was rare for a paramedic to be on one. However, as the paramedics of the sheriff's office, we responded to crashes or to deal with an issue when needed. All our equipment was stored in county station wagons and suburbans. We were the agency with life support at the time, and whenever needed, we rode in the ambulance with the crash victim to provide advanced life support.

With my two roles, I answered two different types of calls. When an emergency call came in and I heard the beep, it meant we had a personal injury accident, and even though I was a paramedic deputy heading out to a call, I was actually a deputy who took on the responsibility of a law enforcement officer. When a different tone rang, we had a medical issue in the jail, and as the paramedic deputy, I addressed that issue. For me, it was the best of both worlds.

The deputies at the sheriff's office answered calls in regular police cars. The only difference when I was on a deputy call was that I drove a patrol car, station wagon, or suburban with all the medical equipment on board. We all worked together as a team.

In the 1990s and 2000s, drunk driving became an epidemic. Those calls were tragic. Oftentimes, when we arrived at the accident scene, we found innocent people who were critically injured or dead because of a crash caused by a drunk driver who often survived it. No matter who causes an accident, we are obligated under oath to take care of any injuries. After a while, I no longer wanted to be the paramedic caring for them. I wanted to be the cop, so I could investigate, seek the charge, and arrest the driver. I was in that role for ten months until there was an opportunity in Delhi Township, one that was officially under and paid for by the township instead of the county. I transferred in 1986.

Then, in 1990, Gene took over Delhi Township, and I was back in the county. Gene recognized the work I performed in all the roles I held over 13 different assignments: paramedic deputy for the jail, deputy patrol for the county and township, detective bureau, and chief deputy for Ingham County. After spending time in our training division, Gene motivated me to explore a sergeant position. I had a lot of exposure through my career to keep achieving new roles and promotions, and I was very blessed. The rest, you can say, is history.

SAM DAVIS, Administrator/Educator (ret.), Ingham County Jail

You don't always know what your calling is in this life. I spent 33 years doing something entirely different than I did during the ten years I was in law enforcement. My greatest lesson was to look at all the opportunities presented before me before closing the door.

I started my career teaching history, psychology, and American government to high school students. Teaching was exciting for me. I slowly matriculated from teacher to assistant principal, principal, administrator, central administrator. Towards the end of my career, I held positions in central administration and became the city-wide athletic director.

Unexpected opportunities arise in all careers, and in education, many times, we are plucked and placed in positions in which the administration believes we will succeed. During my tenure, a principal at one of the middle schools was pregnant and experiencing some complications, and her school was having some issues. She went out on maternity leave. The staff wasn't happy with the administration that was filling in, so I was asked to fill in to help get things back in order.

When I held the central administration role, my superintendent, who I really loved, was retiring. After being in education for so many years, we became attached to the superintendent and other administrators. The "changing of the guard" can be difficult, particularly with the new hires. I wasn't really looking forward to it.

I was at the point where I didn't really want to be a principal again, and I didn't want to go back into the classroom, either. They offered some options. I accepted a transfer into human resources for a district in central Atlanta. My main responsibility was investigating teacher misconduct.

In the administrative positions, I was removed from what attracted me in the first place—being and working with kids. Working with adults and administering the affairs, I enjoyed my career less and less. I wondered about my next step.

While I was back in Michigan, I visited the sheriff's office. I ran into Joel Maatman, who was a major for Gene. He mentioned the sheriff was looking for a jail administrator and that I should think about it. I didn't quite know what to think, so I talked to my superintendent. She advised me to interview. I hadn't needed to interview for decades, and she said, "Test your interview skills and see how it goes."

I submitted my application just for giggles. Then, I was selected to be part of a cadre to do a written interview. And again, I thought, *I'm an educator. I can handle that.* Then, they narrowed it down to four people, including me. Out of the original 24 applicants, it went from eight to four. I still thought, *This is just a great experience for me.*

Strangely enough, Joel and Gene both saw that teaching kids, holding administration positions in schools, and investigating misconduct was parallel to running the county jail. It took me a while to see it and realize that my background was a pretty perfect fit.

The next step was to interview with a panel. I still wasn't sure how I was qualified, but it was a boost to my ego to keep getting reinvited. I thought, *At least I'm competitive.* When I made it to the final four, I was feeling okay and thought, *Even if I don't get this, I don't have a corrections background, a law enforcement background, or a law degree.* I was feeling good because I was still competitive.

We finished the interviews, left, and as I drove about five or six miles north of 27, the phone rang. It was Sheriff Gene. "Hello, Sam. Why don't you pull over?"

Of course, I did what I was told to by the lawman himself.

"How would you like to come work for me?"

I knew Gene as the sheriff, but I didn't know him anymore than most people. "I don't know."

I hadn't talked to my family. I had only told my superintendent that I was going through the process. I needed to talk to some folks and decide if this was what I wanted to do.

Again, Gene encouraged me repeatedly, "You've been able to run a middle school, a high school. You've been citywide athletic director of eight schools: four high schools and four middle schools. You've been in human resources and inspected teacher misconduct. You have a strong command of yourself."

For my entire professional career, I had been in a field with other teachers. When I did my student teaching, I was with other educators, and it was the same when I became a teacher, a coach, and a principal. I was surrounded by other educators who lent their support.

Law enforcement corrections was not in my background. Even though I felt good about getting the opportunity, I still felt trepidation about whether this was something I could do. How would I fit in? I would be an outsider, and I had never been an outsider. I spent 33 years in the Lansing School District. I was an outsider in the first year, but then I did my student teaching.

Long story short, after a conversation with my family and another with my superintendent, I said, "I'm leaving."

My superintendent said, "I think it's a good opportunity for you, Sam."

My family said, "Really?"

I called the sheriff back. "Thank you, sir. I'll do it."

I retired from the school district, and in less than a week, I was at the sheriff's office. I never had even a slight interest; there was no allure, attraction, or anything. It was just fate, then opportunity, and, next thing you know, here I was. The new major.

I've learned that career advancement requires putting yourself in a position where your skills and experience are fitting for new opportunities, you are malleable enough to learn and try new responsibilities, and you're smart enough to know how to say, "I don't know this, but I'm willing to learn and willing to work hard."

SCOTT WRIGGELSWORTH, Current Sheriff, Ingham County

Dad was a role model to me in his law enforcement career. I knew from about 13 or 14 years of age that this line of work would probably be what I would do.

When I graduated from Holt High School in 1988, I attended Michigan State University right away. Through our upbringing, my mom and dad never steered us in one direction or another. They didn't steer us towards police work, though they did not steer us away from it, either. All three boys, at one time in our lives, have been in police work. My oldest brother's been in the private sector for quite a while now, and my youngest brother completed his law enforcement career in 2024. Growing up in a police family, it was natural to become interested in it, and I did.

When I decided to go to MSU, both my parents advised me that there was nothing wrong with a criminal justice degree, but to at least consider getting a degree in something else for three reasons. One, you might want to do something different when you retire from this job. Two, you may decide you don't want to do this job any longer. Three, God forbid, something happens while you're in this job. With a degree in a different field, you have a backup plan. I followed their advice.

In 1992, I graduated with a bachelor's degree in marketing from the MSU Eli Broad College of Business. It was great advice from my parents back in the day, because there are some areas in my career today that relate to my studies in marketing at MSU. Even now, my degree still benefits me in my role as sheriff more than I expected. I have to market our profession. Marketing the agency to recruit new deputies is extremely important and can be challenging given that police, sheriff's offices, and state and federal law enforcement agencies all recruit from the same pool of people. Plus, as an elected official, you must market yourself every day, especially during an election year.

After MSU, I immediately joined the police academy in August of 1992, and I graduated that November from the 51st Mid-Michigan Police Academy at LCC (Lansing Community College).

Then, I started looking for a job, which took 14 months, much longer than I expected. Back then, 100 people might apply for one or two positions.

I struggled finding a job in this area. I had a four-year degree; I thought I was personable and interviewed well. For whatever reason, there were several agencies that chose not to move me forward in the hiring process.

I think, to a certain extent, it may have been a little bit of a political decision to not want to hire the "sheriff's kid." I don't know that to be true, but in my mind, these decisions seemed odd. As much as I wanted to stay in this area while I interviewed with a bunch of different local agencies, it took a while to finally work out.

I landed a job for the Ingham County Parks Police during the summer of '93 as a part-time officer. It kept me busy while I continued seeking full-time employment. Ingham County Parks, which doesn't exist anymore, used to have their own police department.

In late 1993, I received a call that East Lansing was going to hire me, and I started at the East Lansing Police Department on January 3, 1994. When I started police work in 1994, I knew quite a few people still working for local agencies who had worked for my dad when he ran Metro Squad.

Like father, like son. . . I also worked in undercover narcotics for PACT, the Proactive Anti-Crime Team, from 1999–2000. There were four of us in the unit: one supervisor and three officers, one from MSU Police, one from Meridian Township Police Department, and one from the East Lansing Police Department. We handled the small drug cases and transferred the larger cases to the Tri-County Metro Narcotic Squad. During my last week at PACT, I was promoted to sergeant, and then promoted again in 2012 to lieutenant at the East Lansing Police Department, which was the role I had when I retired in 2016.

My first adventure into the political realm was driven by some good advice from my dad. He had been on the Holt Board of Education for about 10–12 years back in the day. I also served on the Holt BOE for six years, from 2007 to 2013.

During my last two years at ELPD, while I ran for sheriff, I also worked as a lieutenant. Then I was transferred to administration. One of my roles was press information officer. That gave me a terrific opportunity to build my relationships not only with the press, but with our local community. It was a good opportunity for the community to become familiar with me as well.

My career path started as a patrol officer, then veered to undercover narcotics for PACT, where I was promoted to sergeant, then lieutenant, and culminated in running for the office of sheriff of Ingham County in 2016.

In 2016, I won the election. After winning, I retired from the East Lansing Police Department and officially took office on January 1, 2017. My third term as sheriff will end on December 31, 2028.

I'm a firm believer that things happen for a reason. Maybe waiting 14 months for an opening at East Lansing set me up for my later career as a sheriff. Seeing it now, the timing was perfect. I spent 23 glorious years at East Lansing PD. I loved that place, and I retired just two days shy of 23 years at the rank of lieutenant.

Our entire community has been great to the Wriggelsworth family, and this is one of many reasons why we keep giving back to it as much as we can. We feel strongly we are making a positive difference in our communities.

JOEL MAATMAN, Major (ret.), Ingham County Sheriff's Office

My career was 41 years long and spanned several quite different positions. I started as a police officer for the City of Lansing, where I wore a blue uniform, and then when I transferred to a deputy position, I wore brown.

As a police officer, I asked to go to Narcotics, and that's when I met Gene. I worked for Gene and Paul Whitford, who were both MSP lieutenants at that time, and they ran the unit. I worked there for almost two years and enjoyed the hell out of both those guys.

After I retired as a lieutenant from LPD, I was the Chief of Police of Public Safety for the PA 330 School District for Lansing schools. Most school districts use private security firms; PA 330 was the only school district in the State of Michigan that allowed citizens to have full police power when they worked on their property and were in uniform.

As private police officers, we were trained and in uniform for the protection of the school students. I had 45 people working for me. They were great, and I loved that role. It doesn't matter where you start in law enforcement, there are plenty of opportunities to try other roles.

DARWIN SHAVER, Chief Deputy (ret.), Ingham County Sheriff's Office

At 21 years old, I worked as a deputy patrol officer for Delhi Township Police Department. From there, while at Delhi, I was promoted to corporal, sergeant, lieutenant, and captain.

I left Delhi for a while and was hired by the sheriff prior to Gene as a chief deputy.

I assisted Gene with his transition to the sheriff's office. He brought his own chief deputy with him. He shared that he had always liked working with me through our many years together, and if I could hang on, he would find a place for me. When he assumed office, as he promised, he hired me as a major.

After Gene's election, I received a nice note from him congratulating us on the election win. He wrote that he appreciated me, and we made a good team. That meant more than anything to me.

As a major, one of my responsibilities was to manage the budget between departments of the sheriff's office. I also was an interim corrections officer during the transition to major, and I was then promoted to chief deputy.

I was and still am immensely proud to say that I worked for Gene Wriggelsworth. I retired as chief deputy with the Ingham County Sheriff's Office, one who held more positions than anyone. In 36 years, I never dreaded going to work. I loved my job.

Note: It was deeply saddening to my family and I that Darwin Shaver passed away during the writing of this book, on June 26, 2025, at the age of 84, surrounded by his loving family.[15] Darwin was an enormous contributor to the success of the Ingham County Sheriff's Office, and I am very grateful to have had him on my team. His hard work and dedication are greatly appreciated.

GENE'S LIFE TIMELINE
(PROOF THAT LIFE IS NOT LINEAR)

November 7, 1944 – Birthday!

1963 – Graduated Owosso High School as a state champion wrestler at 165 lb. weight class

July 1965 – Married my precious bride, Sandy

1966 – Mike was born

1966 – Graduated from Lansing Community College with an associate's degree in business operations and later became a distinguished alumni

September 19, 1966 – Entered MSP Police Academy, East Lansing

December 1966 – Graduated from the police academy and transferred to Flat Rock

1966–1968 – Served as an MSP Trooper located in Flat Rock State Police Post

1968–1972 – Served as an MSP Trooper located in East Lansing State Police Post

1970 – Scott was born

1972–1974 – Served as an MSP Trooper located in Eaton County's State Police Post

1974–1976 – Promoted to sergeant when assigned to the narcotics unit, served in the drug team

1975 – Mark was born

1976–1988 – Promoted to lieutenant in 1976 while assigned to the Tri-County Metro Narcotic Squad.

1978–1988 – Elected to the Board of Education of Holt Public Schools

1988–2016 – Elected Ingham County Sheriff for Seven Consecutive Terms

1994 – Graduated FBI National Academy, received college credits from University of Virginia through the FBI National Academy, and earned bachelor's degree in business administration from Northwood University

+ While sheriff, I was a member of several professional 0rganizations:

- President of the Sheriff's Association
- Chaired the Michigan Sheriff's Training Council
- Chaired Michigan Commission on Law Enforcement Standards
- President of the Michigan State Police Troopers Association
- President, two terms, of the South Lansing Holt Rotary Club
- Chair, Lansing Area Safety Council
- Chair, Ingham County Chiefs Association
- Chair, Mid-Michigan Police Academy Advisory Board at Lansing Community College
- Negotiated and established contracts with Village of Webberville and Delhi Township for Police Services
- DARE, Drug Abuse Resistance Education Program, Sheriff's Office
- Football Chain Gang for Holt High School program for 32 years

*****

2016–Present – Happy Retiree; Retired from Ingham County Sheriff's Office

2023–2025 – Authored my first book, *50 Years of Duty, Honor & Impact*

+ Current volunteer organizations:

- Maintenance Volunteer for Give-A-Kid Projects in Holt

- Board of Directors, The Hundred Club for Ingham, Eaton, and Clinton Counties
- Volunteer Builder, Tuesday Toolmen

CHAPTER 3 LESSON

Each of our lives is unique, and this extends to both our personal and professional paths. No matter where you start, it does not define where you must stay. If you desire to do one thing and change your mind later, do what it is that makes you happy. In law enforcement, the opportunities are limitless when you work hard, operate with integrity, and treat others with respect.

CHAPTER 4

IT TAKES A VILLAGE

"'IT TAKES A village,' they say," and as I reflect on my life, I can attest that it sure does. I've been fortunate from the day I was born to be surrounded by good, hearty, hardworking, and successful people. My parents were the first two most influential people in my life, followed by teachers, coaches, neighbors, bosses, colleagues, mentors, and members of the Lansing and Ingham County communities.

I wouldn't be the person I am today, a retired law enforcement officer who served my communities for 50 years alongside some of the best officers in the country, without having been the father of three wonderful sons and married to Sandy, the best sheriff's wife there could ever be. They also say, "behind every good man (which I hope I am), there is a great woman." That is also true.

I ALMOST DIED

Back in 2020, I might have died if I hadn't been assigned to the top heart surgeon in the state of Michigan. I didn't even know I was sick. I was retired, and customary to retirement, Sandy and I devoted our time to volunteering for many organizations. On one Saturday, we were assigned to deliver furniture to one of the organization's clients. I carried bed frames up the stairs of an apartment complex. They weren't heavy, maybe twenty-five pounds, but I stopped, started, stopped, and realized I couldn't get to the top of the steps. I was winded, weak, and a bit dizzy. I realized something was wrong with me and vowed to see my doctor on Monday. After getting home that day, I felt better, thankfully. Sandy and I walked our usual daily two-mile trek.

My heart doctor, Dr. Paul Zack, ran tests on Monday, reviewed the results, and returned to the room. I noticed his complexion was completely ashen.

"Gene, we must get you to a surgeon, now. You have two blockages at 100%, and two blockages at 80%."

I replied, "Should I go home?"

"No. Don't move. Don't breathe. It's like a time bomb."

I was petrified. Heart disease ran in my family. My dad had it, and his dad, my grandfather, died of a heart attack when my dad was sixteen. The next day, a man of large stature with a dominating presence became my surgeon. Dr. Divyakanti Gandhi performed a quadruple heart bypass surgery at McLaren Hospital of Greater Lansing, Michigan. I was in the recovery room when he knocked on the door.

"Why am I still alive?" I questioned.

"I'll show you why you are still alive," he said as he pulled up the x-rays. "Your heart started creating its own bypass with this artery. It did that because you are seventy-six, in good shape, and you take care of yourself. Your body compensated for the blockages."

I guess the good Lord still had plans for me.

Before the surgery, I researched the good doctor. He was educated in India, licensed in the United States, and came highly, highly recommended. He shared his success rate was 98–99%, and I asked if the other 2% were sporting toe tags. He didn't take kindly to my humor; it's not for everyone. After all, when you are in law enforcement, death is part of our everyday life, and we are accustomed to finding humor in crime scenes. You could say it's a coping mechanism for police officers to avoid suppressing our emotions.

Physical therapy was an important part of my recovery process. During my first session, my PT stressed the importance of staying active.

"Keep going to the gym, do the Stairmasters, treadmills, and whatever else you can to strengthen your cardio." He looked at me, then pointed to the guy on the Stairmaster. "See him? See that guy over there on the Stairmaster? He's back because he didn't do what I just told you."

I was in the hospital for about a week. Talk about a village! Those nurses sure do the heavy lifting. After the doctor cracked open my chest, constructed the bypass in my arteries, and gave me my marching orders, the nurses took over. One was assigned to me for the first 24 hours in the ICU to make sure I didn't code (medical term for "stop breathing," or cardiac arrest) or have any other issues like pain, bleeding, and so on. I guess you could say a quadruple bypass is serious, but they make it look and sound so easy. I am not one who likes people to take care of me; I prefer independence, so it was a bit difficult to depend on others to heal. They nursed me back to health to go home, and to this day, I so appreciate Dr. Gandhi's skill and the nurses' compassion and endless care for my needs.

When I started the physical therapy regimen, the young PT asked about my doctor and confirmed he was the best. "When I was hired, it was required for me to observe Dr. Gandhi in surgery. There is a person who is a 'sprayer' assigned to stand next to every surgeon to spray the doctors' fingers, so they don't stay sticky from the blood. In this case, when he sprayed Dr. Gandhi's fingers, some of the spray went into the body cavity. Dr. Gandhi turned to him and snapped, 'Get out of my operating room.'"

After the PT shared this, I liked the doctor even more because I knew he didn't leave anything in me. Thank you, Dr. Gandhi, the entire medical team at McLaren Hospital, my nurses, and my post-operative home healthcare aides. I wouldn't be authoring this book without you.

FAMILY

When you reflect on your life, who are the people you remember most for the role they played in your development? As I rewind about eighty years, I remember countless people in "my village" who had tremendous impact and influence on me. They shaped the person I am today because of their leadership, kindness, encouragement, reprimand, and belief in my abilities.

My parents, of course, have shaped much of who I am today. Both were very hard workers, committed to each other, devoted to raising a family, and remained financially frugal. Growing up on a farm is like going to kindergarten. Everything you need to learn in life, you learn on the farm. Hard work, time management, life, loss, financial woes, patience, weather patterns and their impact, physical fitness, how to drive tractors, hard labor, animal care, birth, sickness, and death, family values, lifelong friendships, and for me, "international engagement." My parents' experience with prisoners of war from World War II specifically modeled how we all need to welcome, accept, care for, and help all people.

My dad shared stories with me about when I was born in 1944. The war was ongoing, and my parents hosted German POWs (prisoners of war) to work the farm during the day. Dad ran a dairy and cash crop (corn, beans, wheat, hay) farm. When our military captured them during various invasions, they were shipped over from Germany to Michigan and housed at the Owosso racetrack. Each day, they were bussed to work on our farm. Dad and Mom were never afraid of them. Dad said, "They were nice guys. We knew there was no place to escape in Michigan by horseback or slow cars, so nobody ever walked away."

Plus, my mother cooked fried chicken and roast beef, and they loved it. I don't think anyone would refuse my mother's cooking! It was good!

All work and no play makes Gene a very dull boy. Yes, we worked hard and played harder. With the boys in my neighborhood, we played on the hay mounds, rode the rope at the swimming hole from one sandbar to another, and played in the barns; there was always something fun to do. As long as our chores were done, we never let the grass grow under our feet.

Living frugally, my parents instilled proper habits for money management in me. "Always save for a rainy day, and don't live outside of your means."

The years between 1957 and 1973 were consumed by the construction on Interstate 75, which stretched from the Hialeah-Miami border in Florida to the Canadian border in Sault Sainte Marie, Michigan. Gravel was a hot commodity as it was necessary for the roads' foundations.

While digging a ditch on the farm for drain tiles, my dad struck gravel and promptly sold it to be used for building the interstate. They received a fair sum and finally felt comfortable enjoying life a little bit more. My grandmother was a significant role model, too, and I learned how to be strong in the face of adversity, continuously persevere, and be flexible in adapting to unexpected circumstances from her. Despite having only one arm, she proved everything could still be done.

Looking back, I learned more about life from living on the farm than I learned in kindergarten. Yet, both were equally important for my brain, body, spirit, self-confidence, and smarts.

SPORTS AND COACHES

(Trigger warning: readers may find it difficult to read about war events, deaths, dismemberments.)

Baling hay, moving animals, building fences, and all the other hard, laborious chores on the farm contributed to my athleticism. I was fit and loved playing sports. Mom and Dad came to very few of my athletic events because of work, but they encouraged me to keep active and do what I loved.

Gene, senior year Individual State Champion. Class A, 165 lbs.
From left to right: Coach Jerry Alliton, Coach Roger Tavenner, and Gordy Weeks. 1963.

As a 165-pound football player, I was a major contributor as an offensive guard and a defensive tackle. Keep in mind, this was a long time ago. Back then, at 165 pounds, we were the big guys; we didn't have 220-pound players who tackled, and if we did, they weren't fast. In high school, Bill Pike, who became my best friend at 15, was the star player as a tight end and all-conference. His skill and team sportsmanship led us to many unexpected victories and led him to play for Ferris State University. Bill and I are still best friends and share limitless memories about farms, sports, careers, raising families, travel, and life while retired. He winters in Florida with his wife, Wendie, and when he returns home to Michigan, we spend time together enjoying each other's company.

BIG NINE CHAMPS!

VARSITY FOOTBALL: Row 1, Bruce Rubey, Tom Corey, Bill Anderson, Bill Pike, Denny Morris, Gary Palmer, Jerry Vincent, John Gorte, Gene Wriggelsworth, Dick Conklin, Tom Jones. Row 2, Jim Whiteherse, Ron Miller, Jim Noonon, Gordy Weeks, Ed Beamish, Brak Luchenbill, Bill Mack, Neil White, Orval Sater, Norm Eddy. Row 3, Head Coach Bernie Conklin, Backfield Coach Jerry Alliton, Larry Reed, Charlie Lyons, Jim Apsey, Dave Hetfield, Jon Tarolli, Ernie Stewart, Norm Campbell, Carl Hublein and Line Coach Roger Taveoner. Top row, Gary Miller, Dick Thornburg, Tom Gorte, Bruce Haak, Steve Hanzlovic, Jim Gouge, Art Klein, Chuck Jenkinson and Charles Hudecek.

Gene's senior year. Owosso High School Big Nine League Championship.
Gene seated in front row, Number 33. Bill Pike seated in the
front row, fourth from right, Number 60. 1963.

Our first year in the Big Nine League was fun, and we worked hard to place in the League Championship. (State championships didn't exist yet.) In addition to our school, the Owosso Trojans, other high schools included Davison Cardinals, Flint Kearsley Hornets, Grand Blanc Bobcats, Clio Mustangs, Flint Beecher Bucs, Mount Morris Panthers, Flint Ainsworth Spartans, Flushing Raiders, Flint Northern, and Flint Central. Our competition, especially the Flint schools, didn't think much of Owosso High School. They thought we were country bumpkins. When we arrived on buses for their home games, the home fans lined up as a welcome committee and dressed in straw hats. But us country bumpkins kicked their asses. We repeatedly mopped the field with them and won the league championship! Those are *good* memories.

Our winning aptitudes and attitudes were thanks to our coach and history teacher, Bernie Conklin. He was a leader of men. During the war, he served during the unforgettable D-Day in Normandy. Surprisingly, he shared his experiences when he lost one eye and one leg. "It was just hell; just like the movie *The Longest Day*."

You could feel the emotion within him as he shared his story. It was as if he had just returned, even though it had been years.

"People are dying. Limbs are flying. We finally passed the beach and set foot on the mainland. Two guys walked with me, and one of them stepped on a landmine. It killed both of them and took my eye and leg."

Our history class listened in stunned silence.

"We're laying there, and I'm dying. I know I'm going to bleed to death. Here come some German soldiers, and now, I know I'm going to die, but they had a medic with them. They bandaged me up, gave me some morphine, and went on their way."

Wow. He said, "My life was saved by some freaking Nazis."

Coach Conklin was a great guy, an excellent role model for serving our country, a proactive leader, and a talented football coach. He taught us how to build a cohesive, winning team, how to be leaders, and how to be unstoppable despite significant injury, much like my grandmother also taught me. Thank you, Coach Conklin.

Every human being has good ideas and bad ideas. Bruce Ruby and I were both offensive guards and tough kids. Bruce was a little bigger, and I was 165 pounds. One day during practice, Coach calls, "Ruby. Wriggelsworth. Come here."

We both walked up and didn't know what was happening. He ordered all the other players to line up around us for a one-on-one drill. "I want you two guys to try to block each other."

I thought to myself, *What in the hell is this one about?* We rammed against each other like two rams in a movie. *Bam, bam, bam.* I couldn't knock him down. He couldn't knock me down.

After four or five tries, it was over, and Coach said, "That's how you play football."

Okay, I said in my head to avoid another exercise or lecture. A coach always needs to be an example, and show examples, even if they're bad ones. We can't win them all. Thankfully, for safety and health reasons, the rules of tackling have changed significantly to avoid concussions and other brain injuries, so that example would not fly today. The good news was that three guys on our team made all-conference, including my friend, Bill Pike. One player won the All-Conference Honorable Mention.

Coach Conklin's son was our quarterback, which people snickered about when they heard. But he was good; really good. The reason he was quarterback was because he was so good, not because he was the coach's son. To avoid being accused of "playing favorites" or nepotism, Coach announced to the team, "I purposely did not nominate my son because he's my son. I don't want anyone to think I agree with the other coaches who nominate their sons."

It was prudent of him to say so, because it ended up that one of the coaches from a different team nominated his own son, who won unanimously.

*****

Wrestling is a tough sport. To compete successfully, you need to put in a lot of time and hard work. I may have had some natural talent, too. I liked that it was just one-on-one because if I got beaten, I knew it was on me. In other sports, you can blame a team member, but in wrestling, it's just you and you alone. I started wrestling in eighth grade, which warmed me up for freshman year, and I made the varsity team, which was rare. I did well in the 145-pound weight class in my freshman and sophomore years. I was growing like a weed, and the mandatory weigh-in before every match required me to starve myself.

Come junior year, I was sick of the cut weight requirements, so I didn't try out. My coach, Bill Allen, was really perplexed, so he called my parents to lean on them and get me to change my mind. I refused and skipped junior year. I missed competing and later regretted that I took a year off. Then, just before my senior year, Coach left our school to coach at his alma mater, Lansing Eastern High School. Coach Allen was tougher than nails, and I admired him for being a taskmaster who didn't take any crap. Some guys didn't like that, but it didn't bother me. I always figured he was trying to teach me something.

At 170 pounds as a senior, I cut five pounds to 165, and our assistant coach Roger Tavnner replaced Coach Allen. He was a good coach, just as tough as Coach Allen. It was a fun year.

When I competed for the State Wrestling Championship, we were tied. We wrestled in overtime with the winner taking it all. We were both well-matched, and we ended the overtime at a tie, too. In that situation, the rule was that three coaches had to judge us, and the decision came down to who had more riding time. That means which competitor was in the top position over the other wrestler. I did, so I won first place in the state championship! Ironically, one of the three judges was former coach Allen. Fortunately, I've never had to use those skills to wrestle a suspect!

THE REAL WORLD: JOBS AND CAREER

Throughout our lives, I believe people come and go. Some are in our lives to plant seeds in our minds, to help us to learn new ideas, perspectives, or lessons. After high school graduation, I didn't have the money for college, so I entered the workforce, where I made a lot of money. I wondered why my friends all preferred college over making so much money.

However, I admit that question clearly showed my shortcomings at that age, since I didn't understand the advantages of a college degree. I later learned that those who don't attend college have the skills and talents for other types of jobs. I didn't know what I wanted to do, so over the four years after high school, I worked in manufacturing. My supervisor, Pete Harrington, modeled how to trust and be fair to his employees. Being only 20 years old, Pete recognized my integrity and how hard I worked. He trusted us to do what was asked and never had to micromanage us or check in to see that it was done.

Growing up, I learned both on the farm and in school sports how to get the task done. Dad said, "go do," and I did it. I appreciated Pete's leadership style very much. He was one of several people whose approaches I applied to my leadership style.

I did not appreciate the redundancy such manufacturing jobs required. I was bored and wanted something else. Sergeant Craft's words popped into my head again: *You're going to be a state trooper.* With his vision and encouragement, I left manufacturing to enter law enforcement, which I had never considered. That's when I learned, as adults, when we engage in talks with young people about their futures, it's important to plant seeds for positive considerations. You never know what will result. I don't think Sergeant Craft imagined I'd achieve a 50-year career.

When you think about your life, who stands out to you through their positive impact on your life? During my whole life, I learned from people who were younger than me, older than me, and who held all types of positions inside and outside of law enforcement. As a state trooper, undercover police officer, and sheriff, I was a mere cog in the wheel of this village. In each of my roles, the people surrounding me at work and home were and are my "village."

No matter whether my role is that of husband, dad, grandfather, son, friend, officer, sheriff, or retiree, the impact of what I did, and what each of us do in our lives, reaches beyond the squad car, office, and home. It takes all of us to contribute to building safe, cohesive, collaborative, and thriving communities, counties, states, and countries. I could never have imagined such a lengthy career without the people I worked for, worked with, supervised, and served in Ingham County and the State of Michigan. Each day and experience always offered learning lessons that helped me continuously grow in self-development to better serve others.

There are so many influencers and leaders in my "village" who shaped me into the person I am today. Even in retirement, I'm still evolving, learning, building friendships, addressing concerns, changing policies to make sense, working with all the powers that be, and striving to make a positive difference in our community.

During probationary trooper training, Trooper Gordon Smith taught me a particularly important lesson about professional development. When I received my first 30-day probationary evaluation, I was disappointed in how I was rated.

Another trooper, Mike, who had been on the job for three years, had a lot of experience as a former deputy. He shared his marks with me, and he received the highest mark in every category. I was shocked. Even though there were only two categories, "acceptable" or "needs improvement," I was surprised to see that many of mine were "needs improvement." Here I was, the entire time, believing I was doing a great job. I asked Smith, "Am I that bad? Between Mike and me, how could I score such low performance rates?"

He replied, "The difference, Gene, is that you are going to get better, and he isn't."

It really encouraged me, and I've never forgotten that lesson.

Now, when I train people, I identify who has the potential to continuously improve so I know to place them in a supportive group that can guide them along. As an example, as sheriff, I had three undersheriffs who were highly qualified for their role, and while they had more to learn, they quickly grew into their job. As they gained more experience, they excelled.

One of my undersheriffs, Rick Boyd, became the director of the Sheriff's Association. Boyd passed away a few years ago in Tennessee. At home, he fell and injured his head, and then left the hospital at night in a hospital gown, clearly confused. The hardest parts of working in law enforcement are the continuous injury and loss of life of people we know well and with whom we worked. We are all family, and each one hurts deeply.

Jim Rapp was the Lansing supervisor for our Metro Narcotic Squad. When we needed resources to do our jobs, he immediately responded with what we needed. He also functioned as the buffer between the chief of police and our squad, which was helpful in preventing red tape and extensive procedures. He took care of all of that for us; because of what I learned from him, I treated my employees the same way.

Captain Roger Warner was my state police supervisor in the Metro Narcotic Squad. He was the captain of multi-jurisdictional areas outside of Detroit. He started as a trooper and followed the ranks: trooper, sergeant, lieutenant, and captain. As a seasoned officer, he knew things went wrong sometimes, wheels fell off, and he had enough experience and the wherewithal to know we had to fix it and move on, which taught me how to be adaptable to various situations.

In the FBI Academy, I attended that grueling program with fellow sheriff Terry Jungel, who was from Ionia County. We had known each other for ten years. It was the first time two sheriffs from Michigan attended the academy at the same time. It was nice to be able to bounce ideas off each other as sheriffs, along with getting ideas from lieutenants and captains that didn't all correlate to our roles.

VILLAGE, COUNTY, AND STATE INITIATIVES

In addition to all that I learned from my family, colleagues, the people working for me, and those in the higher echelons and other divisions of law enforcement, it was important, as sheriff, to participate in opportunities from various village, county, state, and federal initiatives.

In any town, trains colliding with cars make for tragic accidents. This usually stems from drivers wanting to beat the trains and trying to drive around the train gates to avoid waiting. Don't ever go around the gates to avoid the train. Why risk being the car that loses against the heavier train? Waiting a few minutes for a long freight train is not worth your life. To educate communities on these dangers, the local railroads established a program called "The Sheriff on a Train."

The sheriffs rode the freight train along the sixty miles between Battle Creek and Durand. The freight train traveled about 20–30 miles per hour; those things are big, and they're heavy. It takes miles for them to come to a complete stop, and they are not something to mess with. I remember all the dead deer along the road. They aren't very bright animals.

We recorded the ride on camera to be used later to produce videos. In less than two hours, we observed twelve drivers dodging the gates. Fortunately, for their sake, they beat the train. That doesn't always happen. We shared the recordings with civic groups and schools to educate local community members on how dangerous it was to "beat the train." The local media networks and newspaper also broadcasted the program and video clips to emphasize safety, hoping to deter drivers' bad behaviors and habits at the crossing gates. Since then, the State of Michigan made it illegal to cross the tracks when the gates are down. It is now a ticketable offense with a hefty fine.

Another event happened when the National Guard called and invited me to their annual midair refueling event in San Antonio, Texas, which they do every year with law enforcement officials around the country. It was an experience I will never forget. I took my chief deputy, Greg Harless, with me, and we flew on a military plane out of Michigan to Texas.

When we arrived, there were only six or eight people in total. They led us to the refueling planes, which I'd never seen before. It was a huge jet aircraft with four engines. The plane size was dictated by the engines. We boarded the plane, sat down against a wall, and fastened our seat belts over our heads instead of over our shoulders. They weren't very comfortable, but there was a toilet; it wasn't modest, since it was open for everyone to see the person using it.

We arrived on the runway, walked to the plane, loaded the gear, and took off. About thirty minutes later, a huge jet showed up behind us. The crew dropped a hose that had wings on it for our plane. One of the soldiers laid down on their belly on a big window so he could see the tanks, hose, and connections. We were flying at three hundred miles an hour, and the soldier opened the tanks, inserted the hose, and filled them. It didn't take long; at the most, ten minutes. I don't know how many thousands of gallons of fuel were transferred, but it was a lot in a short period. It was a wonder to see. What an experience for someone who grew up on a farm in a small town.

RETIREMENT

As retirees, Sandy and I agreed to remain active and participate in the community. She was already an avid volunteer with several organizations prior to my retirement, so it felt quite natural to segue into areas where I could continue to be of service.

Many of us have various experiences in any role we hold; it's common to meet and work with someone who you admire. As a member of the Holt School Board, I found Superintendent Henry Sienkiewicz to be a born leader, which should have been tattooed on his forehead. He oversaw 800 to 900 employees and he never forgot one name. He brought the school district into the twenty-first century, and it tremendously benefited the students, teachers, staff, and families. From him, I learned how to run a large organization while remaining engaged with the people.

MY BRIDE

There are times in law enforcement where cases are devastating, traumatic, and unforgettable. The most tragic are when we lose fellow law enforcers or staff in accidents or the line of duty. Then, there are other events that the media learns about, or mishaps in the office. As with every job, it's not always perfect. No matter the crisis, my bride, Sandy, helped me deal with every aspect of my career. Naturally, she knew what I needed and assuaged my hurt feelings, hugged me, and consoled me during the worst days of my career. Her support, love, and encouragement gave me what I needed to heal and continue. Sandy was the center of my village every single day and night, and she remains the center of my life to this day. Thank you, Sandy, my bride.

WHO ARE THE PEOPLE IN YOUR VILLAGE?

In our lives, our paths lead us to different experiences and purposes. We meet all types of people, and we hold dear the lessons we learn from extraordinary people. They say that "people come into your life for a reason, a season, or a lifetime." We can take something with us from every encounter we have that teaches us something new, offers a new perspective, or opens us up to possibilities.

Who are the people who contributed to who you are today? Everyone touches our hearts in some way or another. As I remember all these people who made such a difference in the person I have become, I'm overwhelmed with gratitude. I'm fortunate to have worked with a lot of good people. I could not have done my job without them, and that is why they are my "village." Thank you to all the people who made my life and career a momentous success.

Chapter 4 Activities

1. **It Takes a Village.** Who are the people you consider members of your "village?"

2. **Write a List.** To determine the members of your "village," write a list of people in your life who fill the following roles:

   - Personal Life
     - Family
     - Friends
     - Neighbors
     - Vendors
     - Townspeople (first responders, village officials, teachers, doctors, etc.)

   - Professional Life
     - Coworkers
     - Employers/Executives
     - Bosses/Supervisors/Team Leads
     - Coaches/Mentors/Sponsors
     - Vendors

3. **Give Thanks.** Have you ever considered saying, "Thanks for being a part of my village. This is how you have helped shape me into the person I am today."

PART 2

22 YEARS AS A MICHIGAN STATE POLICE TROOPER

YEARS 1 THROUGH 8

1966–1968
FLAT ROCK MICHIGAN STATE POLICE POST

1968–1972
EAST LANSING MICHIGAN STATE POLICE POST

1972–1974
EATON COUNTY MICHIGAN STATE POLICE POST

CHAPTER 5

THE FIRST EIGHT YEARS FROM FLAT ROCK AND BEYOND

Gene's recruit school graduation photo. 1966.

Recruit school graduation. Gene standing in second row from ground and second from right.
December 1966.

I N DECEMBER OF 1966, I graduated from recruit school and reported to the post in Flat Rock, Michigan. Between 1925 and the 1960s, Flat Rock was home to the Ford Motor Company Factory, which was built along the banks of the Huron River. [16] When I arrived, the small, sleepy town straddled Telegraph Road, which was the previous main artery out of Detroit until I-75 opened. The freeway significantly reduced vehicular traffic through the city. Today, it is considered a small town, with about 10,500 residents. Thanks to the construction of I-75, it is only a 30-minute drive southwest of Detroit. [17]

Yes, progress is good.

As a Michigan State Trooper, I was thrilled to do something more exciting that offered my family and me a future full of opportunities for growth, health benefits, and a retirement plan. We could get ahead, move ahead, and I could even become a corporal! I knew I did not have to be a trooper forever. I also didn't have to stay in Flat Rock forever because, by design, after their first assignment, troopers were transferred after two years.

FLAT ROCK, MICHIGAN

As we drove through Flat Rock, Sandy blinked and missed it. It was a small town, but she grew to appreciate it more than she would have if we were assigned to Detroit or Michigan's upper peninsula.

We found a nice house quickly, but Sandy didn't know anyone. Being ninety minutes away from her parents and alone with our newborn son, Mike, was difficult, considering I was at work on various shifts every month. Severe post-partum depression settled within her, and each day was very difficult. I couldn't tell if it was because of the move, she hadn't made any friends yet, or the post-partum depression. Likely, it was all three. I felt bad about going to work because I could see that she was going to have a distressing day by herself with Mike.

We managed to get through those tough years. Working for the state police was a good-sized pay cut from my previous salary working manufacturing jobs. Money was so tight that on payday, after we bought groceries, there wasn't much left. We even had to borrow money to buy a crib for Mike, but we made it through.

To help steady herself from the PPD and contribute income, Sandy started substitute teaching in the New Boston School District. Mike stayed at daycare with the neighbor across the street. It's hard to be a substitute teacher. She never told them I was a trooper, because they were not well-behaved. The class was so rowdy, one male student even set fire to the trash can in the classroom.

We had two cars; she drove the "good car." When transferred to East Lansing, my car, "the beater," served its purpose and finally broke down. A Brighton wrecking service offered to tow it for free if I gave him the title; I was glad to! After all, it was a 1964 Ford with a different color hood and fender. Who wouldn't want it?

ROOKIE MOVES

FIRST STOP—The first check point in the Michigan State Police safety check lane is to show one's valid driver's license. Trooper G.L. Wriggelsworth of Holt looks for that all important expiration date.

All rookies were tasked with washing the patrol cars. One day, while on car washing duty, a guy pulled into the parking lot with his car and said, "I'm with Sunoco Oil Company and I'm a mystery shopper for the Sunoco station around the corner. I travel to stations to evaluate the attendants' services. They pump the gas until my tank is full, and then I stop at the local state police posts to give the gas away. Do you want some gas?"

I watched the dude for clues and thought, *I'm a rookie. This is a scam or a prank from my fellow troopers. I know it is.* So, I walked inside to the post, where corporals are in charge. Corporal Dave Swanson, an old-time veteran, listened intently and said, "Wait here a minute."

I manned the desk while he checked it out. When he came back ten minutes later, I asked, "So what'd you do?"

He said, "I let him fill my car up."

I was stunned and asked, "Is he still here?"

With a grin, he replied, "No, he left."

Well, I got nothing out of it. It's live and learn.

*****

My first traffic stop is etched in my brain forever and reminds me how naive I was. I pulled a car over with four teenagers in it. They didn't have registration for the vehicle, so my training officer said, "write the ticket for it."

We called the dispatch to run the plate, and they confirmed the car wasn't stolen. He instructed, "Write it for no registration."

I completed the ticket, which is just a form with blanks to fill in. When I came to the part where it said "registration," I left it blank because there was no registration. The training officer, Trooper Gordon Smith, walked up to the car and handed the ticket to the kid.

When he sat back in the car next to me, he called in the ticket, but noticed the registration was left blank. He questioned me, and I replied, "They didn't have registration."

I felt stupid when he looked at me and said, "The registration line is for the license plate, not the paper in the glovebox. Get it?"

The car wasn't too far ahead of us as we watched it take the curve on I-75. As we approached them, we were surprised they pulled to the side of the road, and we watched them remove a case of beer from the trunk for the front seat. Due to my inexperience of leaving a blank on the ticket, they were arrested for minor in possession. It was an interesting situation, and it turned out that Trooper Smith wasn't mad at me, after all.

*****

One day, we had a complaint and drove over to talk with the woman. Now keep in mind, I was just a 22-year-old rookie, so my training officer was with me. We walked up to the door and she greeted us with a package in her hands. She looked at me. She looked at my training officer. She looked at me while she handed him the package and said to me, "You can't see this. Only he can."

It was unsolicited pornographic material, and she didn't know what to do with it. She thought I was too young, at 22, to be viewing such content.

*****

We had a rookie trooper who went on to have a successful career. However, in his early days, he had a major screwup. There was a little round trash burner in the basement of the state police post where we dumped all our trash. Wearing his winter coat, the trooper put his gun inside his coat pocket instead of his holster. He dumped the trash while the fire burned, returned upstairs, and said "I can't find my gun."

Immediately, we heard, *Bang! Bang! Bang!* Apparently, when he bent over to empty the trash, the gun fell out of his coat pocket into the trash burner. That is what we call a hard lesson in gun safety.

*****

When the Michigan State Police was first established, troopers weren't allowed to be married because they were required to live at the state post, which were not equipped for couples. Fortunately, I started after those rules ended. Sandy and I hadn't found a place to live yet. While Sandy lived in Lansing, I had to stay somewhere, so I found "home" at the state post barracks. It wasn't a bad situation, but it was hard to sleep with all the noise. One positive was that I was assigned to training officer Trooper Gordon Smith, who was probably the best trainer I had in my career. He was very patient with me, acknowledged my hard work and potential, and inspired me to improve.

*****

On a memorable traffic stop in Monroe County, Trooper Smith walked to the driver's side, and as his backup, I walked to the passenger side.

"Can I see your license and registration?" he asked.

The driver said to the female passenger, "Glovebox."

She opened it, and I saw a gun in it. I hollered, "Gun!"

We pulled out our guns to order them out of the car. They didn't have paperwork for guns or the car, so they all went to jail.

The next day, we went to court for their arraignment before the justice of the peace. As they sat in the back of the courtroom, they learned the judge's name was Jim Basile. He was a great guy. The two arrestees were obnoxious as they made fun of his last name. When it came time for their arraignment, they paid the price for their comments.

THE DETROIT RIOTS (JULY 23–28, 1967)[17]

The Fourth of July weekend of 1967 came and went. The sweltering summer heat blanketed Michigan. We lived in Flat Rock for six months when a call came on Sunday, July 23. "Wriggelsworth, grab your riot stick and gear. You're going to Detroit."

"All right," I said in a respectful tone as adrenaline pumped through me, mingling with anticipation, curiosity, and fear.

No one in law enforcement or the military wants to be assigned the duty of facing down rioters. It's always dangerous to walk into a lion's den of angry, hungry lions and lionesses. However, we take the oath to protect and serve and uphold the laws of the city and state. We must fulfill our duty and put our training into practice. The most important rule for any officer is to "follow our training." It is designed to prepare us for the worst experiences, and when properly followed, we have the greatest odds of coming home safely and uninjured at the end of our shift.

Detroit Riot damage of Kresge Company. 1967.

10th precinct accommodations for detained prisoners. Detroit Riot, 1967.

Sniper attack. Troopers taking cover on far left, crouched near a car. Detroit Riot, 1967.

That night, 200 out of the 4,700 members of the Detroit Police Department were on duty at the time of a very publicized raid. Together with my fellow Michigan State Police Troopers, we joined forces with the Detroit Police and Fire Departments, the Michigan National Guard, and the US Army. Earlier in the week, at three or four in the morning, the Detroit Police Department raided a "Blind Pig," which was an after-hours drug or drinking establishment. They arrested a bunch of people, a fight started, and that fired up a riot.

The Detroit Historical Society named this event the "Detroit Rebellion of 1967" and the "12th Street Riot" in its historical writings.[1] The five-day event was the largest civil disturbance of the US in the twentieth century. Already a city already divided by racism and long-established segregation, black and white workers from southern states had fled to Michigan at the height of the manufacturing boom. The police raid that night added fuel to the highly flammable discord, and the residents lit the match to fight back. To say the city was scorched would be an understatement.

Trooper Terry Brenay reporting for duty. Detroit Riot, 1967.

The Superior Office Supplies store was ransacked. Detroit Riot, 1967.

Burnt car parked in front of the furniture store and the YMCA. Detroit Riot, 1967.

The pictures show the area of Detroit in which we first reported for duty. For our safety, we first shot out the streetlights at intersections. Being there felt like an unbelievable nightmare. The pictures we took were of some of the buildings that were destroyed by the rioters and the fires. The furniture store above was burned to rubble, while some were not. Many stores were looted, including A&P, a grocery market.

Since we were from Flat Rock and didn't know the city very well, they assigned a Detroit cop to drive our patrol car with three troopers in it. I'll tell you, I'm just a farm boy. We were driving around, and you heard and felt the bullets bounce off your car. I thought, *I've got a wife at home with a brand-new baby. What in the hell am I doing here?*

Those days, I had second thoughts about my entire career. It was frightening, and I imagined that the people who lived there and the store owners had to be terrified. When I could, I checked in with Sandy every day from the pay phone and kept it as positive as possible so she wouldn't worry. I hoped she wasn't watching the news.

Back at Flat Rock and other posts around the state, five troopers were left behind to cover the day and night shifts for the duration of our absence. They were disappointed to miss the "excitement" and thought they were missing out. I had never seen, heard, or experienced anything like the nightmare surrounding me. The Detroit police wore black uniforms so they were easily distinguishable. Some officers were investigated and later arrested for shooting people without cause. The event was so hotly contested, the court proceedings were held in Ingham County instead of the City of Detroit. They were found not guilty. The movie *Detroit*, which depicted the riots, trial, and subsequent acquittal, used the existing county courthouse during the filming for scenes. Thirty years after the riots, as sheriff, I was in charge of courthouse security there, too.

For a week, we took turns sleeping in the front and back seats of various cars. Some of us took our clothes off just so the sweat would dry. We "rendezvoused" every day at predetermined locations. One day, when we arrived, people started shooting at us while we hid behind cars. The Army National Guard was stationed at a school and brought all their weapons and vehicles. The weight of the tanks seemed to create mud everywhere, even though it hadn't rained for the entire week.

"Sleeping accommodations" at the Detroit Riots of 1967.
Notice the MSP officer sleeping in the front seat and his clothes hanging on the line to dry.

We always say, "size matters when it comes to guns." Tanks included.

We were called to a house with an active sniper. As we arrived, our patrol car was hit with bullets from a .22, which is a small caliber weapon with a bullet size about the radius of a drinking straw. You still don't want to get shot with one, because it will kill you. We called for help.

The National Guard came driving down the street with a tank. The street shook and my eyes were wide open. I've never been around tanks in my life, and the top of the tracks were above my head. Suddenly, this little head pops out of the tank's top center. "How can I help you, Trooper?"

"There's a sniper in that house," I pointed. At the exact same time, we heard a "ping" as a bullet bounced off the tank.

That was a big mistake. Our new friend turned around and aimed his 50-caliber machine gun in the direction of the *ping*, fired, and peppered the whole front of the house with bullet holes. The beams on the house were shredded like Swiss cheese. Guess what? The guy came out.

When they assigned us to Detroit, they didn't tell us to pack any clothes. They were totally unprepared for something of this scale, and thankfully, the Red Cross and Salvation Army fed us. Seven days later, I came home in the same underwear, same clothes, and same shoes. We didn't need to use our siren to announce we were arriving because they smelled us coming. It was good to be home, have a shower, and hug my wife and baby. Unfortunately, the Detroit Historical Society reported 43 deaths, hundreds of injuries, almost 1,700 hundred fires, and over 7,000 arrests.[18] I was surely grateful for my safe return home.

50 YEAR ANNIVERSARY OF DETROIT RIOTS

Article reprinted with permission from "WKAR Public Media | Michigan State University"[19]

Black, White and Blue: Two Police Officers Remember 1967 Uprising

50 years ago today, Detroit was in devastation.

The police raid of an after-hours bar on July 23, 1967, triggered a massive wave of arson, looting and sniper fire across much of the city.

The Detroit Police Department, the Michigan State Police, the Michigan National Guard, and even US Army troops were deployed to bring order to Detroit. Their presence, however, only seemed to escalate the anger.

Today, in our ongoing series "50 Years After the Fires," we'll hear the perspectives of two police officers—one black, one white—who were called into service during the uprising.

WARNING: This story contains language some may consider offensive and may not be appropriate for young listeners.

Ike McKinnon remembers the day he decided to become a police officer.

It wasn't an inspiring career day speech at his middle school, or an uplifting TV episode of "Dragnet."

It was the day four white Detroit cops took turns beating him up.

"I was 14 years old," McKinnon recalls. "I knew that someone had to stand up and do something for people like me and the minority community."

Racism in the Ranks

McKinnon turned his anger into ambition, joining the Detroit Police Department in 1965. On his first day on the force, McKinnon reported for roll call. He was the only African American in the room.

"They started calling names out for assignments," he says. "They got to this one officer, they called his name, and they said, 'McKinnon, 2-7.' At that point, this officer yelled out, '(expletive), I'm driving with the n*****.' And everybody started laughing."

Gene Wriggelsworth first donned his badge with the Michigan State Police in 1966. The young officer from rural Shiawassee County was stationed at Flat Rock, south of Detroit.

"We went up there on many trips to the Wayne County Jail," Wriggelsworth says. "So basically, it was a travel through the city where we dropped off prisoners, and returned. Didn't know much about the town."

In 1967, Officer McKinnon and Trooper Wriggelsworth were just starting their careers in public safety.

Six days in July would give each man a baptism by fire.

The Melee Erupts

"I was at home; I'd worked the midnight shift," Wriggelsworth remembers. "We got a call that said, 'Grab your riot helmet and nightstick and report to the Post. You're going to Detroit.' I followed the order thinking a few hours later we'd be home. We came home seven days later."

On the first night of the uprising, Officer McKinnon was driving home after an 18-hour shift. He was still in uniform when a Detroit police cruiser came up behind him.

"And so, I pulled over and they came up with their guns drawn, and I said, 'police officer,'" says McKinnon. "And I stepped out of my car, but I left the door open. The older officer said, 'Tonight, you're going to die,' and he used a racial epithet. It was like slow motion because I could see his hand on the gun and the trigger. As I dove back into the car he started shooting at me. I hit my accelerator with my right hand and steered the car with my left hand as they were shooting at me, and I drove off.

"If those officers were doing that to me as a fellow officer, what were they going to do on the streets of Detroit?"

As the violence exploded, it became clear the city police were overwhelmed.

Trooper Wriggelsworth soon found himself in the line of fire. Snipers had taken up positions in various places in the city.

"The thought that crossed my mind was, *I don't even know these people*," he says. "*What are they shooting at me for?*"

Through it all, Wriggelsworth never fired a shot.

"We had a number of bullets that bounced off the pavement in our area, but you couldn't see where they were coming from, and I'm not one that's just going to crank off a round just for the sport of it," he says.

Looting on Linwood

Ike McKinnon patrolled the streets in his squad car with his partner. On Linwood Street, they encountered a scene of mass looting. McKinnon was shocked when the police sergeant in charge gave a stern order.

"The sergeant stands up to all these people who are black," McKinnon says. "He says, 'G**** all you n*****s, get off this g****** street!' They all heard this guy, and they stopped looting. And I remember this one guy saying specifically, 'What the (expletive) did you just say?' And this guy; this sergeant repeated himself! And they started throwing bricks and bottles at us."

As days and nights wore on, the severity of the crisis in Detroit reached the White House. President Lyndon Johnson mobilized federal troops on July 25.

Assault with a Dangerous Weapon

On one occasion, Trooper Gene Wriggelsworth responded to a report of snipers in a particular building. As he searched for a suspect, a rare moment of levity emerged.

"We had him up on the wall," he remembers. "As I went through his pockets, my hand went into some slime that really made me think, *What have I got here?* He had a hamburger in his pocket, and my fingers went down between the bun and the pickles and all that stuff. And I kind of jumped, quite frankly. It startled me. Here were all these guys armed to the teeth and here I am with ketchup all over my fingers and everybody laughing at me!"

Conflict Fades, Careers Rise

By July 28, the violence had been quelled. The police and soldiers started to pull back. The tragedy in Detroit claimed 43 lives. . . 33 of which were African American.

Stunned, the Johnson administration commissioned a study to uncover the cause of the conflict. In 1968, the Kerner Commission bleakly concluded America was "moving towards two societies, one black, one white—separate and unequal."

The young police officers dispatched in Detroit went on to prosperous careers. Trooper Gene Wriggelsworth retired as sheriff of Ingham County. Officer Ike McKinnon rose to become Detroit's police chief and later, deputy mayor.

> For 50 years, historians have tried to pinpoint the angst that boiled over in the city that summer. For Ike McKinnon—the Detroit native—it's not hard to understand.
>
> "Can people understand what it's like to be demeaned every day, whether it's male or female or black or white or brown?" McKinnon asks. "To be demeaned every day or to be treated in such a way that you're de-humanized. That's the way that I was for all those years in the police department. But I knew that I was going to be there to try and make a difference."

Any career in law enforcement is going to be filled with surprises. I never expected that, within my first six months of service, I would be away from my family for five days in the middle of riots. As officers, we do what we need to so we can protect and serve our community. Every day offered a lesson and I learned something new. Each lesson built the next, and so on, which, unbeknownst to me, led to a larger career than I expected.

CHAPTER 5 LESSONS

1. When starting a new job or getting a promotion in your career, I learned it was best to listen more than talk, observe more than act, and respect everyone. You never know who your next supervisor will be or who will work for you some day.

2. There are a lot of troubled people in our society, and in most cases, they didn't arrive where they are on purpose. It helps you to seek to understand their plight first, see yourself in their shoes, and find out what you can do to serve them. There are some who have no interest in improving their life, and some are looking for a hand up. Be aware of those who need and want a hand up. You will change more lives that way and make the world a better place.

CHAPTER 6

A DAY IN THE LIFE OF A MICHIGAN STATE TROOPER

Gene Wriggelsworth at the East Lansing Michigan State Police Post 11. 1969.

THE BEST PART of being in law enforcement is that every day is different. One day, you are patrolling and writing tickets. Another day, you are chasing a suspect down I-75 through different states. The hardest days are those that involve deaths and notifying family members. The greatest days are those where we save a life. We must take the good with the bad and the ugly. The longer you are in this line of work, it doesn't get easier, but you do learn to handle and manage your emotions and reactions. Fortunately, we have each other to depend on, and we are never alone when we work within our own jurisdictions or with other states, counties, municipalities, and organizations like the FBI. We are united in our duty to protect and serve, and we do the best we possibly can each day, given each circumstance.

EACH DAY IS DIFFERENT

As a Michigan State Trooper, wearing the required uniform meant that we had to wear a hat, too. They still do. It's so problematic, especially when on the freeway. Inevitably, when a semitruck drove by, the hat flew off. It looked like a scene from the TV show *The Dukes of Hazzard*.

*****

The Alcohol, Tobacco, and Firearms Agency (ATF) partnered with the state every once in a while to reduce the trafficking of guns across the border from Ohio to Michigan. Back then, Ohio didn't have any restrictions on owning and carrying guns. Michigan required a gun permit for concealed carry, which you were required to have before you purchased a gun. However, if you bought them, say, in Ohio, without the Michigan permit, chances were you weren't going to get the permit. That's the illegal part of it.

Back then, gun shops in Toledo were like grocery shopping; you could buy anything you wanted. The ATF surveilled the customers at the store, and if the customer traveled towards Michigan, the ATF gave us the car make, model, and description of the people in the car. Once they came across the border, we pulled them over and arrested them. One day, I had 17 concealed weapon arrests!

We had a situation when the ATF guy announced over the radio, "We have a problem. This guy got on a bus with his purchase." An ATF agent followed him onto the bus and told us he was loading the gun on the bus. *Yes, loading the gun on the bus.* We pulled the Greyhound bus over, confiscated the gun, and arrested the guy. I don't know what he was going to do, but he was up to something.

*****

There was a woman who was raped, and I'll never forget her. First, her memorable name was "Miami Florida." I think it was so unusual because she was a dancer at a local bar in Southgate. One night, she was picked up by this guy near Flat Rock, and it turned out he was a pervert. She willingly joined him in the car and planned to have sex with this guy.

The second reason I'll never forget her is because she was smart. When they reached a gravel road, he pulled out a knife, and he planned to brutalize her. That's the kind of guy he was. She saw it wasn't going well. As they sat in the car with the motor running, he saw a car up the road and became confused. Miami Florida reached over, pushed down the gas pedal, and hit the car head on. Fortunately for her, it was the newspaper delivery guy. It was brilliant. It saved her life. Now, that's using your smarts.

*****

I had to go to Charlotte District Court for a preliminary exam on something important. Often, it was typical for defense attorneys to not show or leave us waiting. When I arrived, the judge was also waiting. I saw he was annoyed when he asked the defendant, "Where's your attorney?"

He replied, "I don't know."

The defendant called the attorney's secretary and learned that the attorney was in federal court in Grand Rapids. The judge called the federal court, who relayed they didn't have cases that day. So, then, the judge called the attorney's secretary and said, "If he's not here in one half hour, I'll hold him in contempt of court."

*****

We used to set up a lot of roadblocks in a blockade system here in Michigan for major crimes. For example, if a bank was robbed in Perry, they called out a signal tone, which notified us of something going on, and the blockade covered a 50-mile radius. The location for the blockade was in Shiawassee County.

One night, we had a bank robbery in Saginaw County which required blockades at routes M-52 and M-78. It was a cold, miserable winter day. Blockades only ran for an hour because if we didn't catch them by then, we didn't catch them.

When we covered the roadblock, our job was to block the street with our cars, stand there, and be on the lookout for the "red jeep" or whatever description they gave us until we heard the "all clear" tone. I never cared for this part of the job, but my partner was tickled pink every time. He was either on guard with the shotgun or checking cars, whichever one we felt like doing that day.

We heard the "all clear" tone, and we tore the blockade down as quickly as we could because we were frozen. Then we heard, "Saginaw County canceled. Blockade B, Adam B, Boston in effect for another hour."

That was our spot. That one extra hour of freezing weather made it even more miserable. In all the years I was in law enforcement, I knew troopers who caught suspects with blockades, but I never caught anyone.

*****

We arrested a prisoner for drunk driving. He was so drunk that he couldn't even stand up when we got him out of the car. We dragged him to the patrol car and drove him to the sheriff's office in Mason. Dale Wardwell was a great sergeant at the jail. Dale saw the prisoner was incapacitated and said, "That's okay. I'll book him here laying down."

And he did.

ON THE JOB HUMOR

Some days are harder than hard, and we do have moments where we need to lighten it up. To civilians, the following "humorous incidents" may be gross and uncouth. Please know the mask of humor isn't a sign of disrespect, but it helps us deal with any tough situation so we can do our job effectively and efficiently.

*****

We arrested a guy one night for drunk and disorderly conduct, a minor crime. As we read him his rights, he said in a British accent, "You can't arrest me."

"Why is that?" we asked.

"Because I'm a British citizen," he explained.

I wasn't sure about how being a foreign citizen had anything to do with getting arrested. Just by chance, the border patrol agent for the feds was down the road with the state police. I called him. "Hey, we have this guy here, and he says he's from Britain. Can you come check him out?"

The border patrol agent came over. He was so perfect, I had to hide my laugh. He asked, "Where are you from?"

Mr. Brit replied, "London."

The agent asked, "Did you grow up there?"

He replied, "I lived there my whole life."

The agent continued, "What's the statue in Piccadilly Square?"

He replied, "No clue. No clue."

The border patrol agent looked at me and said, "This guy's not from London. Arrest him."

*****

We had a fatal car versus pedestrian accident on West Road, not far from Telegraph Road. The victim didn't make it. In fact, he was hit so hard that it knocked him right out of his boots. His body was in one location, and his boots were maybe twenty feet in the opposite direction. My supervisor was on site, and as we took measurements and collected the evidence, he started singing "These Boots Are Made for Walkin'." That was one way to lighten up a gruesome and sad scene. It sure was a stress buster.

*****

Every year at graduation time, the high school seniors play a traditional prank on the City of Monroe. Driving down Telegraph Road takes you to downtown Monroe. There's a huge statue of General George Custer on a horse. He was from Monroe. Each year, the seniors paint the horse's balls blue, and it ends up being the topic of conversation at every coffee shop.

*****

One day, in broad daylight, we had a barricaded shooter. As we waited for the SWAT team, emergency vehicles, and personnel to get there, the guy shot off a gun and started screaming at us through the window, "Are you state troopers? My brother's a cop, and he says all troopers are good for is writing tickets and wiping your ass with them."

Clearly, he liked us a lot. We were there probably another half hour, and this guy shows up and introduces himself to me. "Hi, I'm his brother."

I asked, "You're a Detroit cop?"

"Yeah," he replied.

"We heard about you. Would you like one of my tickets to use in the bathroom?"

The look on his face was a Kodak moment; let me tell you.

*****

In the earlier years, when state troopers were transferred, the state had their own moving vans. The truck showed up, followed by a bunch of troopers who would move your stuff. The moving trooper just had to provide beer, so a crew of slightly inebriated troopers loaded the van, often in a disorderly fashion. The same happened at the new assignment where it was unloaded. It was a nice service they had, but now they use common carriers.

I think they changed it because of a particular incident. The state police post was at the major intersection of Telegraph Road and Huron River Drive, which is an uphill climb across Telegraph Road. A trooper's moving van drove up to get gas at the state police post. As he pulled out onto Telegraph Road, he didn't lock the fifth wheel of the trailer onto the tractor. The trailer came unhooked and crashed into the road. To this day, I don't know what was ruined, but it had to be a mess.

*****

The Flat Rock State Police was the first post on 1-75 after the state border. Each company that trucked cigarettes to Michigan had to stop at the post for us to check inventory. I never knew anything about this. One Sunday afternoon, I was on duty when a truck pulled up. The corporal on the desk says, "Hey, go out and count those cigarettes."

I do as I'm ordered. I'm out there crawling around in this truck with a clipboard. I wrote down how many Pall Malls, Chesterfields, and others.

I was out there a long time, and when I headed back in, he said, "Well, what took you so long?"

I replied, "It was a semi full of cigarettes."

He further explained, "All you had to do was go out, take a look, check the mark, and give them the receipts."

I felt like such a fool.

*****

The most senior trooper at the Flat Rock Post was an irascible bastard and did very little on the road. He took all the complaints, and he was good at investigating them. However, he never stopped cars because he didn't like to work traffic. When the post commander realized this, he said, "I want you to write at least one ticket on each shift."

About 20 minutes before his shift ended, he stopped a car for some stupid reason, and he wrote a ticket for not having a registration. On the bottom right of the ticket, he wrote, "panic ticket."

When the commander saw his comment, he called him to his office. They were both smokers. As the commander tried to chew him out for being an idiot, the trooper asked him for a cigarette from the commander and lit it. The commander yelled at him, and the trooper lit another cigarette, but now, he took them out of his own pocket. He did things like that just to screw with the commander.

*****

Near the Flat Rock Police Post, a railway switching yard has about 35 tracks on it. One night, fellow Trooper Terry Brenay and I were partners, and a freight train blocked a rural road. We sat there for five minutes, ten minutes, fifteen minutes. The trains aren't supposed to block a road for more than five minutes. We saw the caboose was about two cars down, so we knew the end was close. Cabooses were small train cars where an engineer was stationed to oversee the train from the back.

The train just sat there with no indication it was going to move. Terry had enough and walked over to bang on the caboose. He said, not so nicely, "Move this train."

The conductor asked, "Who are you?"

Terry replied, "I'm a state trooper."

The guy obviously didn't see Terry's uniform.

"You're going to move this train," Terry demanded.

The conductor grabbed his radio and called the engineer, "A guy back here says he's a state trooper, and we have to move the train."

Terry grabbed the radio, "I am a state trooper; now move the train."

Well, they didn't take kindly to Terry's demands and didn't move the train for another ten minutes. Not everyone is a fan of our work.

THE DAYS I'M ESPECIALLY GRATEFUL TO GOD

Many people have their own faith or spiritual practices, and some don't. For me, I go to church, I pray, and I believe in God. Personally, I think it's a must in our line of work, because we run into a lot of difficult cases and see the worst in humanity. When something does work out and seems miraculous, I attribute it to God's amazing grace. All of us need protection no matter what storm we are fighting.

*****

One night, during an ice storm, I policed a multi-vehicle crash site on I-96 at the big curve towards Grand Rapids. The roads were completely iced over, and when we arrived, there were wrecked cars everywhere. Being the brilliant trooper that I was, I noticed that the centrifugal force had pushed the cars up against the railing on the outside of the curb. There was a bit of bank where the road turned. To be safe, I parked my patrol car on the inside of the curve beside a wrecked car to check on them.

I walked up to the driver and passenger, who were a rabbi and his wife. I instructed, "Have a seat in my car, and I'll write your accident report."

The wife replied angrily, "I'm not getting in your car. You'll get hit."

I politely replied, "No, I'm parked off the side here, and I'm on the inside."

She shook her head, "No, I'm not getting in that car."

Annoyed, I said, "All right, go stand on the other side of the guard rail."

As I wrote the accident report beside them on the other side of the guard rail, I saw a flicker in my peripheral vision. When I looked up, the car swerved, and *bam!* It hit the back of my patrol car.

The wife started in on me. "I told you so!"

That rabbi sure had some good connections with the divine!

*****

We used to have a lot of groups tour the state police post. The Cub Scouts came to earn a patch, and a trooper was in charge of showing them the various weapons. He showed them a shotgun, a pistol, and a 30-caliber rifle. As he carefully showed them each weapon, he pointed the shotgun up towards the ceiling and pretended to shoot it. Well, it went off and blew a hole in the ceiling. The plaster rained down on the kids, and he just kept talking like it was part of the demonstration.

"Next, we have a gas gun," as if nothing happened.

The gun wasn't supposed to be loaded, and we were very glad no one was injured. Back then, it was different times, for sure. In today's culture, the scouts' parents might sue, and the trooper might have been transferred. The scouts should have received two patches that day.

*****

A trooper friend of ours has a son who was also a trooper. The whole family are really good people. When the dad worked the midnight shift, he arrested a juvenile, handcuffed him, and put him in the back of the patrol car. When he arrived at the state police post at the end of his shift, he reported to the shift commander, "I have a prisoner in that car out there. You need someone to take him to the juvenile center. He's handcuffed."

The same day, around 11:00 in the morning, one of the lieutenant colonels barged through the door of the post with fire flying out of his (expletive). "There's been a prisoner in the back of that car for hours."

Thank God it wasn't summer, and the prisoner was unharmed.

*****

Our jobs are wrought with the bad stuff, so we always need to remember to celebrate the good stuff. On I-75, a stolen car hightailed it from Toledo into Michigan. A semitruck had pulled off the road for whatever reason. The driver of the stolen car drove right into the back of the semi without ever hitting its brakes. I don't know if they fell asleep, didn't see it, or thought that was the direction of the road. The impact just demolished the car.

We arrived on the scene, and it was just terrible. People's bodies were mangled, a woman's head was missing, just awful as can be. As we waited for the records and evidence to be collected, a group of us were talking.

"You hear that?" one of us said.

"What?" another replied.

"I think I hear a baby crying."

Quickly, we grabbed and set up the extraction kit. Miraculously, there was a baby who had been in the back seat of that car. When the car hit the truck, it drove that baby under the front seat of the car! The baby was still alive—injured, but is likely still living today. Thankfully, some days, there are unexpected miracles!

*****

The "Detroit Dragway" is just down the street from a gas station. The local kids treated it as a drag strip with a quarter mile raceway. Every Sunday, they raced away. So, if we wanted to get a bunch of easy tickets, we hung out on Sibley Road. Those guys would rip down a 30 mile per hour zone at 90 miles per hour. That was on a Sunday in the summertime. We were always grateful they didn't have any crashes. They were lucky.

*****

In 1968, we had the Martin Luther King riots, and I answered a call to go to the state line on I-75. "You'll meet some Ohio state troopers down there."

They had a march headed from Ohio to Detroit. I drove down, and much to my surprise, they were walking on the freeway. I couldn't believe it. At the same time as I arrived, the Ohio State Police arrived. By then, there were about 500 marchers on the right lane as far as they could get. Traffic was whizzing past them. It was a dangerous situation.

One of the men marching wore bib overalls with captain's bars and was apparently the captain in charge of the marchers. I politely introduced myself and explained I would be their patrol car escort to Detroit. Luckily, I didn't have to walk. We crept along the freeway while these people marched behind me for about three hours. After being involved in the Detroit Riots, it was a much better experience to protect peaceful protestors.

*****

Chasing speeders on I-75 was kind of interesting, because I-75 goes all the way to Florida. Once the driver was south of Monroe County, he was in another state. Occasionally, we chased them into Ohio and called ahead for assistance. It was always a little uncomfortable breaching a jurisdiction where you don't have any power, but considering the possibility of such circumstances, the state police have already worked out those issues.

*****

And, yes, it is by God's amazing grace that the worst didn't happen to these people and so many others who have lived through some of the most horrifying moments in their lives. I'm especially thankful to God for the wonderful life Sandy and I have, and the safety and health of all our family and friends. We are indeed blessed every day.

CHAPTER 6 LESSON

You are going to meet people you like, dislike, love, and hate. Hate is a strong word. Learn to control yourself when you work with or for someone you don't like or get along with. If you must . . . bite your tongue, count to ten, take a walk, do it. It's not worth the risk of getting written up or tarnishing your own reputation.

CHAPTER 7

UNFORGETTABLE AS A
MICHIGAN STATE TROOPER

Anti-war protests on Grand River Avenue in East Lansing. 1972.

TELEGRAPH ROAD USED to be the Main North Road before they put in the freeway. They called it "Bloody Telegraph" because it was a four-lane road, and it was just brutal. About three or four miles along Telegraph Road, south of the state post, there was a Nike missile base. Nike missiles were one of the early anti-aircraft missiles. Occasionally, when you drove by, there were Nike missiles pointed in the air. We were told they were testing their mechanical functions. It was weird and cool at the same time. I suppose the Nike shoe brand was inspired by the name of this missile base.

LOST BUT FOUND

On Old M-78, now I-69, I came across a group of motorcycles on this four-lane road with two lanes in each direction. There were about ten or fifteen of them riding their loud bikes. The front driver didn't have a muffler, so it was even louder. I was on the other side, so I whipped the car around, pulled up alongside them, and passed all of them until I reached the front guy. I pointed out for him to pull over.

Suddenly, in my rearview mirror, I saw all the bikers pull over, and I thought, *This could get interesting.* I called for backup and stepped up to the driver and asked for his license. A big, burly motorcycle guy walked up in his leather jacket and asked, "What did you pull us over for?"

I replied, "I didn't pull 'us' over, I pulled him over. You all followed him over here."

As I glanced at his coat, I asked him, "Are you a deputy in Valparaiso?"

He shook his head. "No."

And I grabbed my handcuffs. "You are under arrest for impersonating a deputy sheriff."

On his jacket, he wore a deputy sheriff's badge from Valparaiso County, Indiana.

I had to haul him to the state police post, so I took a chance that the guys wouldn't try to prevent me from making the arrest. They didn't. Surprisingly, they all followed me into the post with this guy in tow.

I called the Valparaiso County Sheriff's Office, told him about the badge, and he said, "Oh, my God. They were just down here to bond a guy out of a ticket. When they left, they must have grabbed the deputy's badge off his coat that was hanging on a hook."

The deputy didn't even notice it was gone yet. The really odd part about it was the prosecutor wouldn't issue a warrant for his arrest, since he just wore the badge without claiming he was a deputy sheriff. He was lucky.

*****

I used to meet two friends for coffee or breakfast on the east side of town at a restaurant called the M78 Truck Stop. It was usually two or three in the morning. We all hung our coats on the rack, and one morning, as we were leaving, we noticed one of the coats was gone. We couldn't find it anywhere, and we were concerned because it had Trooper Duane Wheat's name and badge on it.

Fast forward to the next fall, when students were back at school. East Lansing PD was driving down an alley behind McDonald's, off Cedar Street. There stood this student wearing a Michigan State Police jacket. The East Lansing Officer walked towards him. "Excuse me. Are you a trooper?"

"No," he replied.

"Well, you're under arrest."

So, he's arrested, and the prosecutor said, "Well, we're not issuing a warrant because there's no way to prove that the jacket came out of inventory. How do you prove that jacket was state police-issued?"

The officer replied, "It says 'State Police' on it, and the badge has the trooper's number."

The prosecutor refused to issue the warrant, and the director of the state police was soon involved. He advised the prosecutor, "If you don't issue, I will call the Attorney General."

Guess what? They issued.

*****

One day, when we were working at the post, one of the troopers used the men's room. The lieutenant had just used the men's room before him, and, to free up his hands, he placed his gun on the back of the toilet. This trooper found the gun and knew exactly what happened. When he came out of the restroom, he walked over to where three of us stood by the sergeant's desk. The trooper announced, "Hey, I don't know what's going on. Somebody up here left their gun on the back of the toilet, and it looks like it's a lieutenant's gun."

You could say it was a "Kodak moment."

*****

EXTRACURRICULAR ACTIVITIES

One night, I was assigned to patrol around the State Capitol of Michigan. At two in the morning, I noticed a light on in one of the offices. When I walked into the office, I saw that the state representative was hosting a romantic interlude with his secretary. He wasn't happy that I was so bold as to enter his office, but I told him, "That's my job."

His wife was not happy when she found out about it, but I wasn't the one that told her.

*****

In Lansing Township, there was a bank robbery just before closing time at 3:30 p.m. They sent me. "Go patrol the area and see if you can find the stolen car."

I drove around the railroads, and I found some tire tracks where a car drove off the road. I followed it, walked up to the windows, and it was the mail carrier and some female in a compromising position. They seemed to be a bit too occupied to have robbed the bank.

What does Forest Gump say? "Life is a box of chocolates. You never know what you are going to get." It's true, especially for police work.

*****

Lieutenant Dick Coleman, a friend of mine, was an undercover guy. One night, he worked the Michigan State campus to get intelligence on student rioters to identify assembling points and hear what was being said about plans to burn down a building and shoot cops.

All of a sudden, someone shouted, "Hey! I think that guy's a cop!"

They chased him clear across campus to his car. Dick jumped into his car, and as he tried to leave, the kids raced to the back of the car and lifted the back wheels off the ground so Dick couldn't reverse. But Dick was a bit of a genius. He started his car, put it in reverse gear, and revved it as fast as it would go. The tires were rolling, and the students couldn't hold it up anymore. They begged, "Please take your foot off the gas."

If he didn't, he would have run into them as soon as they put the car down. That's called "thinking on your feet," for sure.

Dick was a lieutenant at the time, and unfortunately, they chased him because they didn't want him knowing anything about their plans. I don't know what they were going to do to him; beat him up or kill him. I mean, who knows? But you never want your cover blown. These are the types of scary situations law enforcers get into every day. We always have to keep our head on a swivel and be ready to take action.

*****

Two troopers reported to work at 4:00 p.m. and noticed one of the post commanders leaving. The one trooper said, "Nice to be the boss and leave whenever you want."

Since it was nighttime, there were two officers in a car, so he and his partner jumped in the patrol cars to start their shift. As they drove through the small downtown area of Munising, they saw the commander at a pay phone. They said to each other, "That's bizarre. He just left the post. Why is he at a phone booth?"

There happened to be a local phone company down the street where we used to pay our bills (Remember, it's the 1960s). They walked in and one of the troopers asked the desk attendant, "There's a phone call coming from that phone booth down the street there. Where's it going?"

The operator replied, "Your house."

Everyone was taken aback.

Turns out, the boss was having an affair with this trooper's wife. He waited an hour, went home, and caught him in the act. He was required to attend what they called a "deputy director's hearing." The commander walked into the hearing with a Bible under his arm. Like that was going to save him. I, personally, thought you needed to read and practice what it preaches, not just carry it around. He ended up getting demoted to trooper. I thought he should have lost his job. The poor trooper was transferred even though he didn't do anything wrong.

*****

THINK AGAIN

On I-75, near Southgate, a semitruck was stopped on the side of the road. It was sitting there and running, so I grew curious about the driver. I figured he was doing something stupid or may have been dead. I jumped up on the step while cars zoomed by at high speed and peered through his window. He was slumped over the steering wheel. I wanted to make sure he wasn't dead. I opened the door, reached in to shake him. *Bam*, he swung at me and hit me. Clearly, he wasn't dead, yet. Since I disturbed him, I didn't write a ticket, but I did tell him, "Don't sleep on the side of the road. Next time, go to a rest stop or truck stop."

*****

A call came in from a guy on I-75 who said, "I noticed a car in front of me that suddenly veered off. He hit the median and went out of sight."

This particular freeway median was probably a half-mile wide and heavily wooded. We went to check it anyway, and found they had a stolen car chop shop set up inside the trees on the median. Motors and car parts hung on the trees; they were a well-oiled operation with easy entrances and exits. It was a smart setup, and still illegal. We broke it up, and once again were reminded that people will try anything. It's always good to say something if you see something. Many of the tips we receive from citizens are from people who recognized that something didn't look right and called it in. We always play it safe rather than sorry.

*****

There was a big factory just outside of Flat Rock that manufactured human-sized mannequins. There was a lot of wood and flammable material inside because of the lacquers and other stuff they used in making their products. One night, the factory caught fire at oh dark thirty. When we arrived on scene, it was an inferno. The back part of it and the office up front weren't on fire yet, but it wasn't far from it. The owner and his wife were there watching. She was crying because Fifi (not her real name; protected for her privacy), the dog, was still in the office.

So, my partner, the hero that he was, ran in and retrieved Fifi. We finished our shift and headed back to the post about the same time as the post commander walked in. My partner addressed the commander, "Can I talk to you?"

"Yeah," the commander said.

My partner explained, "I want you to know that we had a fire last night."

"Yeah. They called me at home and told me about it."

"The owner was really happy because we saved her dog. I wondered if you would want to put me in for an award for it."

Turning red, the commander tried to keep his cool. "Put you in for an award? For saving a freaking dog? I ought to trial board you. Do you know how much. . . You know how much we've got invested in you? And you go into a burning building to save a dog?"

I guess he wasn't going to get that award. Rookies, take note: don't run into a burning building to save pets!

*****

One of my many bosses was a major in the state police, and he was a great guy. They called him "Black Dan." He was about as mean as he looked, and I don't think I ever saw the guy smile. But I loved him, and I'll tell you why. He spoke to us at a recruit school graduation. He said, "I'm going to tell you all something right now. When it comes to officer safety, I would rather be tried by twelve than carried by six. Remember that."

*****

A gas station on Telegraph and Sibley Roads near Flat Rock was owned by George Corder. It was a typical gas station with a two-bay station, and on the side, he fixed cars. The poor guy had been robbed on numerous occasions. He was sick of it, so he put a bed in the back of the station to spend the night, and he had a shotgun. We received a call one night, "Go to George Corder's gas station. He just shot and killed a guy."

Sure enough, these guys came through the front door, and he let them have it.

*****

MURDERS

In 1970, I received a call on a Saturday around 3:00 in the afternoon. I drove over to meet a guy in Holt because he found a body in this field. Her name was Marie. We walked to the wooded area off the road, and a naked woman laid there on the ground. Her bra was the only clothing around, and it was up around her neck. It was still cool outside, so decomposition hadn't started, but an animal did take some of her nose. I called the dispatch, "I need the detectives and crime lab out here."

It was a sad sight. And when we are in this line of work, it's always hard to see another human who has died. However, we do grow immune to what other people would call gross and disgusting. We're used to it. The most important part is solving the crime. Who is she? How did she get here? Who did this to her? That's what I was focused on.

Around 4:00 p.m., the crime lab arrived and everyone assembled. I'm always in awe of these guys because they are the ones who catch the bad guys. Watching them is interesting. They reach a whole other level in their roles as they see the worst of the worst and have to handle all the evidence. So, they are even more immune to the gravity of the situation. But it still shocked me that when they arrived, they put a boombox on the hood of the car to listen to the rest of the Michigan vs. Ohio State game. Distraction can help with emotions, for sure. For you young people, a boombox is a portable stereo that plays cassette tapes, CDs, live music, news, and sports from the local radio stations.

They finished collecting the evidence as it was getting dark, and the team filed it to start searching for the perpetrator, or "perp." I was called to report back to the post, and when I arrived, two bigwigs from the university police walked right up to me, got in my face, and said, "What the — are you doing on our property? That's our side."

My boss just sat there and didn't say anything. He let me take the ass chewing.

"I apologize," I replied, "There wasn't a fence; no sign. Nothing was around that said it was university property. How would I know?"

They eventually backed off.

Unfortunately, the case of this poor woman who was murdered was cold for more than 25 years. At that time, my friend Jim Dunlap became chief of police at MSU, and I was the sheriff. We received a tip that the guy might be down in Florida. The team reached out to authorities, but it turned out that he died in jail or prison. They had his DNA in the system, and it was a match. It was long overdue, but for loved ones, this result is always bittersweet. At least it offered them some closure. Hopefully, it helped Marie rest in peace.

*****

TRAGIC

I'll never forget the call we received one afternoon from a dad. His son came home from school and went to take a shower. The dad called because he had been in there a half hour. He checked on him but couldn't get the door open. He kicked the door open and found his son lying on the floor. He had put a belt around his neck and hung it off the door.

When I arrived on the scene, the son was lying on the bathroom floor. I dragged him out to the hall and started CPR on him even though his body was already cold. I was pretty sure we had already lost him. He was only fifteen, just a kid. There I was, working on this young kid who was naked as a jaybird while I waited for the ambulance to get there. This was an apparent autoerotic death. Then, I saw his mother coming down the hallway, and I just about lost it. Can you imagine seeing your son like that? I'll never forget her facial expression.

The worst part of social media and the internet is that the kids don't even know what they are doing or the tragedy they cause. As a kid, I never even knew what an autoerotic act was, not to mention autoerotic asphyxiation, and that death would result. Whether it's that kind of death, or dying from trying a drug that's laced with fentanyl, or pulling a prank on a friend that goes too far, these kids are just too young to die. They don't realize the finality of the decisions they make until it's too late. And that's the saddest part. No parent should have to bury their child.

SUICIDES

During my second year as a state trooper, there was a major summer thunderstorm, one that sent lightning strikes across the sky. A farmer complained about a pickup truck parked in his bean field. I arrived on the scene with a partner who was senior to me by five years. As we approached the truck, we noticed the driver's side door was open. The man had shot himself in the side of the head, so the left side of his body hung out of the truck secured by his seatbelt. The rain and the heat of the hot summer day accelerated decomposition; there had to be 6,000 mosquitoes on his open head wound. One of his eyes bulged out. Those types of images were seared into my mind then and are still unforgettable.

While we waited for the coroner, the trooper and I inspected his body and the car. The rain came down hard, thunder erupted, and lightning crashed around us. We returned to our patrol car. Suddenly, the largest lightning bolt strike I ever saw in my life lit up the sky, and the man's face lit up like a horror movie. Both of us big, strong, and brave state troopers there on the scene, armed with our guns, nearly jumped out of our own skin. My partner reached over and locked the door.

*****

A couple who lived in a large house in a very ritzy subdivision fell into really hard times. They lost their business, had to file bankruptcy, and were selling their house. They had a showing at noon with a realtor. While cleaning up the house, the husband took the trash out. We believed, on a whim, he opened the trunk of his car, saw his .22, climbed inside the trunk of his car, and shot himself in the mouth. The house was so large that no one heard the shot. The wife couldn't find him, searched everywhere, and finally found him in the garage. She was beside herself. It was a horrific scene and a very difficult tragedy.

PROGRESS IS GOOD

Wayne County Jail in downtown Detroit used to be like something out of a movie. We called it "The Catacombs." Once in the building, we surrendered our guns and locked them in a locker. Then, we started the walk down the stairway to the elevator, and then went down another hallway. It was a never-ending maze, which likely made it impossible for prisoners to know how to escape. I never knew if I would ever get out of there.

*****

When I was at the post, we had 1967 Ford patrol cars, and they had a louder muffler system on them than most hot rods. It was embarrassing. When we drove through Flat Rock on Telegraph Road, the noise echoed off the mirrors and the windows of buildings. They were high-performance engines, and I think they needed a less restrictive muffler system to make them high-performance. Those Fords went up to 120 miles per hour, and we had a Plymouth with a speedometer that showed 140 miles per hour.

As a trooper, I went on many high-speed chases, and 120 miles per hour is way too fast, even though I drove at that speed many times. When driving that fast, my blood pressure increased to the point where I could feel it, and the pressure sucked the windows out of the patrol car a little bit. With all the wind noise, we never heard the radio. I would never drive that way today, and I'm really glad the speedometers are not set at 140 mph anymore.

Our modern-day traffic doesn't provide space for safe driving at those speeds. Our training taught us that to have control, we were to drive at 80% of our capabilities. If we drove at 100% of our capabilities, we would get in a wreck. In high-speed chases, tunnel vision is a problem because the focus is on the car running through traffic in all directions. It's easy to lose sight of what is in your peripheral vision, and you need to be cognizant of everything in all directions. I took part in many high-speed chases and never wrecked. To tell you the truth, I can't remember anyone who escaped from me.

It is crazy. Even back then, I would never do 140. If you hit a deer at 140, you're going to die. Even if you hit a pheasant, 140 miles per hour can kill you if the bird goes through the window.

*****

The LEIN system, which stands for the Law Enforcement Information Network, has been implemented nationwide. If I stopped you today for speeding, I could run your plate in LEIN and get reports on whether it's a stolen vehicle, whether you're wanted for an arrest, and a lot of other information. It's tremendously increased our safety and subject awareness before we even exit our patrol cars.

Like most subjects mentioned in this book, we didn't have LEIN or any similar technology when I started. When we pulled someone over or saw something suspicious, we called it in on the police radio. Then, dispatch looked it up and told us what they knew. Worse was that when we left for patrol, they gave us a "stolen car sheet" on paper which came from East Lansing. All stolen cars were phoned into the State Police Headquarters, who distributed a list. It sounds pretty archaic now. What's even worse was that it was always 8-12 hours behind. When we pulled a car over, we had to call it in to dispatch and check our stolen car sheet. I never had any stolen vehicles, but it was great progress when LEIN came on deck.

*****

Justices of peace were elected officials, and they were everywhere. Every township had one, and some had two or three. They were considered the first step before the judge. Each time we wrote a ticket, we had to send them to the JOP for a little hearing. If we had a suspect arrested for felonies, they would go before the JOP to determine whether they would get kicked up to the circuit court.

They did away with JOPs when they changed to the district court system in Michigan. It was antiquated, and the people didn't have the background to hold hearings. Today, when people talk about going to the JOP to get married, they actually go before a magistrate judge in Michigan.

TRANSFERRED TO NEXT POST

My first transfer was due in late 1968. Per the process, I was asked to submit eight location requests for my next transfer in rank order of preference. The word around the post was to put your first choice last, so I tried to tailor my list with psychological prowess. I listed the East Lansing Post as number eight, my last preference.

My partner and I had just finished a stop, and I was writing the notes. The radio came on with an announcement. I wasn't paying attention, so when my partner finished the call on the radio, he hung up the phone and said, "You just got transferred to East Lansing."

"What?" I asked.

"Yeah." He kept saying, "You're transferred to East Lansing. You're transferred to East Lansing."

I hoped he was right because nothing would make Sandy and me happier.

CHAPTER 7 LESSON

The hardest part of your job will be the losses you endure. Each one of us deals with grief differently. There are books to help you process grief, there are therapists to help you deal with grief, and so many other resources. No matter which paths you choose, just be sure that you keep yourself from stuffing it all down and ignoring it.

CHAPTER 8

IN MEMORIAM

THE ULTIMATE SACRIFICE, 1966–1974

AGAIN, I CANNOT express the impact we experience when one of our officers is injured or killed. There just are not enough words.

During my 22 years as a Michigan State Trooper and undercover officer, I lost many law enforcement friends and colleagues.

Back on New Year's Eve in 1971, two of our troopers were shot on the same day. Trooper Charley Stark and I were in the Troopers Association together. He and his partner, Trooper Gary Rampy, pulled over a suspected drunk driver who pulled into a citizen's driveway. Charley walked to the driver's door to get his license. The driver pulled his gun on Trooper Stark, and both troopers were tragically killed during this traffic stop.

The resident of the driveway they pulled their car into opened his door, turned on the outdoor house lights, and shouted, "Hey, what's going on there?"

Then he saw the gunfire and called the state police post. "I think two of your troopers just got shot in my front yard."

The suspect and his girlfriend, who sat in the passenger seat, took off down Red Arrow Highway. Down the road, the driver realized that the trooper he just shot still had his driver's license. So, he turned around to retrieve it.

Well, that was a dumb mistake, because the other troopers were driving at 120 miles an hour towards the scene and his escape route. They came in so fast that as the bad guy pulled away from the scene for the second time, the troopers couldn't stop their cars quickly enough. They flew past the scene, and as soon as they could, turned around, caught up to him, and rammed into his car. The guy jumped out of the car and took off running. During the chase, they shot and killed him.

They returned to their cars. One trooper had stayed back to grab the girl and arrest her. He threw her in the back of the patrol car. While they were tying up the details, she started climbing over the front seat of that patrol car to get the trooper's shotgun out of the boot. To this day, state police don't have cages in their cars to separate the front from the back. They may want to rethink that. Fortunately, she didn't get it unlocked.

Both Charley's and Gary's funerals were on the same day. Charley's services were in Muskegon. His dad was a minister, and he wrote and read the eulogy. About a thousand police from all over the country attended that day. At the end, the minister said, "Now as for the man who shot my son, I think he got what he had coming."

It was odd to hear the minister say that, but it made me want to stand up and applaud him.

Trooper Gary T. Rampy, age 27, served the Michigan State Police for five years and seven months, and Trooper Charles Stark, age 32, served the Michigan State Police for seven years and six months. Their watches to protect and serve ended on December 31, 1971. They were both survived by their wives, children, and loved ones.

Trooper Charles Stark's funeral. 1971.

*****

On his first day back at work after a family vacation, Trooper Steven B. DeVries of the Michigan State Police Niles Post pulled a driver over for a traffic violation on October 12, 1972.[20] Since the bank alarm hadn't sounded yet, he was completely unaware that this was the suspect who just robbed a bank. When he walked up to the driver's door, the suspect pulled a gun on him and shot him in the chest, stomach, and leg. Then, he escaped down the road.

The "Officer Down Memorial Page" reported on the tragic incident:

> Responding officers found that during the course of the stop, Trooper DeVries had written the man's name and address on a note pad which provided the details which led to his arrest. Not only was he the suspect in a bank robbery but had kidnapped the owner of the vehicle who was restrained in the trunk during the shooting.[21] The suspect was sentenced to life, escaped on March 21, 1975, and was captured by FBI agents in Los Angeles three weeks later. He escaped prison again in 1987; later that same year, he was shot and killed by deputies in Mississippi following another bank robbery.[22]

Equally shocking to all of us was that the newspaper printed the photo of Trooper DeVries lying on the pavement surrounded by blood after his shooting. They usually don't print what I consider private and intrusive photos. We need to remember that this man was a son, a husband, a father, a friend, and a trooper. He was loved. I hate to think of how horrible it must have been for the family to see that on the front page of the paper.

When we confronted the paper about it, the editor-in-chief justified it with a reply in the following day's paper saying something to the effect of, "we do not regret printing this photo because we hope it prompts justice to be done." Sure, that's one way to look at it, and justice was served in the end, but I still can't get the picture out of my head. If I was his wife or family, I know I wouldn't ever want to see it.

SANDY

"So many people assume that I was most worried when Gene was undercover and going on raids. I was never worried, because they over-planned for every single scenario for weeks or months before they kicked in the door. It was when he was on patrol throughout the state that I worried most. Just like how we lost Trooper DeVries, some fool could pull a gun on him at any time without Gene even knowing. The grieving of our lost officers is the hardest part of Gene's job for both of us, and we don't ever forget them or their families."

Trooper Steven B. DeVries was killed at the age of 32. He served and protected our state of Michigan until Thursday, October 12, 1972. He is survived by his wife and two young sons. Part of US 12 was renamed in his honor on May 19, 2016.[23]

*****

My good friend Larry Forreider was also a state trooper who I worked with at the Flat Rock Post. He started as a rookie, maybe one or two recruit schools after me. He was such a great guy. Sandy and I became good friends with him and his wife, Betty. He was transferred to Alpena. In those days, we didn't have issued body armor like we do now.

Before Christmas, he and his partner pulled over a car for a defective taillight at 2:30 in the morning. Larry approached the driver's side, and his partner approached the passenger's side. His partner observed a gun, and before the troopers could have the subjects exit the car, the driver retrieved a second gun and opened fire. Even though Larry was struck twice in the chest,[24] he still pulled out his own gun, shot all his bullets into the car, and struck one of the subjects. Unfortunately, they drove away. However, luckily, the team captured them within a few minutes. To add to this tragedy and heartbreak, his wife had a bulletproof vest for him that was wrapped under the Christmas tree.

Michigan State Police Trooper Larry Lee Forreider's tour was seven years, and his watch to protect and serve ended on December 5, 1974, at age 33. He is survived by his wife, two children, parents, two brothers, and three sisters.

CHAPTER 8 LESSON

We often say "life is too short," and it is. In law enforcement, I can't stress the devastation we endure when our coworker wakes up one day and doesn't make it home the same night. The lives of their loved ones will never be the same. And it happens in other fields, too. That's why I firmly believe it's worth making the effort to never go to bed angry, never end an argument without an apology, share your love and feelings with everyone you care about, and always kiss and/or hug goodbye. Be grateful every morning you are gifted another day, and every evening you make it home.

PART 3

22 Years
as a Michigan State
Trooper, Undercover

Years 9 through 22

Undercover Supervisor
for the
Tri-County Metro Narcotic Squad

1974–1988

Undercover

Sergeant | Lieutenant

CHAPTER 9

DAD AND HUSBAND BY DAY/DRUG BUSTER BY NIGHT

Gene's new style for Tri-County Metro Narcotic Squad. Mid-1970s.

Goofy photo of Gene; Gene's code name in Narcotics was "Goofy."

Gene's Lucious Locks, Tri-County Metro Narcotic Squad. Late 1970s.

1968–1972
EAST LANSING STATE POLICE POST, MSP TROOPER
(HEADQUARTERS)
1972–1974
EATON COUNTY STATE POLICE POST, MSP TROOPER
(TROOPERS RELOCATED FROM HEADQUARTERS)

Flat Rock was home for Sandy and me for two years. In 1968, my partner had been right about preference order for location transfers. I was transferred to the East Lansing State Police Post. Hallelujah! We were both very happy to know we would be near our families again. Sandy was ecstatic because we figured they would send us further away again.

During reassignment, there were lots of arrangements to make. Sandy stayed in Flat Rock until we found a house in East Lansing, and I lived in a single house at the post for transferred troopers. I bunked with six to eight guys again. It was impossible to sleep while everyone worked different shifts. It was like being in a hospital, where sleep is pretty much nonexistent.

It was very difficult being a long-distance couple and away from my family for three months. As soon as I received my paychecks, I knew Sandy needed the money in Flat Rock, so I mailed them to her.

When we called Sandy's parents to announce my transfer, they were very happy, too. Sandy's mom and stepdad suggested we look at houses in a brand-new subdivision.

"They look nice. I think they're affordable," Sandy's mother explained.

The next day, we found a house where we knew Sandy could easily make a home for our expanding family. She was always good at making our houses a home. We went to the real estate office to sign the papers with all the money we had: $500.

As we sat there in the real estate office, the secretary stuck her head in and said, "Gene Wrigglesworth? Major Avery is on the phone and wants to talk to you."

I thought, *That's not good. Majors never call state troopers.*

In the end, he was the major in charge of transfers. I picked up the phone, and he asked, "You sign anything?"

"Yes, sir. I signed for a new house, and I put every nickel I had down with it."

"Let me call you right back." He called me right back, and said, "We've sent someone else to Flat Rock, and you'll get to stay there."

Well, good, I thought, because moving to Lansing really buoyed Sandy's spirits. Her mother and stepdad were close, her dad was in Muskegon, and she had a lot of friends in the local area. I would have been hard-pressed to tell her we were moving back to Flat Rock.

In September of 1968, Sandy and I settled in Holt and expanded our family. We had two more sons to keep Mike company: Scott and Mark. Sandy was at home alone with the kids a lot. Mike was only about two when we moved into the new house. In 1970, Scott was born, and in 1975, Mark was born. Two-thirds of my shifts were afternoons and nights. I worked one of three different shifts, and the sequence changed every month: 8 p.m. to 4 a.m.; 4 p.m. to 12 a.m.; or 12 a.m. to 8 a.m. Sandy probably would not admit this, but it was hard on her, understandably so.

SANDY

The school I attended did not allow me to continue my studies since I was pregnant with Mike. Thank goodness times have changed since then. It was frustrating because I still had nine months of classes to complete, plus student teaching.

The boys were young, and there was no way I was going to leave them. When the time came, I went back to college, and Gene covered the kids for me. For student teaching, I was assigned to a school in Mason to teach fourth and fifth grade. My biggest fear was that I would get some young twenty-something as my mentor teacher, telling me what to do. It was hard enough to go back to college as a forty-year-old. I didn't think I could handle a mentor younger than me.

Fortunately, Mr. Berger, a wonderful gentleman, was two years older than me. He taught fourth and fifth grade. Later in my career, I ended up getting a split class (combined classes) one year, and it was just wonderful having that experience behind me on how to run a classroom. I enjoyed it thoroughly.

After I received my degree, I started substitute teaching. I applied for several open positions but was never hired. At the end of every interview, I asked if there was a conflict of interest since my husband was on the school board. I interviewed in front of all eight principals. Only one principal had a problem with it, and he nixed me every time. But I didn't know that was the situation, so my self-esteem kind of went into the toilet during the three years I subbed. I couldn't understand why I wasn't being hired. Then, when Gene was elected sheriff, I was hired as a full-time teacher. Interesting, yes?

Actually, I was hired in a hurry by my principal who I loved. We had so much fun. It was a wonderful 20-year career. It really was. My financial contribution helped get my boys through college and enabled me to have a life outside of doing monotonous housekeeping.

I didn't realize that Gene's position as sheriff would impact my life and career so much while in a school setting. It was so funny because, at lunch, people would ask, "Sandy, what's happening over on 'such and such' corner? It looks like they're tearing down a house."

I had to remind them, "We are not in the building department. My husband is the sheriff, and I only know about law enforcement issues."

They kept asking. So, I said to the group, "On the first Monday of every month, you may submit to me, in writing, a question. And I will bring you a written response. I really don't want to spend my lunch talking about what crime is going on in the community."

My teaching experience was wonderful. In my last year, I don't know if they were handpicked for me or not, but they were wonderful girls and wonderful boys. We had so many great times. I took on things like safety patrol, student council, anything extra I could, because I really enjoyed the time with them. I still encounter my students all over the place. When I hear "Mrs. Wriggelsworth," I know that I've had them in school. That makes me smile every time.

BUILD AND LEVERAGE RELATIONSHIPS

Since East Lansing was Michigan State Police Headquarters, all the divisions were together in one complex. It was the only post where all the "big shots" were mixed in with the troopers. I didn't think I would like the culture because we saw the director of the state police and his underlings everywhere. Pretty soon, they were calling me "Gene" when they saw me at the gas pump and in town. It seemed very informal.

However, I learned soon that, just like in any career, building relationships is important for a healthy career and future opportunities. It became a great benefit to meet, spend time with, and get to know the people at headquarters.

When the state police post opened in Owosso, the major in charge of transfers approached me one day and asked, "Aren't you from Owosso?"

"Yes." I replied.

"I heard that you want to go?" he insisted.

I chuckled. "No, I like it here."

So, it was that kind of contact I wouldn't have been able to circumvent without being at headquarters.

The conversations and connections forged the beginnings of my reputation and recognition by the higher-ups.

PATROL

My first patrol in East Lansing marked me as the target for good old cop humor. Each district and state police are assigned a number for communications. Flat Rock was the second district in the state, so all the posts of District 2 started with 2; Flat Rock was 25, which meant that all the patrol car numbers started with 25. For the fleet of fifteen cars, the number ran 251 through 2515 in sequential order: 251 for the first car, 252 for the second car, 2515 for the fifteenth car.

After being in Flat Rock for two years, I was used to listening to the radio for cars called "25. . ." when we were called to the scene. On my first patrol, the radio dispatched car 117. No one answered. It went on for a couple of hours, and I thought, *Somebody's going to be in trouble. They're not answering.*

Then it occurred, *Holy shit. It's me. It's me.*

I drove right to a payphone, since we didn't have cell phones. I called the folks at dispatch, "You've been calling me."

"Yes, we have been. We were worried about you and were going to send out people to look for you."

"Gosh, I apologize," I replied as I thought, *My mind was on 25.*

I wasn't going to announce that over the radio for everyone to hear. Regardless, the news moved around the office pretty quickly.

*****

I survived the on-the-job cruelty of my brothers and sisters in uniform during that first month. It was a fairly warm day in September. The call came in that they found a car just off the road in Eaton Rapids with a dead guy. When I arrived on the scene, I saw he'd been there for a few days. There were signs that rigor mortis had set in, as the body was bloated into the steering wheel, and his skin changed from white to black because of the decay. When it's decayed badly, limbs and body parts come off as easily as if they are well-basted chicken legs. We ran into this stuff all the time.

The coroner arrived. "Well, Trooper, I don't know how we're going to get him out of here."

I looked at him, shocked. "We? You're the coroner, I'm the trooper. I'm not dragging this body out."

It was one of those times when I was able to pull rank, and I was grateful.

*****

About three months into my new post, I headed to Flat Rock on business. When I walked in the door, I didn't recognize anyone from the state police force.

"You Wriggelsworth?" The trooper at the front desk asked.

"Yeah."

"You're the reason I'm sitting here."

It is a small world, and most everything comes around full circle. Since I had signed our life away on the house and was able to stay in Lansing, this poor guy was assigned to Flat Rock.

*****

A call came in from Clinton County on Christmas Eve. When we arrived, it was a nightmare. The husband beat the shit out of his wife. He was drunk, the kids were crying, and the Christmas tree was knocked over. Back then, we didn't have domestic violence laws. Since we didn't see the assault take place, we had to goad him into taking a swing at us. To mess with his head, we goaded him, he took a swing, and he went to jail because of it. It was a sad situation, but the wife and kids were going to live in peace and be safe for the next 24-48 hours. I hoped they had a better Christmas than if he had been with them.

*****

Leslie is about 15 miles south of Lansing. A burglar robbed a drugstore and they called it in right away. The drugstore didn't know for sure the car description, but it was "like a red Chevrolet Caprice or something like that." One of the deputies was on a freeway ramp when the red Caprice drove past. The chase was on; it was a high-speed and tense kind of a chase. Well, to assist, MSP sent a car to join my deputy on the chase. He lined up behind our deputy. On the radio, I heard the MSP trooper address my deputy, "Pull over and let me take this over."

I thought to myself, *Well, you (expletive).* He knew our deputy heard the call, but he refused to back off. Luckily, our deputy caught the guy. We won.

*****

The kinds of chases we did back then are not what they do today, thankfully. It's too dangerous. The OJ Simpson high-speed chase was one of a kind. Back then, we had one chase that started in Mason and ended many miles later at the Detroit Metro Airport.

As humans, each of us only has so much capacity to pay attention to and coherently process our surroundings. In training, we learn that our brain capacity during urgent matters is only 80%, versus 100%. So, if you drive 100 miles per hour, your brain isn't equipped to handle all that you need to pay attention to. Best practice is to operate at 80% of capacity.

Nowadays, when they start a chase, a supervisor oversees the process from the road or office. He monitors it for the safety of pedestrians, other drivers, and officers. Once it gets dangerous, he'll say "terminate," which calls it off. We don't want any collisions, or to hurt or kill any kids walking to school, or something like that. Then, the supervisor puts out an APB to local police departments with the description of the car. Often, they get caught anyway, and people are safer in the meantime.

There were just way too many cops driving 100 miles per hour through a subdivision. You can't do that. When we had the Plymouths with the turbocharged engine, we hit 140 miles per hour. They were scary fast.

*****

Promotion to undercover sergeant in the Tri-County Metro Narcotic Squad, 1974–1988.

The annual State Police Post Christmas Party in 1974 was one of my favorites. Between 1968 and 1972, I reported to the East Lansing Police Post "Headquarters." However, in 1972, they relocated the troopers to the new Eaton County State Police Post, which was where the Christmas party was held.

Our spouses were invited, and it was always a nice time for us to celebrate the year. During the announcements, I heard the post commander say, "We have some important announcements to make. Wriggelsworth and Simmons, you are promoted to sergeant. You're getting transferred to the narcotics unit."

I was quite surprised. Both Simmons and I liked the idea of the promotion, but I wasn't excited about the narcotics thing. I didn't have any experience in that arena.

My hair was the length of the skin on your teeth; it was really short. Undercover meant a whole new makeover for me. I didn't know anything about narcotics. They sent us to a two-week long drug school to learn about the paraphernalia that goes with the drugs. Needles were one thing I knew about, but we had to know about the glass bowls, the scales, the packaging, the appearances of drugs, and the slang names. I adapted really quickly and loved it.

You could attribute this promotion to the relationships I built at East Lansing Headquarters. For some positions, they appointed people that they thought would do a good job. Once you were on that list, you went where they wanted you. Fortunately, this promotion didn't take me to St. Ignace, Gladstone, or anywhere far away. Neither Sandy nor I wanted to go to the UP (Upper Peninsula, Michigan), so it worked out. I was lucky to stay here in Lansing when I was promoted to both sergeant and lieutenant of the Tri-County Metro Narcotic Squad. When most people were promoted, back then, they sent you somewhere else. For me, there happened to be positions open when I was promoted that kept me here, and I'm grateful we never had to transfer.

When I was first transferred in 1974, it was with the Tri-County Metro Narcotic Squad. They used to call it the "intelligence section." Now it's called the "narcotics unit." Our crew covered everything from Lansing and north, where there are still a lot of small towns, which made the territory seem even larger.

Working north was interesting, and we had a lot of fun. When anyone was promoted or transferred into the narcotics unit, they assigned a "probe name" for your undercover persona. Disney characters were the theme when I started. They named me "Goofy." I didn't pick it; it was derived from a couple of guys who were higher up in the state police. They were leery of me because of my union connection. So that was their idea. I actually liked it; people called me "Goof."

*****

One thing about police work to remember is that the hierarchy is important, and if you breach it, they will let you know. They put the intelligence people together in temporary trailer housing until a permanent structure was built. One day, we were working in the office, which was also in a trailer. One of our guys sat in a chair behind a desk with his feet up on it. The major walked in, never said a word, and walked towards his desk. He kicked the guy's feet off the desk and said, "There's one guy in this organization who puts his feet on the desk. It ain't you."

Everybody laughed. I never tried that myself. It wasn't my style, but it was so funny.

The sheriff in De Tour called us to assist with problems at a bar. It's a nice drive north on the freeway over the Mackinac Bridge. The road leads right to it; just take a right turn at the end, and you run into it. The town is set beautifully on the lake. I organized a crew and headed up. Remember, we were undercover, with long hair and beards. When we walked into this southern, blue-collar-type bar, they looked at us like we were cops. Ouch!

BEYOND THE JOB

Involvement in our community has been an important part of my life, and both Sandy and I devoted any time we could to giving back. For both of us, it seemed like a natural extension beyond our family and our careers in law enforcement and elementary education. One endeavor I enjoyed was teaching elementary students about law enforcement and police work. Each year, over the course of ten years, one of the teachers in Clinton County asked me to present to four of her classes. I've never been a schoolteacher, but by the time I was doing the third class for the day, I felt dumb. It's hard work repeating the same material, fielding their questions (and there were many), and managing the students. As part of our Drug Awareness Program, I also taught high school students about the different types of drugs and showed them what they looked like in a locked glass display case. I often wonder if we prevented anyone from trying drugs. When I was elected sheriff, I decided I wouldn't teach students any longer. That was hard work, and I have a profound respect for teachers, especially my wife!

Gene takes time to read a story to Sandy's fourth grade class. 1994.

Gene reconnects with a former student, Mary, the front desk associate at Residence Inn, East Lansing, Michigan. Mary was a student at Okemos High School when Gene presented his drug awareness class. She fondly remembers Sergeant Wrigglesworth wearing his suit jacket and showing the glass display case that held samples of various drugs. She is proud to say, "I am a law-abiding citizen. I have a spotless driving record." 1981.

*****

The "Blood Relays" was a service the 11th Post offered that was interesting. The hospitals called us with emergency orders to pick up a package at the blood bank and drive it to State Police Post #1 in Brighton. We had to get there quickly. At the post, most of the time, someone would drive it to the University of Michigan for a surgical operation. Sometimes we picked up a kidney or heart, so it made you feel good that you were helping save lives. Now, they have helicopters and vans to transport blood and organs, so it's not a duty of the state troopers anymore.

*****

At the Tri-County Metro Narcotic Squad, I also presented narcotics training to our departments. One of our directors, George Halverson, was a friend of mine. One day, an instructor from a company that provided police training called me.

"I want to hire you to do some narcotics training for me in New Mexico," he offered.

I didn't quite understand his request, so I said, "You want to hire me to go to New Mexico?"

"Yeah, we do."

"Where in the hell did you get my name?" I asked, surprised.

He responded, "From George Halverson. He said you are 'the guy.'"

I thought to myself, *The state police director said that about me?* I was pleasantly surprised because, I mean, it made me feel good.

The drive to New Mexico was not exciting. I mean, it's a desert. It's all cacti and tumbleweeds rolling around. I was down there for a week, and it was a great bunch of guys. I taught a surveillance class. Trying to be funny, I said, "You know, I don't know how you all will do surveillance around here. I mean, it's pretty desolate. I guess you can hide behind a tumbleweed or something."

As I've mentioned before, not everyone appreciates my humor.

Family photo. Back row: Mike, Scott, and Mark. 1980.

CHAPTER 9 LESSON

I definitely recommend honing your skills to build relationships from your first day on the job with every level of any organization in your career. At first, I was very hesitant about being in the same building with all the state trooper supervisors and directors because I just wanted to be left alone to do my job. I assumed I would be "hounded" or micromanaged.

However, it ended up being quite the opposite. Instead, I found shaking hands and passing by people at all levels put a face to my name, and they remembered who I was. It also carved the way for me to make opportunities to share the cases I had and build my reputation. I believe being amongst the leaders also prompted me to stand a little taller, kept me on my toes, and raised my level of professionalism around the office.

When my supervisors and even the director of the Michigan State Troopers observed or heard about an accomplishment, they kept it in mind and later referred me for special assignments, like training in New Mexico, placement in the Tri-County Metro Narcotic Squad, and promotions.

Look for opportunities in your job that put you in front of others and that will get you recognized for your achievements. It greatly improves chances for later opportunities.

GENE'S UNDERCOVER DAYS AND NIGHTS

Tri-County Metro Narcotic Squad, Mid-70s.
Front row: Jim Trieweiler, Gene, Joe Duby, Rick Cook, and Dave Ruiz.
Back row: Stan Granger, Bill Trap, and Sam Tomlin.

Metro Squad East Lansing drug bust. 1980.

Marijuana harvest in Eaton County, MI. Mid-1980s.

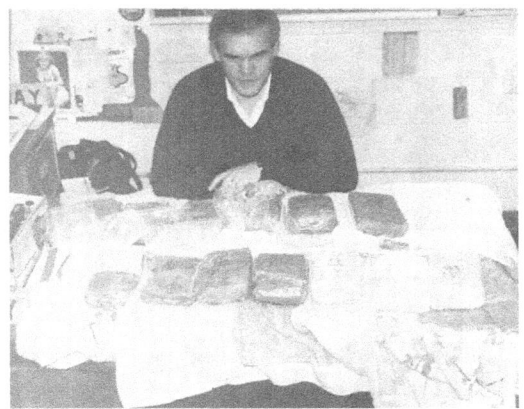

The largest cocaine seizure in Michigan at the time. Circa 1977.

Tri-County Metro Narcotic Squad team.
Front row: Jose Estrada, Paul Whitford, Gene, Cassie Alley, and Joel Maatman.
Back row: Jill Pierce, John Rojeski, Patti Nowak, Russell McKenzie,
Tom Reich, and Bruce Holiday.

Vintage photo of Gene at MSP Post 11, East Lansing, MI. 1968.

Metro Narcotic Squad staff. Mid-1970s.
Back row, left to right: Sgt. Ron Floyd, Off. Dale Metts, Dep. Dale Lauerman, and Off. Craig DeSonia.
Front row: Sgt. Paul Whitford, Off. Don Gilbert, Sgt. Gene Wriggelsworth, and Off. Fred Schnarr.

Hanging out at a raid. Gene, undercover for Metro Narcotic Squad,
sitting next to and working with the Ingham County Sheriff's Office. Mid-1970s.

Thursday, March 19, 1981, Lansing, Michigan

Staff photo by GINGER SHARP

Marijuana seized

Lt. Gene Wriggelsworth of the Tri-County Metro Narcotics Squad displays 130 pounds of marijuana confiscated during arrests in Delta Township Tuesday. The illicit weed carries a $30,000 street value. Also seized were a handgun and a van used to transport the marijuana. Examination for three suspects in the drug bust has been scheduled for March 27 in Eaton County District Court. They are Oscar Cantu, Jr., 25, of 1623 Martin; Jose Munoz, 27, of Detroit, and Gabino Jasso Guzman, 47, of Laredo, Tex. They were arraigned Wednesday and remanded to the Eaton County Jail in lieu of bond.

Lansing State Journal/EILEEN BLASS

Tri-County Metro Squad Detective Lt. Gene Wriggelsworth collects some of the marijuana plants during a raid Tuesday in southern Eaton County.

March 19, 1981.

A-2   JACKSON CITIZEN PATRIOT, TUESDAY, JANUARY 15, 1985

Gene Wriggelsworth, left, and Sgt. John Rojeski of the Lansing Metro Narcotics Squad, display the unusually long "rap sheet" of Larry Steed.

Lansing State Journal/GINGER SHARP

Lt. Gene Wriggelsworth stands with some of the drugs and weapons that were confiscated Tuesday from an Eaton County house.

Rap sheet of local convicted drug dealer. January 6, 1985.

Detective Lt. Gene Wriggelsworth displays seized cocaine laboratory — UPI PHO

A cocaine lab? MSU student is accused

Student chemist in off-campus drug operation. Late 1970s.

Lansing State Journal/GINGER SHARP

Lt. Gene Wriggelsworth (left) and Detective Lt. Paul Whitford of the Tri-County Metro Narcotics unit show off some of the drugs and $114,266 in cash, confiscated during a raid Thursday night.

9-5-1986

Paul Whitford and Gene Wriggelsworth. Metro narcotic drug bust. Cocaine and proceeds. 1980s.

THE TRI COUNTY METRO NARCOTICS squad arrested two Hubbardston men for possession of approximately $250,000 in cocaine and marijuana, the largest single haul by the squad based in Lansing. (Photo by Rus Gregory)

Metro Narcotic Squad makes "largest ever" bust in Hubbardston.

Smuggling operation in Miami, Florida was thwarted by information Metro Narcotic Squad provided DEA. 2.5 tons of cocaine seized.

Tri-County Metro Narcotics officers (from left) John Reisdd, Paul Whitford and Greg Wrigget.

Inmate called 'mastermind' of busted cocaine operation

CHAPTER 10

THE DRUGS, THE RAIDS, AND THE ODDITIES

SCOTT

"All I remember from my childhood was that Mom was a stay-at-home mom, and my dad was a cop. But from the time I was four years old, he was undercover for the Tri-County Metro Narcotic Squad. I saw my dad in uniform for the first time when he took office as the sheriff in 1989. That was also when I started my first year at Michigan State University. Until then, my dad was out of uniform doing the undercover thing. It was a pretty neat experience to be his son and watch the work he was doing. My buddies in high school all thought it was really cool, too.

"Undercover was always Dad's thing when it came to police work, and I think that's why he lasted fourteen years, which is unheard of. Usually and today, undercover assignments last for two years at a time for our safety. There are a lot of people who can't handle it for various reasons. It takes a lot out of a police officer personally, professionally, and family-wise. Dad handled it like the pro he is, and he also had tremendous support from my mom. The two of them together are what, I believe, contributed to Dad's successful long-term career."

THE DRUGS AND RAIDS

When the Michigan State Police promoted me to sergeant for the Tri-County Metro Narcotic Squad, I was surprised, to say the least. The two-week narcotics training was critical to prepare us, especially since I had never been around drugs except for during patrol duty. Even then, we never encountered all the drug paraphernalia we learned about. It was interesting, but nothing could have prepared me for the number of raids we would plan or the amounts of marijuana, cocaine, heroin, and other illegal substances we seized. Any cash seized at the raids was added to the legal drug proceeds forfeiture budget for the seizing agency.

The cash was a perk for the seizing agency's budget, and the successful raids were big wins for the team. The drugs are entered into evidence and eventually will be destroyed after the case ends.

The tragedies that accompany production, use, and sales of illegal or underground prescriptive drugs infiltrate our community, tear apart families, steal our friends, and increase crime all around us. Raids are one of those necessary evils to keep the bad guys from committing crime.

The real wins were, and still are today, that in all successful raids, we prevented the drugs from getting to the streets, ruining lives, and in some cases, we took down the drug ring. Perhaps we can't crush all crime, but any crime we do matters, because at the end of the day, we reduce drug distribution, which ruins people's lives.

*****

There are so many names for various drugs. You could be having a conversation with someone, and they ask, "Do you want some honey?"

You say "sure," thinking that it's honey. Soon after, they hand you a bag with marijuana in it and charge you the "market rate." The slang terms for all the drugs covered here were taken from BHDDH.ri.gov. [25]

Marijuana

A.K.A. weed, hash, grass, Mary Jane, reefer, cannabis, hemp, herb, skunk, pot, boom, chronic; **Synthetic Marijuana:** K-2, spice, fake weed, gold spice; **Marijuana Concentrates:** hash oil, 710, dabs, dabbing, amber, honey[1]

Our first raid of marijuana included the grower and operator who happened to be right down the street from the offices of our local newspaper, *The State Journal*. The house caught fire. The police and fire department arrived and put the fire out before it burned down. The reason it caught on fire was because the owners grew marijuana in their attic using a fully-operating hydroponic system. You know something is wrong when your neighbor has grow-lights and a watering system in their attic. The weights of the marijuana and water-filled hydro system caused the ceiling to sag. Then, the lights caught fire. Sometimes, the stupidity of criminals is comical. They didn't see the ceiling caving in before it caught on fire?

*****

Marijuana calls regularly came in from neighbors, as did tips about fraternity houses on college campuses. At a frat house behind a bar in Lansing, we found huge marijuana plants, so we started pulling them out. Two guys came out. "What the (expletive) are you doing?"

"We are police officers, and we are pulling this marijuana."

"Well, I don't know whose it is," they claimed.

It's hard to prove whose it was, so we just pulled it whenever we found it. They would have to find other, more productive ways to pay their tuition.

Cocaine

A.K.A. Blow, C, candy, coke, do a line, freeze, girl, happy dust, Mama coca, mojo, monster, nose, pimp, shot, smoking gun, snow, sugar, sweet stuff, and white powder[26]

There was an Ingham County Health Department inspector who inspected restaurants to make sure they were compliant with health rules. He had a side job where he delivered marijuana and cocaine to his "elite customers." We heard about it and investigated for more information. We learned he drove a Chevy Suburban, and we asked the car dealer if he knew who bought that particular one and how much he owed. Turns out, the suspect paid cash for it.

We also learned that he stored his money at his grandma's house in Eaton Rapids. While we interviewed him, the phone rang. It was Paul Whitford, who informed us, "Okay, we're in the house. We found the money. Everything's good."

I looked at the suspect and said, "You're going to tell me where you keep your money."

He replied, "I don't know what you're talking about."

I replied, "Just so you know, we just took it out of your grandma's house."

The poor grandma. She was a sweet little lady who had no idea. She just loved her grandson.

He was arrested and sent to jail. The funny part was, we drove his car for a couple of years as an undercover buying car. Who would suspect a Suburban as an undercover sting? Well, one day, the officer who was driving noticed that the blower on the defroster didn't work anymore. I told him, "Really? Take it in the garage and get it fixed."

While it was getting worked on, we received a call from the mechanic. "You have to come in and see this."

We showed up, and there was $30,000 in cash stuffed in the vents.

Heroin

A.K.A. Big H, brown sugar, antifreeze, junk, mug, tar, train, skag, horse, cheese (when mixed with cough medicine)

We had a case of a mother who called about her 15-year-old daughter's experience while babysitting. The daughter pulled a tab off of a posting for a babysitter job in Tulsa Township. She called and found out the parents needed a babysitter to travel with them to the Caribbean and watch their two kids. The mother called me to explain the situation, and explained, "My daughter is petrified. She said people are using drugs, and she saw the husband beat the wife."

We investigated and learned their return flight information to Detroit. We set up surveillance at the airport and monitored his car. While I sat in my car waiting for action, suddenly, a hand banged on my window. A Detroit Metro airport police officer demanded, "Who are you? Identify yourself."

I showed him my credentials and explained the case. He wasn't happy. "You're supposed to tell us when you come in here."

I replied, "Sorry."

The family landed, and we followed them back to Lansing. Along with the babysitter, the mom, dad, and two children were in the car. We didn't want to do anything until the babysitter and his kids were out of the car.

I'll never forget him because they called him Nano. We searched him and all he had on him was an ounce of cocaine. It wasn't a lot, but enough to get him in jail. He started complaining about how he couldn't go to jail because he owned a company in Massachusetts and didn't want to go to prison. He was petrified. I thought, *You should have planned better than this.*

"I think I can get you a big score," he said.

"Well, what's a big score?" I asked.

"A boatload."

After getting more information, we put him in touch with the Miami DEA. They ended up hauling in two and a half tons of cocaine on a ship called the "Galaxy." When it went to trial, I had to go to court in Miami and testify. The Feds loved us.

*****

It's pretty surprising how many people use the United States Post Office for special deliveries. PCP was often transferred to cartoon characters on paper.

*****

THE ODDITIES: I CAN'T MAKE THIS STUFF UP

Gaylord, Michigan is a beautiful resort town directly north of Lansing. We did about a dozen buys during a particular week and decided to bust the dealers. I offered to get the warrants from ***, about a two-and-a-half-hour drive.

I walked into the prosecutor's office in my undercover style, which I forgot about. As I approached the pretty secretary at the desk, I identified myself as "Lieutenant of the State Police. I need to talk with the prosecutor."

She looked at me like she had never seen anyone like me. I was out of the norm for Gaylord, so it was funny.

"Just a minute," she replied before walking down the hall, opening an office door, and saying, "You've got to see this."

They had never seen a cop that looked like me. After receiving the warrants, we then met with the local police. Their eyes were as big as saucers. It was so fun, and it's what we had to do for the job. I had to blend in with my 1970s goatee, which my wife hated. "I have to go in public with you looking like this," she often said.

One day, I decided to shave it off, so I did. I walked downstairs to the kitchen for breakfast. She didn't notice. Breakfast was served; the kids came down. "Oh my God! Dad shaved his beard!"

Dressing undercover could be a nuisance and hindrance. People are very judgmental. Sandy and I wanted to buy a lamp for the house, so we went to a store in town called Robinson Super City. It was a big furniture store. We found a lamp we liked, but it didn't have a price on it. I asked the salesperson, "Can you tell me how much this lamp is?"

He said, "You can't afford it."

I replied, "You're right. I'm not buying it here, dude."

*****

Sometimes, our egos and bravado get the best of us. We had a bust in a dorm on campus. We coordinated with the campus police, and a campus police officer who looked like he was 13 years old walked up to the door. He was really young, and we guessed he watched too many TV shows. He walked up the door, leaned back, and kicked his foot to bust open the door. *Bam!* He kicked the door. Campus doors are steel.

"Oh, my knee!" he shouted. He was clearly in pain.

My partner walked over to the door. "Let me show you how we do it."
He turned the doorknob, and we walked in.

*****

We raided a house on the southwest side of Lansing. One of our undercovers gave us the map of the house, so we knew the location of the bathroom. He told us when we hit it, they would flush the drugs. I walked around to the back of the house and spotted the window with a curtain. I was pretty sure it was the bathroom window, so I was ready with my nightstick. All of a sudden, I heard "Police officer, search warrant!" and they hit the door.

I took my nightstick and busted that glass out. As I looked through the broken glass, there was a guy and a girl sitting in a bathtub. Their eyes confirmed they were as shocked as I was!

*****

Hubbardston is a rural area north of Lansing, and I was assigned surveillance for a drug house there. In my undercover car, I sat in a farmer's driveway to observe a house about half-a-mile away. All of a sudden, I sensed that somebody was watching me. Cautiously, I looked to my left, unsure what I was going to see. There he was, a dopey looking Great Dane with his face inches from mine. His face looked like he was asking, "Who are you?"

*****

Joel Maatman was undercover on a deal to buy drugs off the guys in a house. I was nearby with the surveillance team so we could see and hear the action. Joe wore a body transmitter so we could hear everything. He was in the house, making friends with the drug dealers. Apparently, he had to go to the bathroom. He didn't think to reach down and turn off the transmitter. We heard all kinds of disgusting sounds. Next, he shouted, "Hey! You got any toilet paper up there?"

We about fell out of our cars. Years later, I shared that story at his retirement party. The people in the room laughed hysterically. They loved it.

*****

I'll never forget this! We raided a house by Potter Park because this kid was dealing dope out of his bedroom in his mother's house. We arrived right at 6:30 at night.

We kicked in the door and found the mother having a Tupperware party. I went in to get the kid from his bedroom, and I shouted to Joel, "Get me a 'Sip and Seal' or two." All those women went home with a hell of a story that night.

*****

Joel Maatman raided a house in Lansing with a brand-new van. The first night in commission, SWAT rode in it with the sliding door open so they could quickly exit. The house had a lamppost right at the corner of the sidewalk in the driveway. They drove too close to it and ripped the door off that brand new van.

At the end of the raid, my friend, Bill Trap, said to Joel, "You're coming with me, my friend, to the head of SWAT?"

Joel informed the director in a very nonchalant tone, "Hey boss, just so you know, we ripped the door off your brand-new van."

*****

I had a raid on Serpentine Drive in Clinton County. The house lights were turned off, and it was pitch black. We had several cars that showed up. I opened my car door, and the next car drove up without seeing my door and ripped it right off. So much for a surprise raid!

*****

Oops. There was a huge surveillance team for a guy that was riding a cattle bus. They are pretty big objects; one you wouldn't likely miss. The team was divided, with some undercovers riding on the bus with the suspect and some scattered around the blocks. One person is called "the eyeball" and reports everything back to the rest of us.

We sat there and sat there. Nothing happened. By now, the bus should have moved. I turned on my radio and bumped the eyeball. "What's the deal?"

"What do you mean?" he replied.

"Where's the bus?"

"The bus left," he casually mentioned.

"The bus left? You didn't tell us?" I asked, stunned. "It's gone. We've got nothing on this guy now."

*****

Bill Trapp, a good friend of mine, had a raid on the north side of town with a front door crew and a back door crew. Bill entered the front door without any difficulty, but the back door crew had trouble with the entrance. One of the officers used his gun to smash the glass out of the door. As he reached through the glass to unlock the door from the inside, he pulled his hand back and sliced it open significantly. When he did that, it touched his gun off and shot Bill in the upper arm. I thought he was going to lose his arm, because there was blood everywhere. It took a chunk of bone out, and we saw everything in his arm. We didn't have time to wait for an ambulance, so we threw him in the back of the patrol car and raced to the hospital. It took him a while, but he made a full recovery.

Now, my friend who was shot in the leg in a story to come, Dick Cortwright, didn't fare so well in recovery. He survived, but he ended up being off work for a long time.

*****

Sault Ste. Marie is a city in the Upper Peninsula, and it's a nice drive. Out of nowhere, a shadow came over my car, which was weird, because it was a clear and sunny day. As I tried to figure out what it was, I remembered that there was a B-52 army base nearby. It was pretty neat.

*****

I called the prosecutor's office in Detroit to pick up warrants for about 25 people. It was a big raid for acid and cocaine dealers. He offered to meet us at the Ramada Inn. He walked into our room with a case of beer and snacks, and his secretary followed him holding a typewriter and warrant forms. He said, "We'll type these up right here."

So, while she typed them all up, we had some beers and snacks.

*****

As we followed a drug dealer in Mackinac Island, he led us onto the north side of Mackinac in the Upper Peninsula. We followed him to his house somewhere near Gillard. To keep our cover, we had to stop and pay at the toll booth like everyone else. I stopped, showed the attendant my badge, and he still wanted me to pay him. We headed down a country road, a two-lane dirt track, and up the hill. There was a house trailer in the middle of nowhere.

We walked up to kick the door in. That didn't work, because house trailer doors swing outward when opened. We stood there in a quandary for a couple of minutes wondering how we were going to get him out, because he wasn't coming to the door. We finally said, "Look, either open the door or we'll have the SWAT team come and blow this door right off the side here."

They let us in.

*****

One of the first raids I did when I started at the Metro Squad was over on Baker Street. It was a beautiful home with an oak front door that was probably three inches thick and had oval beveled glass. One of the officers tried to kick in the glass but cut his foot and hurt his knee. So, we had to hit it with the battering ram. It was a shame to ruin such a beautiful door.

*****

Our team on the Metro Squad was from all over the tri-county area, and each of us had our own expertise. One of our guys was an LPD sergeant. While undercover inside the homes we planned to raid, he memorized the layout of the house in his head. He then wrote it down for us, so we became really good at doing raids whenever we knew the layout. He gave us everything, including front and rear exits, bathrooms, and bedrooms.

However, for one particular house, no one had ever been in it. Our undercover officer made all the buys at the front door and never went into the house. Just before we headed in, we called LPD, and they sent a sergeant who assessed the situation and determined we weren't going in. "You're not going in because you don't have this. . . you don't know that."

Here we were, ready to raid the house, and we were going to waste it all. So, I called his boss, who was also my boss, so he could make the decision. "Just so you know, here's what we got. He's refusing to cooperate."

The LPD replied, "Let me call you right back."

Next thing you know, the sergeant asked, "Can you feel your way through?"

I confirmed, "Yeah, yeah."

We got it done.

*****

We banged on the door—"Police officer, search warrant!"—for a house on the west side. The suspect started shooting his gun towards us from the basement. There were shots going everywhere. Simultaneously, everyone called for backup on the radio. Dick Cortwright tackled him, and while they were wrestling, he was shot in the leg.

The chief called me the next day to his office. "Gene, I heard the tapes of yesterday's raid. It was a cluster (expletive)."

I explained, "There were multiple shooters, every one of our officers called for backup at the same time, and no one at dispatch could hear anything. One of our guys got shot."

The chief responded, "I'm sending one of my sergeants with you on every raid."

"Yes, sir," I replied. I knew he was serious. "Thank you. We could use all the help we can get."

It didn't do any good for me to stand there and try to explain it. What he may not have realized was in a situation like that, an extra sergeant wasn't going to be able to do anything.

*****

Michigan winters are not for the weak of heart. They are cold, freezing. One winter night, we kicked the door in for this raid. We collected evidence for about an hour or so and we arrested the guy. We took him to the car to go to jail. The officer started the car, and a scream like you've never heard before breaks the silence of the night. Well, after the door was busted open, the guy's cat left the house and must have crawled up in the engine because it was warm.

"You kicked in my door, and now you killed my cat!" He was furious.

*****

At one point during my career, when we lived on Schoolcraft Street, there was a contract put out on my life, according to some informants. The contract was for $1,000, which kind of pissed me off. I thought I would be worth more than that. That night, we talked about it at the dinner table and, of course, our sons heard us. We probably shouldn't have said anything in front of them. After dinner, they headed down to their neighborhood friends' houses to play. They must have said something because after that, they wouldn't let our kids play with their kids because it was too dangerous.

*****

I was a runner until much later in my years. One day, I jogged down our street. As I rounded the corner, a car was parked on the side of the street with four people in it. I jogged by and smelled marijuana. I thought, *C'mon. This is supposed to be my day off.* I was in a T-shirt, shorts, smelly, sweaty, and didn't want to deal with it.

They knew who I was, so I stopped and asked, "What's the deal, guys?"

I didn't have my phone with me, so I thought I would wave down someone driving by and they could call the sheriff's office to pick these guys up. So, one of the neighbor ladies drove by, saw me, waved, and kept on driving.

I opened the door. "Slide over, you're coming with me."

And I took them in.

*****

We did a raid in Ann Arbor. It was what we call a "buy-bust," which is when you buy the drug from the dealer and then arrest them. You end up busting your cover, so then your undercover is blown. We surveilled a biophysics student, and he drove an old beat-up Cadillac with the continental kit on the back trunk. Since we were state police, we didn't have radio capabilities to contact local police. I told my guys, "We're going to do a Starsky and Hutch move on them."

This was in reference to a TV show about two officers named Starsky and Hutch; they often did a rolling stop on the suspects. One car would drive in front of the car, and then two cars drove beside him, one on each side.

While we arrested the suspect, a lieutenant from the Ann Arbor PD showed up. "Hey, are you in charge here?"

"Yep." I replied.

"We have an ordinance against making rolling traffic stops." He explained.

"Okay," I said respectively. "But I'm the state police. I'm not obeying your ordinance. I'm just doing police work."

He took exception. "You're breaking ordinances. What are you getting him for?"

"Selling drugs. Cocaine." I replied.

"Oh, okay, all right."

At that point, he had no problem with our Starsky and Hutch move.

*****

A few of us had to extradite a prisoner from Idaho. It was a long time ago, before TSA and concealed carry. We were pretty saucy before the plane took off. I pulled the flight attendant aside and said, "We're police officers, and we are armed."

She replied, "Okay, just tell the pilot you have a gun."

As we settled into our seats, the pilot was there, and I said, "Hey, we're pretty saucy. We have guns."

He surprisingly replied, "Shoot to the back, not towards the cockpit."

*****

We had an alcohol, tobacco, and firearms guy signed to our unit for a couple of years. He was a godsend, too, because every time we confiscated a gun on our raids, they prosecuted him federally. That was nice, because state courts which handle drug convictions don't prosecute guns. It's not the same situation today.

*****

East Lansing's Cedar Village has a lot of student housing. It was early morning as we walked down the street with a two-hand battering ram, about six inches in diameter and about six feet long. It requires two or three people to carry because it's so heavy. Two of our guys carried it as we walked down the street.

Students were in the street, on the sidewalks, and near the houses. A group of students walked toward us, saw us, and said, "Oh my God! They have a bazooka!"

Everyone ran for cover. Then we saw the pizza delivery guy. We were going to the same house! We kicked the door down.

The pizza guy said, "I suppose they're not going to take the pizza now, are they?"

"They're all going to jail." I replied.

"Oh, here, you might as well take it then," he said as he handed us the pizza.

*****

Whenever we raided a house, we were required to take pictures of everything, including any damage incurred. We had a very expensive 35-millimeter camera that was left behind on one of our raids. When we arrived in court, we told the defense attorney, "Just so you know, we left our camera behind."

He said, "I heard that. The lady that lived in the house you raided thought it had a hidden microphone in it. Were you bugging the house on this camera?"

I earnestly replied, "No, we were not bugging her house. We would really like to get it back."

Luckily, he gave us back the camera. Poor lady. She thought we were bugging the house with a camera the entire time.

*****

In a beautiful subdivision of Williamstown Township with big houses, we planned a small marijuana raid. It's not an area where you expect to find a drug dealer. The undercover had long hair and was creepy looking. He knocked on the door under the pretext of buying weed. It took him a while to convince the dealer, but he did. He was a university adjunct professor. We arrested him, and while we searched his house, we found seven pounds of cocaine worth $200,000 in street market value in his basement. It was a big deal.

*****

I wasn't undercover for very long for this case, but I was in pretty good with this crew who sold meth in Jackson County. I had been buying marijuana from this guy, and I asked if he could get me other drugs.

"Well, I can get all the methamphetamine you want," he said.

"How much?" I asked.

Confidently, he replied, "Ten thousand hits."

We pulled some money together, about $8,000, and went down to bust him. He lived in an old schoolhouse with a dirt driveway. It was a dump. A dog was chained up in the front yard and ran back and forth.

The code phrase was, "Gene's gonna like this, guys." He didn't know me as Gene, so it fit. I handed him the money; he gave me the stuff. He kneeled on the floor and counted it right in front of me. As I waited for him to finish counting, I said, "Gene's gonna like this, guys," which was the cue for the guys to come in.

His dog started barking, which indicated someone was there. It was the rest of the team. When he looked up at me, he only saw the barrel of my gun as I pointed it at him.

"Don, you're under arrest." I said.

Shocked, he replied, "Aw, Gene, how could you do this to me?"

I told Sandy it was the greatest compliment I ever got. I completely fooled him.

*****

There was a guy named Jimmy, and he was married to Rosie. We bought cocaine from him for a while. He lived right by our guy who ran the Metro Squad. We took him down, and she went berserk and screamed in horror. As we walked out the door, she screamed at me, "Hey, Wriggelsworth, suck my womb, you (expletive)."

I'd never heard that one before.

Fast forward six months. Jimmy was in prison. We needed a $3,000 flash roll, which is when the dealer gets to see the money before the buy. My LPD boss says, "Go to this bank, and they'll have the money waiting for you."

When I walked into the bank, there was Rosie. I can't say I was happy to see her. Ironically, she worked at the bank and handed me the flash roll.

*****

During my first year in narcotics, I worked in a state police team. We had a deal down in Battle Creek and headed back around noon to Lansing. There were six cars of us speeding up Old M-78, going about 80 or 90 in a 65-mph speed limit zone. It was a four-lane highway, two lanes in each direction, divided by a median. Unbeknownst to us, the then-current sheriff was headed in the opposite direction. He saw us but didn't know who we were. He called for a patrol car to stop us. Suddenly, I saw an Eaton County car coming, and he hooked around the median. I knew he was coming after us. The lieutenant driving behind me announced on the radio, "You guys keep going because he can't stop us all. I'll take the heat."

I thought that was the end of it.

The next morning, the captain called. "I received a complaint from the county sheriff that you guys were speeding up the road yesterday."

"Yes." I stood there and thought to myself, *Well, he didn't catch me. On the other hand, if I tell him I didn't do it, I'd be lying to him. He knew we were all together.*

So, I said, "Yeah, boss, I did. I think Bob stopped and talked to the sheriff about what we were doing, and that was it."

He said, "Okay, here's what we're going to do. I'm going to give you a written reprimand that will stay on your file for one year. And if you don't do this again in one year, it comes out."

True to form, he took it out after one year, and that was the end of it.

Gene's rise in the trooper association. 1972.

CHAPTER 10 LESSON

Don't do drugs!

CHAPTER 11

UNFORGETTABLE AS AN UNDERCOVER LIEUTENANT

NICE TO HAVE FRIENDS

A GUY NAMED Larry was a long-time drug dealer around Lansing, but he was kind of a likable guy. We chased him around for quite a while, and we finally took him down at a traffic stop. It was a Starsky and Hutch move, where we had a bunch of cars swoop in to stop him. He had a passenger with him. As we cuffed him, he told his buddy, "Well, this is Gene Wriggelsworth here, and this is John Rojeski."

He's cuffed, and he introduced us to each other like he was at a cocktail party.

"Larry, good to see you. Maybe find something a little more productive to do than dealing marijuana," I encouraged.

He went to prison.

*****

We had a female undercover officer who worked for me and was the wife of the police chief. We took her down to buy drugs in a bar in Detroit. As surveillance, we sat in the parking lot with our motor running. With it being fall, the steam came off the hood of the car. So, she's in this bar, and I'm listening to the radio for her signal. I looked out of my window, and a tall and large sergeant stood next to my car. "Who are you?"

I replied, "State trooper."

He seemed annoyed. "What are you doing here?"

"Well," I replied and pointed to the building, "I have a female undercover officer in that bar right there buying drugs."

"Lieutenant, you get in there and get her ass out of there, because if you don't, she's going to get murdered," he said without pause.

The team extracted her, and we all went home safe and sound. Nobody knew the area better than him. We knew how to listen to him.

CLEARING THE STREETS

We had a big raid from a bunch of undercover buys. We had over sixty dealers we had bought from and obtained the warrants. That day, we raided 62 and arrested 62, so it was well-planned and successful. For this size of a raid, we needed uniforms to help serve the warrants and arrest them. The uniform guys love that kind of stuff because they didn't get to do it very often.

We met for a briefing and distributed the packets with the names, addresses, photos, and warrants. Each of them had three warrants per packet. Once they had them in custody, they took them to the jail where they were processed.

It was the biggest drug bust that year, and the media hyped it a bit, too. That's always a good thing when it's a good result.

FOLLOW YOUR INTUITION

One night in Lansing, we had a raid. We were well stocked with weapons, including shotguns. As I stood in position, I looked over to my left and saw a guy over in the weeds. I thought, *This guy doesn't belong here.* Then, the guy came out of the weeds, he was lucky I listened to my gut, and he was lucky we didn't shoot him.

We always have to think fast on these jobs, listen to our intuition, and be prepared not to shoot anybody without cause. We have a lot of cases when we walk through the yard or kick in a door. We had a couple of accidental discharges from the same uniform officer. One of them happened when he touched the shotgun and it blew up into the roof of the house, and another time he did it outside.

You can't put your finger on the trigger when you bust into a house. There could be kids in the houses. That's why it helps you to be keenly aware of the surrounding area as you walk up to the house. If there is a kid's bike, or balls, or a chain for a dog, those are all clues that kids and pets may be in the house. If your finger is always on the trigger, you could accidentally shoot the wrong thing.

When it comes to kids at raids or crime scenes, I've even changed a few diapers in my career because the baby was crying while we took the mom to jail. We had to wait for grandma to get there. We always need to use caution and look for ways to serve that may not be what we expect.

VERY UNFORTUNATE

Mona was a well-known prostitute in the area, and she was picked up by a guy in Williamstown. He took her to the rest area on I-96 to do whatever they're going to do. They were both drunk, and they passed out. She got out of the car after she pulled herself together and walked out on the freeway. We don't think she knew it was the freeway because it was so dark. Unfortunately, she was hit by a truck and was repeatedly hit by several more cars. Someone finally called us, and when we arrived, we realized Mona had probably been hit 30 times. A dark night with a 70-mph speed limit made it hard for even semitrucks to see anything. That was a hard way to go. Pretty sad.

*****

We arrested a group of guys who were manufacturing PCP and recruited a chemist who was a 22-year-old Fulbright Scholar genius. He didn't have an ounce of street smarts. He was hooked up with these guys as their chemist and ended up in prison. Such a shame.

14 YEARS IS A LONG UNDERCOVER CAREER

I loved the fourteen years I spent undercover. I was growing older and felt myself getting tired from the grind. It was a lot of night stuff; one shift might start at eight in the morning and end at four the next morning. Then we had to get warrants, do raids and arrests, and complete the processing.

The time had come when I told Sandy I was getting tired. Though rewarding, it was a very demanding position with a lot of responsibility. Plus, as you get older, you do get tired, no matter how much you don't want to admit it. The shifts could be 12–18 hours long or more, and I felt that it was time for something new. When I shared my thoughts with Sandy, she was fully supportive, and I decided to run for sheriff. I told her, "If I don't get elected sheriff, I'll ask to return to uniform, where I'll have a little more of a 'normal' life."

Little did I know how the next 28 years would unfold.

No. 41   Wednesday, Oct. 12, 1983

QUIET REPOSE—Gene Wriggelsorth, field supervisor of the tri-county metro narcotics squad, enjoys a quiet Saturday afternoon at his peaceful home, away from the sometimes da....id dangerous world of drug trafficking.

Gene posing for a photo for the Ingham County News on the deck he built with his three sons.

CHAPTER 11 LESSON

Sometimes, when in a difficult or long-time role, it will feel as if it's time for a change or new opportunity. I loved being undercover for Metro. I did it for 14 years and had the pleasure of working with the best of local law enforcement. The time had come when I told Sandy I was getting tired. It was a very demanding and rewarding position with a lot of responsibility. Plus, as you get older, you do get tired, no matter how much you don't want to admit it. The shifts could be 12-18 hours long or more, and I felt it was time for something new.

At any stage of your career, be sure to check in with yourself, because you may be faced with changing circumstances, such as your age, life balance, finances, health, or family, that make it so you desire to advance or change your career. Don't hold yourself back from exploring that next step and do what is best for you in your life.

CHAPTER 12

IN MEMORIAM,
THE ULTIMATE SACRIFICE, 1974–1988

Trooper Larry Lee Forreider, Michigan State Police

AT 33 YEARS old, Trooper Forreider died in the line of duty. He served in the Michigan State Police for seven years and was a United States Air Force Veteran. He was my partner at the Flat Rock State Police Post prior to his transfer to Alpena, where he pulled a car over for a defective taillight at 2:30 a.m. With three passengers in the car, he was shot with a gun and struck twice by the driver. He bravely returned shots as the subjects were fleeing and struck one of the subjects who was apprehended at the scene.[6]

For any person in law enforcement, losing one of our own is more than difficult. Losing a partner or former partner is even worse. With any partner, we work so closely with each other that a special bond develops, because we must work together in synchrony on every call.

What makes this even sadder, Trooper Forreider was killed before body armor was issued for protection. His wife had already purchased a vest for him, wrapped it, and put it under the Christmas tree.

On Thursday, December 5, 1974, Trooper Forreider's watch to protect and serve tragically ended. He is survived by his wife, two children, parents, two brothers, and three sisters.

*****

Police Officer Mac J. Donnelly, Jr., Lansing Police Department

At 35 years old, Officer Donnelly died in the line of duty. He served in the Lansing Police Department for nine years and was a United States Coast Guard Veteran. During a bank robbery, Officer Donnelly attempted to rescue four hostages and was shot and killed by the bank robbery suspect. He was able to return fire and wounded the suspect. All the hostages were freed.[10]

Officer Donnelly's watch to protect and serve sadly ended on Thursday, June 16, 1977. He is survived by his five children.

*****

Police Officer James Spencer Johnson, East Lansing Police Department

At 44 years old, Officer Johnson died in the line of duty. He served in the East Lansing Police Department for 11 years and was a United States Army Veteran. Jim worked for me in the Tri-County Metro Narcotic Squad. Attempting to arrest a resistant woman for auto theft, he was shot by her male companion who emerged from the bathroom.[7]

Officer Johnson's watch to protect and serve ended on Thursday, October 25, 1984. He is survived by his wife and six children. As a result of his death, The 100 Club of Greater Lansing was formed to support families during their time of crisis.

*****

Police Officer Dean A. Whitehead, Lansing Police Department

At 30 years old, Officer Whitehead died in the line of duty. He served the Lansing Police Department for nine years. He was on air patrol with his partner when they spotted a burning motor home. They began to ascend after fire units arrived on the scene, but the helicopter struck electrical lines, then descended rapidly and struck the ground. Both officers fled the aircraft, and Officer Whitehead was killed instantly when struck by the rotor blades.[13]

Officer Whitehead's watch to protect and serve tragically ended on May 9, 1985. He is survived by his wife, parents, and three brothers.

*****

Police Officer Julie Engelhardt, Lansing Police Department

At 34 years old, Police Officer Engelhardt died in the line of duty. She served the Lansing Police Department for 14 years and previously served the Ingham County Sheriff's Office. Two boys reported a man had taken their sled away, and as she responded to that call, the man shot her as she approached. Officer Engelhardt returned fire, critically wounding the suspect.[5]

Officer Engelhardt's watch to protect and serve tragically ended on Friday, February 12, 1988. She is survived by her two sisters.

*****

CHAPTER 12 LESSON

Every day, the media reports on tragic and fatal events. Most of us are desensitized to the tragedy of it and move about our day. Next time you hear about someone injured or killed, just pause without judgement or negative thoughts. Think about the victim and those who survive them. Remember that anyone who is injured or dies is loved by someone and deserves respect, and their loved ones deserve empathy. If you are a praying person, send them all a little prayer.

PART 4

28 YEARS
AS THE SHERIFF
OF
INGHAM COUNTY, MICHIGAN

1988–2016
INGHAM COUNTY SHERIFF
ELECTED FOR SEVEN CONSECUTIVE TERMS

CHAPTER 13

A DAY IN THE LIFE AS THE SHERIFF OF INGHAM COUNTY

I WON! IT was a remarkably close race; in fact, it was so close that the *Lansing State Journal* printed the morning edition of the paper showing my opponent as the winner. Later, they corrected the announcement. I eked out the win by one-tenth of one percent, by 882 votes out of 110,000 votes cast. That's about as close as it gets.

Gene's first swearing-in ceremony as sheriff of Ingham County. Gene shakes hands with his father, Gerald Wriggelsworth. 1988.

Sandy and Gene Wriggelsworth. 1990.

SANDY

When Gene approached the boys and me about running for sheriff, I said, "Okay. I'll support you."

I was relieved we could return to a more normal schedule, sort of. However, I never had a clue it would be so political. It shocked me that everybody wanted the sheriff at every event happening in the community. It was hard to teach students all day and attend events at night. Mike was in college, Scott was in high school, and Mark was in middle school, so we didn't have to be home for the boys, but we were gone almost every night.

I attended all the events until I saw that the attendees looked right through me and didn't care if I was there or not. They wanted Gene, so I started picking and choosing which to attend. As a sheriff and spouse, we were very much the center of attention; more Gene than me, of course. I just never realized how much people relied on the sheriff as a presence. I really liked going with him, so I went to a lot of things and made a lot of good friends.

THE EARLY DAYS AS SHERIFF

January 1, 1989 was the date I assumed my new position and office. I used the two months before to prepare my remaining investigations for my successor, who would replace me as a lieutenant for the state police. Around Thanksgiving, I started making appearances at the sheriff's office to meet the people and get the lay of the land.

The incumbent sheriff never returned to the office after I won the August primary, so the undersheriff stepped in to assume his duties. He was instrumental in the transition. Darwin Shaver, the previous chief deputy, was also invaluable for the first few weeks and kept us out of the minefields. I knew Darwin throughout my entire career and working with him was always an excellent experience. Even though I announced I was bringing in my own team, I wanted him to stay.

I submitted my proposed new organization of personnel to the board of commissioners, which included Undersheriff Rick Boyd, Chief Deputy Matt Myers, and two majors, Darwin Shaver and Joel Maatman. It was approved, and Darwin was happy to remain on staff. The team assumed many responsibilities in addition to their primary role assignments:

- Undersheriff Boyd was my right-hand person to run the day-to-day operations.
- Chief Deputy Myers oversaw the uniform personnel, including road patrol and jail employees.
- Major Shaver oversaw central records and was in charge of recruiting, interviewing, doing background checks on, and hiring new employees.
- Major Maatman addressed personnel issues and oversaw the building inspections and operations.

I was lucky to have an extremely hard-working team whose dedication, morals, and values mirrored my own. Together, we served the communities of Ingham County with duty, honor, and respect, and I do believe, together and individually, we made a positive impact.

It is with deep regret I share that we lost Major Darwin Shaver during the writing of this book. Darwin Shaver retired from the Ingham County Sheriff's Office as chief deputy. He passed away on June 26, 2025 at 84 years old.[27] He will be greatly missed.

*****

As a newly-elected sheriff, my law enforcement background allowed for a smoother transition than if my career had been in another field. That being said, there was still a lot to learn. The first rule for myself, as a leader, was to observe the current happenings, solicit feedback, assess, and then consider changing protocols and processes. It was important to me to first build relationships with my team, then with other employees, and then with our external partners, like the board of commissioners, the Fraternal Order of Police, the local police departments, the judges at the courthouse, and the prosecutors. I wanted them to get to know who I was, hear my goals, and understand the differences between me and the former sheriff.

In my opinion, his immediate exit from the sheriff's office after losing the election seemed true to his form of leadership. Fortunately, his previous undersheriff and chief deputy welcomed me to the office and helped me become familiar with the daily operations. Their camaraderie and hospitality were in alignment with how I operated, and it was a smooth transition.

Building trust is the most important step in my style of leadership, so I started with what I thought were small changes. However small the changes seemed, they had an enormous positive impact on my deputies and staff. I made it clear when I ran for sheriff that I would not be the "white shirt" type of leader. I chose to wear the same uniform as my staff instead of the traditional white shirt the previous sheriff wore. The term "uniform" means we all look the same and we all work together. That change alone seemed to endear a few deputies to me.

When I heard there wasn't a recognition program for "outstanding service," I was stunned. It was such an integral part of boosting morale at the state police post. When we did good police work, we received medallions to put on our shirts for recognition. The captain had been there his entire career, so I asked him, "What do we do for recognition?"

"What are you talking about?" he asked.

"How do we award our deputies and staff for outstanding service?"

"We don't," he answered.

In law enforcement, most of the work we do isn't ever recognized because it's just part of our job. However, when someone goes out of their way to do something good, they should be rewarded for it. I put together an awards board. I didn't want to be the guy who determined who was recognized, so I told them, "You are in charge of selecting those who you believe should be recognized."

They liked the process, it worked well, and it's still in effect today.

I also wanted people to feel comfortable stopping by to ask a question or talk about different situations. I instituted an "open door policy" so they could walk in any time. Deputy Ted Harrison, who had a good sense of humor, frequently stuck his head in the doorway of my office and said, "I noticed you're a little late for work today, Boss."

That struck me as funny. They embraced the changes because it built trust between us. They must have felt comfortable with this change since that wasn't something deputies would usually say to the boss. They knew I was available to them, and that we worked together as a team.

Sheriff's office administrative staff photo.
Front row: Allan Spyke, Gene, and Greg Harless.
Back row: Sam Davis, Kathy Cole, and Joel Maatman.

2009 Christmas card photo on the field of the MSU Spartan Stadium.
Pictured from left to right: Chief Deputy Gregory Harless, Undersheriff Allan Spyke, Administrative
Assistant Kathy Cole, Sheriff Gene Wriggelsworth, Major Joel Maatman, and Major Sam Davis.

BUILDING BRIDGES

I hadn't been a sheriff for more than a year when there was a barricaded shooter situation in the middle of the afternoon. The sheriff's office in Delhi Township was in charge, so I grabbed a couple of guys to check out what was going on. We were new, and I wanted to see if the responders needed anything.

I'll never forget this day. Sergeant Dick Fitzgerald stood at the blockade in the road, and when we pulled up, the look of dread on his face seemed to say, "What the (expletive)? Not these guys."

I walked up to him. "Hey, Dick, how are you doing?"

"I'm doing all right," he replied. "I've got Tactical coming."

"Do you need anything?" I asked him.

There was quiet. He didn't reply.

"You need anything? You need food, water? You need barricades? Can we call somebody else to help you out here?"

"No," he said, "We're good."

A couple of days later, he called. "When I saw you pull up, I told the guys, 'Now, the Old Man is here. This is going to be a cluster.' But it was so refreshing having you come up to see what we needed without taking over, which isn't what used to happen."

I only went to the call as a positive gesture. Dick was a veteran sergeant who retired as a captain; what could I tell him to do? Just because I had more stuff on my collar didn't mean I was smarter than anyone else. I worked every day to convey that to my troops, and it went a long way to build morale.

As crimestoppers, investigators, and law enforcers, trusting each other is the greatest asset we have, whether in the office or in the field. We need to know that the people who surround us have our backs.

Gene's first year as Ingham County Sheriff. Picture includes all of the
Ingham County deputies, canine unit, and fleet of vehicles in 1989.

Sheriffs are responsible for arranging for security and transportation for any political leader. Gene welcomed Illinois Senator Barack Obama, who was campaigning for US president at the Lansing Center. 2008.

Field trip with Grandpa! Gene with his grandson, Andrew, when he was called to testify before the Michigan Senate.

ADVANCED EDUCATION

Finished My Bachelor's Degree and Graduated from the FBI National Academy

By the time I became a sheriff, I only had four or five classes to go to receive my undergraduate degree in business administration from Northwood University. However, I wanted to complete the FBI National Academy training. The University of Virginia ran the program for the FBI, but if I completed my degree at Northwood University, my credits would transfer, along with those they called "life experience credits." All the credits went toward finishing my bachelor's. My business administration degree was a perfect complement to my current role, and I highly recommend getting one to anyone in law enforcement who desires to become a good leader. Finally, I was equipped to start as a senior college student at 50 years old. It was a long way from being "cool in school."

After the application and acceptance process, I was assigned to the FBI National Academy in Quantico from April through June of 1994! There were officers from all over the country in the program, and even from Russia, and FBI agents from all over the world taught our courses. I met many interesting people over the twelve-week long academy.

The FBI training was more about the types of crimes we encountered. For example, the class about serial killers was fascinating, and I shared our case on the serial killer crimes we solved. The Bureau now uses it in their classes as an example. We learned the best practices to work with our agencies, how the FBI supports local governments, and how agents can collaborate with state and local law enforcement.

My roommate was Joe Ventura, a lieutenant from Visalia PD in California. He arrived the day before me, so when I walked into our dorm, he was lying in bed. We became pretty good friends. He didn't have a car, and since I drove down, he relied on me, borrowing my car to run errands.

There was a building at the academy campus called "The Boardroom," which was the local bar. Drinks were cheap, and we hung around after classes or took a drive into town. I've never been a drinker, so for me to drive into town to have a beer was not exciting. A lot of guys' lives were centered around drinking, and they indulged whenever they could. The parking lot became the "hot spot" because they saved money from The Boardroom with cases of beer instead of drafts. It was similar to an MSU tailgate. Guys sat around with their car trunks opened and drank beer. It was too rowdy for me, so I opted out.

One morning we were called to report to the auditorium. That never happened before, and we wondered if the POTUS was shot. Instead, we received instructions. "Guys, we need to start acting like adults here."

I woke up that morning and there were beer bottles on everybody's antenna in that parking lot, and I guess the general of the base didn't want us behaving that way. It wasn't me, I might add. Common sense seemed to evaporate when guys drank large quantities. There must have been a lot of cases of beer they consumed that night. It was funny, and we all laughed when we were dismissed. (For the younger folks reading this book, each car had a straight aluminum rod attached to the car for radio frequencies. Now, the "antennas" are baked into the windshields.)

About halfway through the first week, everyone was called outside for agility testing. They divided us into groups by age. We had to run around the track for about a half mile. It wasn't long, but that's how they determined our ability to run. Then, they broke us into five different groups by ability. I was in a red shirt group, which wasn't the slowest or the fastest.

For eleven weeks, each "challenge run" was different from the last and was progressively longer and harder. We started at one-and-a-half miles, then two miles, then two-and-a-half miles, and so on.

The Quantico grounds are very hilly and the paths curve back and forth. Given the nature of the base, we heard weapons going off all day long. Rifles make a distinctive sound, and artillery is even more distinct. We didn't think much about it.

During our three-mile run, we ascended from the top of a hill. All of a sudden, a marine jumped out of the weeds. "What the (expletive) is going on here?"

He scared us to death, so we stammered, and I answered, "We're doing our run for the FBI National Academy."

Alarmed, he responded, "This is a live fire zone today. Get the (expletive) out of here."

He didn't have to tell us twice.

The names of the runs were unique to the objective. The "Flora and Fauna Run" led us through the woods on what looked like a deer path about twelve inches wide. Everybody ran in single-file. Since we were fairly close together, they did not tell us that it was not smooth running. The roots were brutal. Just like that, I stepped on a root and rolled my ankle, and it instantly blew up. I was almost certain it was broken. I limped back to the academy as my fellow runners passed by as if I wasn't there.

When I arrived at the base's medical station, the doctor said, "Oh boy. You would have been better off to break this."

The x-ray showed it wasn't broken, but it was a fourth-degree sprain—whatever that was. By then, my ankle was enormous and purple. How was I going to finish the series of runs to graduate from the academy?

To succeed, the runs were necessary to get the achievement of accomplishment, a "Yellow Brick Road" award. No one attending wanted to leave without one. My ankle had no chance of healing to run the next day or for any of the following weeks. I asked the instructor, "What are the rules to win the yellow brick?"

He replied, "You just have to do it."

"So, I can crawl on my belly if I need to?"

"Yeah."

Fortunately, I wasn't alone; another guy was injured the same day on the same run. We walked the rest of the courses and graduated with a yellow brick! My son, Scott, also earned one during his time at the FBI National Academy. By the time he attended, the curriculum was only ten weeks long, versus my 12-week stint.

My family came down for the graduation ceremony. For Sandy, our family, and me, it was very memorable. I appreciated my family feeling so proud. We had about 250 people at the Academy that autumn. The director of the FBI, Louis Freeh, presented us with our diplomas. It was very special. The program wasn't really designed for people my age, but for sergeants and lieutenants to get ahead in their careers. I was proud that I finished, especially because, at my age, I was a bit more physically challenged. It's never too late—even at 50 years young!

Gene graduates from the FBI National Academy on Jun. 24, 1994.

https://www.fbi.gov/investigate/how-we-investigate/training

VICTORY PARTIES FOR ALL

Every four years, I had to run to be reelected sheriff. After the results were in, we always had a victory party to thank our supporters, friends, and family. The parties were a lot of fun because they were attended by people who liked me, and that's always good. We had one of my later victory parties at the Electricians' Union Hall, and we invited a group of people for food, drinks, and celebration. They were coming and going all night.

One of our lieutenants brought me a bottle of Crown Royal because I enjoy a glass every so often. He set it on the table with the other congratulatory items people brought. As we were readying to leave, I asked, "Where's my bottle of Crown?"

Sometimes, people come in for free food even though they didn't work on the campaign. I remembered this one man who came in. I didn't recognize him, but I noticed he hung around the front of the hall, ate some food, and stayed near the front door. I don't have a problem with people who do that. I noticed he didn't speak to anyone, and he didn't stay long. I suspected he grabbed the bottle on his way out to have his own party. That's what we call a "dine, grab, and dash."

Gene's family has a victory party to celebrate winning a later election for Sheriff of Ingham County. Pictured left to right: Mike, Scott, Gene, Sandy, and Mark. 2012.

Swearing in for Sheriff of Ingham County by Judge Tom Boyd. 1992. Pictured in back, left to right: Kathy Cole, Sam Davis, Mark Wriggelsworth, Mike Wriggelsworth, Scott Wriggelsworth, and Joe Maatman.

Mike Wriggelsworth

After Dad became sheriff, our interesting life as kids continued. "Wriggelsworth" is an unusual last name, and I couldn't go anywhere without somebody asking, "Hey, are you related to the sheriff?" or "Are you the sheriff's son?" Even today, I'll run into a customer who works two hours away who asks, "Are you related to that sheriff up in Lansing?"

"Yes, he's my dad, but he retired." I always reply. Then I add, "The current sheriff of Ingham County is my brother."

It usually takes a second to click in. It's pretty funny.

When Dad was sheriff, I think my experience growing up was different from other kids'. I was never picked on or bullied, because everyone knew my parents' professions. As kids, we met a lot of interesting people, especially through Mom and Dad's tight-knit group of friends who were at our house a lot. They were from the sheriff's office, Dad's narcotics days, or from the neighborhood. It was always a lot of fun because they were the type of people that you liked immediately and could trust. If you were a good person, they welcomed you into the fold. Those lifelong friendships are still with us today.

I credit both of my parents with surrounding us with good people and providing a stable and nurturing environment. They both gave everything they could to us boys. Mom sacrificed her teaching career to become a wife, a stay-at-home spouse, and to raise us three boys. Dad worked hard to keep getting ahead so we would have the essentials, plus a college education. Both of them took us to all our sporting events, helped us with homework, and did whatever else we needed.

Personally, they've been a big rock for me my entire life. To this day, if I need a shoulder to lean on or to talk through something with someone, I don't ever hesitate to talk to Mom or Dad. No matter what it is, they never judge what we do, they strive to understand us, and they ask how they can support us.

They are both inspirational, too. After the three of us were raised, Mom finished her undergraduate classes, completed her student teaching, taught for years as a substitute, and started teaching full-time at the same time Dad became sheriff.

Dad also didn't let anything slow him down or keep him from learning and achieving all he could to protect and serve our communities. At 50, Dad graduated from the FBI National Academy and later finished his classes to get his bachelor's degree.

They both retired, and I think they are busier now than when they were working. They go to the gym every day to work out, volunteer for at least a dozen non-profit organizations, are very involved in our families, and spend as much time as they can with their grandchildren.

I'm inspired by them every day. I'm not sure I've ever thanked them enough for being such wonderful parents, and if I didn't. . . Thanks, Mom and Dad. I wouldn't be the man, husband, and dad I am today without you.

Love,
Mike.

Crime prevention marketing strategy for local merchants.

CHAPTER 13 LESSON

Whenever you start a new leadership role in your career, these are the most important steps in the first weeks:

1. Build relationships with your:
   a. Core leadership team
   b. Direct reports

    c. Remaining staff

    d. Peers in other divisions, offices, or departments

2. Set the example you want employees to follow, such as:

    a. Communications styles, tones, behavior

    b. Dress, style

    c. Decorum in behaviors and interpersonal skills

    d. Timeliness, schedules, benefits

    e. Influence between internal and external interfaces

3. Establish and explain:

    a. Expectations

    b. Acceptable and unacceptable behaviors

    c. Individual and team responsibilities

    d. Divisions of duty

    e. Expected routines, processes and procedures

    f. Technology use and abuse

4. Prepare your own:

    a. Expectations

    b. Operations, plans, processes, and procedures

    c. Schedule

    d. Timeline of opportunities for self-development and career advancement

CHAPTER 14

ADVANCEMENTS FOR THE INGHAM COUNTY SHERIFF'S OFFICE

AMBITIOUS PROFESSIONALS USUALLY desire to use their role in life and their career to make a difference and leave the place in a better position than when they arrived. Holding the position of state trooper for 22 years and then sheriff for 28, I led several initiatives to advance the services we provided the county and for our deputies and staff. Many of the innovative advances we implemented were copied by several of the sheriffs in Michigan. Author Oscar Wilde always said that "imitation is the sincerest form of flattery." We were humbled and honored that our work was respected and implemented across the state.

SCOTT

Dad's schedule didn't get any easier when he became sheriff. You think a dope schedule is complicated? Imagine being an elected official pulled in a million different directions. Dad seemed like he was everywhere, but he never wavered on his commitment to his family. He was still at home a lot and attended our sporting events, birthday parties, and all the other family events. Cops talk about all the stuff that we miss. While Dad didn't attend everything, especially when he was working dope, he was still a very present dad, even when he was implementing various programs in the sheriff's office and Ingham County community.

Gene with son, Mike, at seven years old.

Softball Coach Wriggelsworth.
Scott standing in back row on right. Mark kneeling in front row, third from right.

Gene with son, Mark, 16 years old, in his Explorer uniform for the Ingham County Sheriff's Office.

THERE'S NO "I" IN "TEAM," BUT THERE IS INCLUSIVITY

In sports, it's often said that "there is no 'I' in 'team.'" That is true. It takes all of us to successfully perform our roles. Yes, even in law enforcement. The most important part of my job was building my team. Increasing and maintaining a high sense of morale, strong integrity amongst everyone, and unwavering trust in each other was important and pertinent to the safety and protection of each deputy and staff member. We knew we had each other's backs in every situation. We knew following our training was the only way to perform our roles.

During my years in law enforcement, there were many movements to improve the civil rights of minorities and women. Inclusivity always made sense to me. I think it had to do with my upbringing because my parents never differentiated us from other people. As far as I was concerned, we were all the same. So, when we received assignments to protect and serve at marches and riots, it was important to me to maintain objectivity and uphold the law. When the media portrayed the stories about fairness, rights, and advancements for minorities and women, it always made sense to me that all people deserved to be treated the same. Plus, I already believed the only "I" in "team" was "inclusivity." No matter the role or rank.

Within a short time of assuming my role as sheriff, I promoted the first woman in the sheriff's office with the rank of "chief deputy." Subsequently, over the years, I promoted several people from various genders, backgrounds, skill sets, and ethnicities to command lieutenant roles and other positions that had never been held by people of their demographics in the sheriff's office before.

LOGO

The Michigan's Sheriff's Association updated their logo to include the shape of Michigan behind their star. I liked how it looked, so I incorporated the shape of Michigan into our star logo, too. I appreciated the cohesive brand that showed unity between us. Afterward, several other counties implemented the change as well.

VICTIM ADVOCATES

Between 1988 and 1990, we established the Victim Advocate Program, headed by Mrs. Patty Thayer, to support families of victims and facilitate any necessary processes to be followed after the incident. We were grateful for the many advocates who volunteered their time, including one who remains dear to us today, Linda Dennany. When we received a call in the middle of the night about a fatal accident, the advocate arrived at the scene to tend to the survivors of the accident. They did whatever was needed. Sometimes, that meant taking them home, getting diapers or food for any children, and even babysitting while the parents went to the hospital to deal with the tragedy. Sometimes, they were asked to watch the kids while the parents attended the funeral. It was a successful initiative for both our deputies and the public, and it received notoriety across the state. It is still in existence today and has expanded to other divisions of law enforcement to support victims of crime and other offices in the judicial system.

SHOP WITH A HERO

Serving everyone in our communities is the most important aspect of the job for those in law enforcement and public safety. Yes, we address unlawful behaviors and actions and put out fires. We are also looking for opportunities to serve people who abide by the law and those who may face difficulties and hardships. Christmas is one of my favorite times to show our support and give back to the community.

Chief Deputy Gregory Harless proposed a special holiday program for our community; I liked it very much and inaugurated the annual "Shop with a Hero" program. We assembled both police and firefighters to participate. Each child from an economically depressed area of Ingham County was partnered with a police officer or firefighter for a shopping spree at Meijers in Mason. We had a steady 30 children participate each year. Each child received $100 to spend on their family for Christmas. It was a very touching and heartwarming event.

My first little boy, sadly, wanted to go to the meat department because his family didn't have any meat to eat. Meijers always gave a complete turkey dinner, so he was covered. The most interesting part was that the child shopping always bought the other family members their gifts first. They shopped for themselves last. It was one of the greatest acts of selflessness and love I've ever seen. Many times, the police officers and firefighters always chipped in extra cash to make sure the child shopping also received a nice gift!

DARE

The Drug Abuse Resistance Education program—DARE—was held each year for fifth grade students. We even had a graduation ceremony with many classes and large numbers of fifth graders. It was a well-received program by all the parents who attended.

One school year, we had several overdose deaths in the area that were well publicized, which they continue to be today. That year, I wanted to make a point to our students at graduation, so I brought a prop. It was a body bag used at scenes involving death. I unfurled it, held it up, and asked, "Does anyone know what this is?"

As anticipated, no one did. I explained it was a "body bag" and one size fits all. It created quite a buzz with those in attendance, which was my hope. I was happy to learn that it was a memorable lesson many years later when, during my time as sheriff, one of my former students mentioned remembering the graduation with the body bag. I wish I knew how many students it may have kept from using drugs.

LACTATION ROOM

It's no surprise that women employees oftentimes become moms during their career. We learned that the greatest challenge young mothers faced once they returned from maternity leave was whether to continue breast feeding. We didn't have anything in place to assist them in that part of mothering, and I received pushback from people who thought I was "unconventional" for allowing "time off" for feeding their baby. However, we still converted an unused room into a private lactation room with comfortable seating and supplies so moms could nurse their babies or pump their breastmilk in private. To me, it wasn't any different than people taking smoking breaks several times a day. As time passes, different needs arise. I don't believe they have the lactation room anymore, but there are gender neutral locker rooms. It's always important to research opportunities on how to successfully meet the needs of staff and emphasize inclusivity in any organization.

CAMPUS POLICE

When I was sheriff, the local police, county deputies, state troopers, and campus police all worked on cases at Michigan State University. They were called the Department of Public Safety, and to work as a campus police officer, I continued to deputize them.

Finally, a few years ago, some law enforcement agencies applied to the legislature for a change in the law. Now, each university has its own police department, which makes sense and saves a lot of time and effort.

VOLUNTEER DEPUTIES

The Mounted Unit

The Mounted Unit of Ingham County was comprised of dedicated men and women volunteers who supported our team whenever needed. On many occasions, they provided search and rescue services, managed ceremonial details for parades and other celebrations, and served as crowd control during local and state capitol events and riots.

These volunteers were made up of a variety of business and private sector professionals who made a difference. Each volunteer provided all their needed equipment, uniforms, guns, horses, trucks, trailers, and fuel. They even had uniforms for their horses!

The mounted unit leader was Captain John Causie, owner of Causie Construction, a road building and repair company. He and all our volunteers were invaluable to the success of many outcomes. Unfortunately, John passed away a few years ago.

The Motorcycle Unit

Seeing how successful and helpful the mounted unit was to us, I deployed a motorcycle unit of volunteers who also wanted to support us in various efforts. Each volunteer also provided their own equipment, including expensive motorcycles, guns, uniforms, and fuel.

Captain Gary Rutherford, the owner of a local automobile dealership, led the motor unit, which provided escort services for presidential visits, led parades, assisted in search of rescue needs, and supplemented our security needs at various large events, including demonstrations that turned ugly.

The Disabled Parking Spaces Unit

On a daily basis, in any county and state, many disabled parking spaces are occupied by people who are not disabled and do not have the appropriate state-provided disabled sticker or placard. I commissioned one of our cars to be detailed "Disabled Parking Enforcement" and recruited a group of volunteers to drive around the parking lots to ensure these spaces were appropriately occupied. They did not carry weapons for protection and were only responsible for writing tickets.

DART TEAM

Despite the concern and consternation of the Dart Corporation, which makes styrofoam containers in Mason, we initiated the DART team. That acronym stood for "Dead Animal Recovery Team." It was created because the road commission complained about the roadkill on all the roads, mostly deer. As a problem solver, I worked with my volunteer teams to explore ideas. They said, "Why don't we get a trailer for our pickup truck and deploy our deputy volunteer units to supervise our trustees in jail while they dispose of the animals into the trailer? Our motorcycle unit could help supervise."

I thought it was a fantastic solution.

The trustees were a small group of people who were in jail for less serious offenses and identified by our corrections officers to be trustworthy individuals. Over time, they were slowly granted more responsibility to use their time wisely and develop new skills. Being that DART required this group to be on the highway was a fitting addition to their responsibilities. I'm not sure they appreciated the skills learned by picking up dead carcasses, but it greatly enhanced the aesthetics of the Ingham County roadways. We had both the mounted and motorcycle division assist them.

Shortly after we rolled out the program, two of our volunteer deputies reported, "We thought we lost your inmates today."

"How did that happen?" I asked.

"Well, they were picking up a dead animal. Next thing we know, we can't find them," one deputy replied. "We found them in the woods, vomiting."

Now *that's* a punishment. The press supported the efforts in a positive way. There are all kinds of costs to committing crime. This was probably the most disliked task among them.

*****

The volunteer programs lasted through my terms until I retired. Their service benefited both the citizens and law enforcement professionals of Ingham County and the State of Michigan.

All of the time, work, and contributions of our volunteer members and the leadership of Captain John Causie and Captain Gary Rutherford will always be greatly appreciated.

When my son, Scott, prepared the sheriff's office for his term, he made a good point, one with which I agreed. The volunteers were getting older. All held guns, except for the volunteers who handled disabled people parking spaces. Possible risks were that they could be overpowered and suffer unnecessary injury or tragedy.

When Scott assumed his role as sheriff, he disbanded the programs out of concern for the safety of our volunteers. The road commission assumed the work of the DART team. Disabled parking spaces are covered by regular patrol. The work of the mounted and motorcycle volunteers was transitioned to deputy employees. They were all terrific programs during my tenure. Today, safety and crime are much different than they were then, so it was the best solution to return the work to our trained, hired deputy personnel.

VOLUNTEER CHAPLAINS CORP

In times of tragedy, many people call upon their faith for comfort and guidance. It seemed natural to me to form a corps of chaplains to lend support to our deputies and staff during times of hardship caused by the work they do. I called upon chaplains in the community from various faiths so we would always have the counsel we needed for different people of different faiths.

The chaplains loved the idea because we assigned them a uniform and a gun. They were led by Captain Reverend Daryl Franzel. At first, when they went on ride-along patrols for education, they didn't have guns, until one of them mentioned the dangers they encountered while in uniform at dangerous traffic stops. To assign them guns, we had to clear it with our insurance company, who required us to train them like we train our deputies. We trained them and guns were distributed.

Most people who are not in law enforcement don't realize the difficulties of our jobs. The value the chaplains imparted to the staff was immeasurable. They filled so many needs and comforted us during times we didn't even think we needed comfort and counsel. Like the victim advocates, they, too, served our public.

Separation, divorce, illness, or loss of a child or family member are struggles we all endure regardless of our professional roles. Our deputies and staff also witness, view, and process scenes that would put the worst movie scenes to shame. It's our job, but it affects us. I was pleasantly surprised that often, my teams called the chaplains of their own accord, which emphasized the importance of such a program.

During two of the worst experiences I had as a sheriff, the chaplains were paramount to our recovery and healing. They were a godsend at the scenes and on our campus when we lost two of our own. On Sunday, October 6, 1996, while responding to a call, Sergeant Paul Cole, 40 years old, swerved off the road to avoid a deer and hit a tree. When I arrived back at the office from being on the scene all night, it was around 5:00 a.m. A lot of our staff were huddled in our meeting room in various stages of grief. It's not often you see grown adults visibly crying on the job.

On December 7, 2014, we lost Deputy Sheriff Grant William Whitaker, who was only 25 years old and on the job for only 18 months. During a high-speed police chase, his patrol car left the roadway and struck a tree.

During both tragedies, we were all shattered by the loss of important members of our law enforcement family. In times like this, I can help console people by hugging and listening, but the chaplains supported us at a much higher level. Their presence, prayers, and counsel led everyone to calmness so we could do our job. They were instrumental during my terms in office and remain so today under the new administration.

A LEGACY MEMORIAL STATUE TO HONOR THE FALLEN

The Ingham County Memorial for fallen officers. The two statues are life-size replicas of Lieutenant Danielle Patrick and Captain Steve Ryan. Danielle presents the flag to Steve, representing the fallen officers. The names and dates and dates for each officer who died in the line of duty are mounted around the base of the monument. Dedicated August 1, 2000.

Honor. Respect. Remember. With sorrowful hearts filled with gratitude, we remember those who have fallen in the line of duty while serving the citizens of Ingham County.

As a result of Paul Cole dying in the line of duty, it became abundantly apparent to me there was nothing in Ingham County to memorialize police officers from any law enforcement organization who were killed while serving on the job. It took some doing, but we made it happen.

My vision was a large base topped with life-size statues of two deputies: Lieutenant Danielle Patrick presenting a flag to Captain Steve Ryan. Around the base, we added names and dates for each officer who died in the line of duty.

Once I knew what I wanted to do, I initiated the process with a signed note and our own money, putting down $115,000. When I went home that night, I said, "Sandy, just so you know, we're in debt now, but we'll raise the money independently to pay for the memorial."

She was in full support, and the community wrapped its arms around it and fully paid for it with contributions. Our largest single contributor was El Dorado Golf Course in Mason, who sponsored a golf outing exclusively for the monument. All proceeds were donated to the cause, and Mike Bell, the general manager, made it happen.

It was important to me that the statue be located at the sheriff's office so it wouldn't get vandalized. A local police union gave me some heat because they thought it should be located in Lansing. We worked through it, and today, it stands in the center of the square before the sheriff's office.

With the construction of the new jail and sheriff's administrative offices, we also wanted to pay respect to all the sheriffs who ever served Ingham County. On the largest wall across from the main entrance, we relocated all the pictures of former sheriffs from the previous building to the new building. There were six photos missing, but retired Captain Versil Babcock asked for something to do for the sheriff's office.

Retirement can be boring. He was a photographer, so he was the perfect candidate to curate those last six photos.

In addition, Scott wanted to memorialize two fallen deputies during my term, Sgt. Paul Cole and Deputy Grant Whitaker. Inside the lobby of the front entrance, he commissioned lockers to be built for each one, with glass fronts to display their uniforms and the belongings they had stored in the locker room.

All three initiatives are timeless reminders of those who protect and serve our communities and unexpectedly pay the ultimate sacrifice.

Bulletin Honors Sheriff's Office on the FBI Law Enforcement Bulletin's (LEB) website (eb.fbi.gov).

In 1998, the Ingham County Sheriff's Office began fundraising for a $115,000 Ingham County Law Enforcement Memorial. Private donations from local businesses and the sale of commemorative bricks were used to construct the original memorial. Bronze plaques display the names of the 12 fallen law enforcement officers who served departments throughout Ingham County. The monument features a hexagonal block base supporting a granite top, which includes two life-sized bronze statues of Ingham County Deputies in Honor Guard uniforms ceremoniously presenting a flag. Construction was done by the local brick layers' union at no cost.

In 2018, Ingham County voters approved funding for a new Ingham County Justice Complex. In 2020, construction began, and the memorial was carefully dismantled and preserved for relocation. In 2023, it was reconstructed as the centerpiece of the courtyard to the entrances of the Sheriff's Office, Correctional Facility, and 55th District Court. The memorial is surrounded by the flags of Ingham County, the State of Michigan, and the United States of America, as well as benches and a donor plaque.

In 2023, the Lansing Police Department discovered two additional line-of-duty deaths were not recognized on the memorial. On May 6, 1901, 45-year-old Officer George Brown died from a heart attack while struggling with an intoxicated inmate at the Lansing jail. On December 24, 1947, 37-year-old Detective Sergeant Homer Hatt died from a heart attack shortly after being struck in the chest while attempting to stop a fight between two men. To ensure their sacrifice was never forgotten, the Ingham County Sheriff's Office added both names to the memorial in 2024, 123 years after Officer Brown made his sacrifice.

The memorial serves as a solemn reminder of the ultimate sacrifice made and the services provided by local law enforcement officers. A county-wide law enforcement memorial ceremony is held at the site every May.

Bulletin Honors: Ingham County Law Enforcement Memorial — LEB

PLANTING THE SEED FOR A NEW JAIL

Around 2010, it came time to replace the jail that was built in 1963. The bricks around the entire building were falling apart and needed to be tuckpointed, which is a very expensive process. Additionally, it's not a permanent solution, because tuckpointing would be required for years to come. Tuckpointing is a construction technique on the exterior of brick buildings where masons (expert builders for brick-and-mortar products) improve their look and duration. They chip out broken mortar (a hard compound) and fill the joints between bricks with new mortar. Additionally, the jail was showing extreme wear and tear on the interior and was quite outdated for the current needs from facility and technological standpoints.

To me, it didn't make any sense to me to invest taxpayers' money into something that was a temporary solution. I met with the county controller. He updated me with their plans: "We are going to have the building tuckpointed. I have companies bidding. It'll be a 15-year fix."

I asked, "Why wouldn't you do a 50-year fix?"

He said, "Gene, are you going to be here in 50 years?"

"No."

"Well, I'm not either." he concurred.

Then, I replied for emphasis, "We need a new jail."

"Boy, I think it's going to be a hard sell, Gene. You need to put together a presentation for the board of commissioners."

We discussed it further, and he was convinced. We put together a presentation for the commissioners, went before them, and presented it for approval. I thought they would simply take a vote for yay or nay. However, they didn't. They said, "We want to study this a little bit more."

They studied it for quite a while. It's a full jail; they weren't going to let it fall down.

The county moved forward with the tuckpointing on the then-current jail. I was encouraged because the longest serving commissioner Mark Grebner mentioned, "Gene, just so you know, it'll pass."

With his political prowess and knowledge about our voters, he felt that law enforcement and criminal justice issues were important to the people of Ingham County.

Unfortunately, we didn't get it approved for the vote during my term. When Scott was elected sheriff in 2016, he continued to advocate for the new jail and administration complex. After many months of discussions, the board of commissioners agreed to place the issue on the August 2018 ballot to let the voters decide. Prior to the vote, Scott rolled out a massive campaign to educate the public on why it was needed.

On the 2018 ballot, citizens voted and, sure enough, it passed. It passed handily, too. Not by a little bit, but *handily*, to the tune of approving an $80 million bond. It's the most expensive building project the county ever had. Fortunately for the incoming sheriff, Scott, and all the employees at the sheriff's office, Granger Construction built a beautiful, state-of-the-art facility that meets today's needs for both the inmates and the staff.

Sandy

With Scott, we gave many tours of the new sheriff's office and jail. I enjoyed seeing and hugging everybody that I knew for years. When I saw the young deputies, I thought, *Are you old enough to have a gun?* They looked so young to me. I guess that's part of getting up into the later years.

I'm proud of Gene, and maybe I was over-involved, but I wanted him to know that I supported him and what he was doing. There were a lot of rocky moments, as there always is when dealing with employees, the public and crime.

Chapter 14 Lesson

For many of us, it's important that we leave the place we live or work better than when we found it. Initiating these advancements for the sheriff's office and Ingham County citizens was an absolute honor. However, the reason they were successful and impacted our communities so much was because of all the people involved, who also made a difference in their career, life, family, and community. It certainly takes a village, and these initiatives sure did, too.

Where in your life, family, or community can you improve the lives of others? I believe part of the reason we are here is to do exactly that. You don't have to create your own initiative or reinvent the wheel. There are plenty of community events within your town, county, church, school, and social organizations. Sandy and I have found that it is very helpful to pick the activities you enjoy and to prioritize the types of contributions you want to see make a difference.

CHAPTER 15

UNFORGETTABLE AS THE SHERIFF

Mark Wriggelsworth

Careers in law enforcement are unforgettable. We have really funny experiences, and we witness horrific scenes that sear themselves into your brain. Cop humor is a necessity of survival, even if it seems morbid or inappropriate to civilians. We just need to stay on task and get the job done.

Eaton County, where I worked, is a busy county, and we dealt with a lot of death and injuries. I believe a lot of people don't realize how many natural and unexpected deaths law enforcement personnel encounter and must address. Every death is difficult for us, the parties involved, and the surviving loved ones.

Natural deaths, expected or not, are part of all our lives, and a little easier to process than an unexpected or tragic passing. Gruesome, unthinkable deaths are a part of our day, week, month, and year, and include accidents around the home with chainsaws and other objects, gruesome car accidents with fatalities, and suicides. Unlike natural deaths or accidents, murders are inflicted upon the innocent. During my last year as captain in 2022, we had eight homicides, of which two were triple homicides. Over my 25-year career, I wish the numerous homicides, fatal crashes, and suicides never happened.

There are also people, like my mom mentions, who are mentally ill, drugged, or incoherent. When my dad was at the hospital visiting someone, a woman approached him and said, "You know, they are listening to us right now."

My mom said, "Call the police."

"They won't come anymore." the woman responded.

Unlike what people see on TV, it's not wrapped up in a 60-minute drama, and it's not just about the crime. As first responders, it's our duty to determine the cause of death and support the living family members. On Thanksgiving, a person has a heart attack and dies. It's a horrific event for everyone involved. We might discover a suicide or the untimely death of a child. We are not only there to oversee the deceased, we are there as advocates to help whoever needs support. Sharing resources of supportive organizations to guide them through the experience is always important, and we hope, given the excruciating circumstance, we can ease their anguish just a bit.

When we leave that call, it sticks with us, it repeatedly plays in our minds, and it is unforgettable. And that is why we value the uplifting, positive, and extraordinary events that also happen to us.

It's a career where the good outweighs the bad, which is why we take on these careers, because we truly care about people and want to make our communities safer.

DROWNING

In Holt, there is an *esker*, which is a gravel pit filled with water. It runs all the way north to St. Johns and all the way east to Mason. During the summer, it's common for the kids to swim in it, but it's not the safest thing to do. One day, a group of kids decided to swim across the lake to the opposite shore. Three of them made it, and, very unfortunately, one did not. We had the dive team out there all day searching for the missing boy. The family was beyond emotion; as expected, everyone was extremely distressed.

As night fell, our sergeant commanded the dive team to end their efforts and return in the morning. The parents had no way to understand how impossible it was to see anything in the dark water. Understandably, they were irate and didn't hold anything back in their outlash. It's one of those situations where anything we did was never going to be enough, and we were still criticized. And while it's difficult to say—we always want to do the right thing, recover their beloved child, and finish the search properly—we also must ensure the safety of the responders. In that particular gravel pit, there was abandoned mining machinery and a car sitting at the bottom. Anyone could get tangled in it. It was dangerous for everyone. The next day, the boy's body was found. A child passing away is always the most difficult part of our jobs.

TORNADO

There was a tornado that traveled through Williamston, and it caused a lot of property damage. Unfortunately, two people died as well. The couple was building a house and temporarily lived in a modular home, which is prefabricated in two parts and secured with equipment. They dug a large pond next to both the modular home and the home under construction. At night, while they were sleeping in bed, the tornado ran through the town, picked up the modular home, and threw it upside down in the pond. The divers found them in the pond under the bed. The tornado came in so quickly, they didn't even have time to get out of bed. It appeared that the installation and securing of the modular home was not yet completed. When it comes to trailers and prefabs, it's absolutely necessary to complete the entire installation before occupancy.

LOST BUT FOUND

A mother arrived home in a local trailer park and reported her daughter was kidnapped. The daughter was a teenager, and as we investigated the scene, there were indications of a possible struggle. We couldn't find her, so we called the FBI and state police. They came out, set up their equipment, and a command center in the training room of the Sheriff's office. It was quite an effort to observe. To everyone's relief, we found her the same day. She took off with some guy. I was proud of how our teams collaborated with other departments. Continuing efforts on our part helped find the missing girl.

*****

When our son, Scott, was an East Lansing Officer, he called me one afternoon.

"Hey, Dad, there's a guy working at the 7-11 store, and he's wearing an Ingham County jail inmate uniform."

Surprised, I asked, "Really? What color?"

He replied, "Orange, and it says 'Ingham County' on it."

I thought, *That wasn't good.*

"Go over there and grab the guy up," I directed.

It turned out he was a former inmate that was in our jail, and he explained, "Well, when I was released, nobody paid attention. I took it and walked out the door with it."

We learned a valuable lesson and tightened up the exit process. He was the son of a lieutenant in the East Lansing Police Department. However, he stole the uniform, which was a crime.

SHOOTINGS

One of the female undercover officers who worked for me was driven to be the first person at everything. When you raid a house, the uniforms are positioned in the door first so the people in the house know they're police officers. If I went running in with just a police jacket on, I would get shot.

We raided a house on Johnson Street; it had a set of stairs on the outside of the house. She ran up the steps and kicked the door down before everyone else was in place. The guy shot her right in the forehead, right at the hairline. She went down like a bag of potatoes. He shot her again in the back of the leg. Surprisingly, it was the wound in the leg that took her down. The bullet was a low power gun, it traversed under her scalp but above her skull, and out the back. We recovered the bullet. After it went through her head, it went out a window and ended up in the eaves of the house next door.

They rushed her to the hospital, and I was glad to hear she survived when I got there.

"Where is she at?" I asked the desk nurse.

She pointed to the room and said, "She sure is wound up."

I saw her young ones nearby and walked into the room. They had her stripped to her waist as she laid there. "Hey, Boss! How are you doing?"

I cleared my throat and looked in another direction. "Well, seeing this much of you, I'm not sure. But I'm glad you are okay."

I think she was more worried about the wound than her boobs being exposed.

"I'll tell you; you are the hardest-headed woman I ever met."

The leg laid her up for a long time, but she eventually made a full recovery. Thankfully.

*****

In 2012, we had about a half-dozen shootings along I-96 all the way through Ingham County and southwest into Oakland County. A sniper, while driving, randomly shot at other drivers. It took a while to figure out the shooter's location through the firing of their gun. Fortunately, no one was killed, but many cars had bullet holes. A shooting on M-52 at Williamston Road even took out a windshield. It was dangerous.

Our detectives were sharp, and I told them, "Start walking about a mile down Williamston Road, and search the soil for any brass from a gun."

Sure enough, they found the brass laying on the gravel along the road. We were the only police department that found evidence. Oakland County chased down a suspect, grabbed him, found the gun, and connected it to him. He was convicted of 25 felonies and one count of terrorism, which landed him in prison for 40 years. Ingham, Livingston, and Oakland counties worked together to solve the case and prevent further shootings.

MURDER

When we live and work in the same county, we are bound to cross paths with people we know. I just always hoped it would be under positive circumstances and not felony crimes. David was a local guy who worked in the volunteer fire department with our oldest son, Mike. He had been to our house several times. While he was a big guy at 6'8", he was innocuous to me. He was pleasant, and I never thought much about him.

A local woman named Jeanette was reported missing, and her body was found at a park in this township. She was found bound with flex cuffs, naked—upon further examination, we learned she was sexually assaulted—and she had been murdered. There were zero suspects, as no evidence was found. Her elderly mother, Muriel, was a nice lady and understandably distraught. We did everything we could to find something that would solve it. A few years later, it was designated as a cold case. Muriel was very upset with me and went to the media. The media reported we weren't doing anything, which wasn't true, as I had people assigned to it the whole time. We can only do so much with so little.

A few years later, luck, if that's what you want to call it, turned up some evidence related to Jeanette. David attempted to kidnap a woman in Traverse City. He was caught and arrested. Grand Traverse County called us to report the subject was wearing an Ingham County Sheriff hat. He was a local guy; his name was familiar. We started reinvestigating cases. In the meantime, her mother met with the State Attorney General to report we weren't doing anything. The AG called me. "I know this is a problem for you all. Do you mind if I assign a couple of my investigators?"

I knew the officers he assigned because they were former local officers.

"Send them down, we could use all the help we can get," I replied, hoping something would surface.

They were great cops and did what they could. Eventually, one of our detectives, Peter Ackerly, started reinterviewing people and reviewing the case file.

Peter interviewed one of the former firefighters who worked with David and said, "You know, I had an old state police car that I bought at an auction. David asked me if he could have the flex cuffs that had been left in the trunk of the car."

Peter had it pulled in for inspection to look for clues. The team found flex cuffs in the wheel well of the car. We compared them to those used to tie Jeanette.

We found the smoking gun. There was a little bitty metal clip on the flex cuffs found in the auctioned police car, which was only manufactured on flex cuffs used by law enforcement. The clip prevented people from removing them. We had an officer travel to Mexico and meet with the manufacturer of the cuffs. They compared their machine markings to the machine markings on the flex cuff to confirm that's where they came from. That was the nail in the coffin for David. He pled not guilty and went to trial. He was convicted and is in prison for 60-90 years, the equivalent of a life sentence. Unfortunately, in the meantime, Jeanette's mother passed away and never saw the conclusion of this case.

Prior to Jeanette's murder, we also learned that he sexually assaulted the daughter of one of our staff members. That story was covered in the media for a couple of years, too, especially when we made the arrest.

When we arrested him for his arraignment hearing for Jeanette's murder, I wanted to humiliate him as best as I could. Our smallest female officer cuffed him up and walked him into court. I knew it bothered him that he was marched into court by a very petite woman lieutenant.

*****

During the Fourth of July weekend in 2005, the parents of a little boy named Ricky reported that he was kidnapped. We deployed a massive search with people from all over, including different police departments, Boy Scout Troops, and volunteer citizens. You name it, everyone was there who was available. The family lived by the Red Cedar River, and the searchers combed rows of corn in the farmers' fields and the riverbanks to no avail. The logistics to manage everyone was a nightmare given the search area parameters. Fortunately, for two weeks, one of the farmers lent us part of his yard for our setup and parking.

My team started knocking on doors and landed upon a house trailer with a guy living by himself. From the doorway, the deputies could see he had a stash of newspaper clippings stuck on his wall about the missing child. We thought he was suspicious and investigated him. He came out clean, just eccentric.

The neighbors next to Ricky's house mentioned the family dog that previously died before Ricky went missing. They saw the dad digging in the back yard. We found the area and dug the dirt up to reveal bones of the dead dog.

Through interviewing the parents and the neighbors, we learned of unspeakable acts and behaviors that happened in the victim's house. While in his basement, one neighbor heard noises above. When he went to the first floor, he found Ricky rummaging through his cupboards. Upon asking what he was doing, Ricky answered, "I don't get fed anything at home. I don't think my mother likes me."

When it came to the parents, we couldn't get anything out of them, and we didn't find clues to find Ricky.

A few months after his kidnapping, the father came to the sheriff's office. Apparently, the mother was in complete control of the family, including her husband. The father shared that Ricky's favorite meal was chicken nuggets. When the mother made them, she fed them to the other children but made Ricky sit in the corner and eat carrot sticks, which he hated. With Ricky's absence, the mother transferred her hate to one of her other sons. As Ricky's dad sat before us, he buried his head in his hands and said, "I can't go through this again. I can never kill another one of my kids."

He told us how much the mother hated Ricky. One night, she was mad at him. She hit him in the head with a hammer. It didn't kill him, and he ended up in a coma while he laid in bed until he died two days later. In his short seven years of life, he endured horrendous torture at the hands of his own parents.

After the father relayed the story to us, he had an epiphany and took us to find Ricky's body. We found him in a plastic trash bag, and he had decomposed quite a bit. According to the coroner, he had a dent on his head where she hit him with the hammer that caused a brain bleed. There was damage to his elbow, nose, shoulder blade, and his upper jaw was broken, all from previous injuries. That poor little boy. It just tore your heart up.

Without the dad, we never would have found him in a swampy area along Williamston Road. We charged them both with murder, they pled "not guilty," and we went to trial in front of a judge, no jury. They were both tried at the same time. I found it strange that they didn't separate them. The husband took the stand, testified against his wife, and admitted culpability. He was the one that really solved the case for us, and he went to prison for a while. Ricky's two brothers were placed with a family member.

The judge was disgusted with the case and sentenced them with these haunting final words: "You buried your dog in the back yard, and you threw your son in a trash bag into a ditch."

*****

A 19-year-old woman named Amanda broke up with her boyfriend. She traveled to Florida for spring break with a group of female and male friends. Her boyfriend was not happy she was with other guys. During the trip, she sent him a picture of her lying in bed with two guys. It infuriated him.

Soon after her return home after the vacation, she was reported missing. We found her car not far from her home. Then, some joggers ran near the railroad tracks in rural Ingham County and found the body of a dead woman. Her throat was cut from ear to ear, through the neck to her spine.

As we investigated him, we found a video of him killing his dog in his backyard. Clearly, he had all the makings of a serial killer. When she came back from Florida, and when we found her, she wore a parka jacket called a "jarka." We found the fibers from that coat in the trunk of his car. That was really the smoking gun, in my opinion, and we charged him with murder. During the jury trial, they found him not guilty. He walked out of court like a fancy rooster. Even more disturbing was that he was a good-looking kid, and a couple of girls hooked onto him after they saw him on trial.

I was devastated and really felt for the victim's parents. We put a lot of time and effort into this case. The crime lab did an outstanding job identifying those fibers. One of the jurors asked one of our detectives why we didn't put him on the polygraph. We ran him on it, and halfway through, he stood up and walked out. The polygraph examiner said he flunked it so badly that it could have been used as a good example for other examiners to compare. Unfortunately, polygraphs are inadmissible in court.

*****

In Holt, a woman named Wanda worked her first midnight shift at a local gas station. We received a call about a dead woman at the gas station. When we arrived, her son was there with the man who found her. Right away, it seemed suspicious, but later, the son was found not to be involved. She was shot once in her head. We retrieved the video from the camera system that showed a man wandering around to confirm the store was empty. He pointed his gun at her, made her give him all the money in the cash register, and shot her. There was no reason. He ran out of the station.

The video was all we had for evidence that just showed the headlight and maybe part of the front door. Of course, it was pre-digital, and the store owner had inserted a previously used tape that had his kid's baseball game on it. The recording of the shooting was poor quality, and the crime lab could not fix it. However, they referred us to a company in Jackson that fixed the film on the Hubble Telescope.

The work to repair it was amazing. Our guys determined the type of car and with the renewed quality, they saw the license plate. We arrested the suspect, and he went to prison for murder.

*****

In 1996, a man named Mitch was involved with a woman named Christine. Their relationship went sideways because she also had a husband who was in prison. She called her husband in prison and told him Mitch wasn't treating her well. So, he escaped prison and brought a buddy with him, they kidnapped Mitch, and beheaded him. Gruesome.

Of course, we were involved since his head was buried in Delhi Township in a swampy area. The media picked up on the fact that there were a bunch of uniforms around, so they were snooping for the story. We were trying to keep it on the downlow because we didn't have the body yet. However, the buddy confessed, so we knew the body was in Jackson County.

The team brought the gurney out, and even though they only recovered the head, they made it look like the shape of the body. The last thing we needed was the media picking up on it. One of our detectives walked up to me, "Boss, we're done here. We're going to go get the body."

One of the reporters heard him say that, and he walked over to me, "I heard what he said to you. The body isn't here?"

Now, I always promised that I didn't lie to the media, so I said in a stern voice, "The body is not here. But if you release that news to anybody, you'll never, ever get another story out of me. But I promise you this, as soon as we recover that body, you will be my first phone call, and you can have the scoop and put it out first."

He nodded and agreed with that deal. And that's exactly what he did. As soon as the body was in Jackson County, I called him. "Okay, you can put it out now."

We convicted both the escapee and his buddy. It was just a brutal murder.

SEXUAL ASSAULT

Around seven in the morning, there was a rape in southern rural Ingham County. While we interviewed the victim, the officers learned the victim had answered a knock at the door, and a guy assaulted her. As she described the car he drove, she looked out the window, pointed, and shouted, "There he goes."

We dragged the suspect back to the scene where he was identified by the victim. He was arrested and taken to jail. It doesn't usually happen like that, but it sure was a nice and easy way to apprehend the suspect.

REASONS I'M GRATEFUL TO GOD

There was a huge garage behind the sheriff's office used for vehicle repair. Sometimes, we used it for employee training. While training, one of the trainees was handcuffed, his hands secured behind his back with flex cuffs, which are a plastic handcuff that doesn't need a key to be removed. For some reason that day, the trainee learning to remove them couldn't get them off his fellow trainee. No one had any wire cutters, so the sergeant used a knife to cut them back and forth. Accidentally, the sergeant drove the knife blade right into the trainee's back. They transported the guy to the hospital immediately, where they sewed in a few stitches, gave him a pain pill, and sent him home. Fortunately, that's all he needed. It was just a surface injury. Thank God.

CHAPTER 15 LESSONS

SPECIAL SAFETY TIPS

I do believe any upstanding and law-abiding citizen would be stunned at the number and types of crimes that are committed on a daily basis. Oftentimes, "staying safe" seems like it would be so simple. In reality, so many people don't know how to report crimes or suspicious acts they see, or how to keep themselves safe. Here are some tips which I hope you find helpful to keep yourself, your family, and your community safe.

HOW TO REPORT OR RESPOND TO A CRIME OR SUSPICIOUS ACTS

When we get a call from dispatch, there are many physical, emotional, and mental reactions we have as we respond. Each situation is unique and calls for different reactions. If 911 tells us there is a homicide or domestic situation in progress, we drive very fast, with our blood rushing and mind planning our approach: do we run into the house or wait for backup?

When a car is stolen or there is a robbery or a mugging, and they dispatch the description, we drive cautiously to keep an eye on passing cars or injured persons.

If we are merely driving or on patrol, we keep an eye on everything to ensure proper order in public situations. Being on alert is natural for law enforcers because we have to always be ready to intervene. I might be on personal leave or off for the day. If there is an emergency or crime, I must intervene as a part of my oath.

HOW CAN YOU HELP US FIGHT CRIME?

When you are suspicious of behavior or witness a crime, try to gather as much information as possible. When you write down information, type it into your phone or take pictures; it is the best way to help us and reduce the stress from having to remember it.

- For vehicles: With as much detail as possible, describe any people, vehicles, directions headed, and location. On vehicles, it's best to get a license plate and/or the make/model/color of a vehicle. For instance, black Chevy SUV and license plate number. If you notice anything unusual like tinted windows, a dent, or a smashed light, that will be helpful, too.

- For people: Document anything you see or remember, including gender, height, age, colors of hair, beard, mustache, eyes, and skin color. All are important. Any clothing, masks, or unique shoes that stand out and are easy to remember—a gray hoodie, black jeans, red tennis shoes. Don't forget to mention any tattoos, scars, or odors, like perfume, bad breath, cigarettes, or drugs. If they are with other people or children or pets, that is also important information.

- Lastly, the location and direction the vehicle or person was seen in and where they went next helps us zero in on finding the perpetrator. We had one brave victim who shared a bunch of information she remembered with us, and the guy passed by the scene as we interviewed her. When she pointed him out, we grabbed him immediately.

CHAPTER 16

IN MEMORIAM,
THE ULTIMATE SACRIFICE, 1988–2016

SERGEANT PAUL LAWRENCE COLE,
INGHAM COUNTY SHERIFF'S OFFICE

ON SUNDAY, OCTOBER 6, 1996, at two in the morning, the phone at our house rang. When I answered, my son, Scott, said, "Dad, I don't know what's going on, but I think an officer got killed."

Immediately, I wondered why my son was calling me and not the sheriff's office. I soon learned the office was too busy handling the scene and waited to call me until they knew more.

Paul Cole worked for me for several years. He was a great guy and a terrific sergeant. He was called to a domestic violence call with a guy who chased after his wife with a gun or knife. As he drove to the scene, a herd of deer ran in front of him. He swerved to avoid them, which caused his car to leave the road and hit a tree. We were grateful he didn't suffer as his death was instant.

I sprinted to my car and sped to the scene. It was the first "in line of duty" death since I became sheriff in 1988. He was one of our family, and when I arrived, our staff understandably were standing around and crying. Paul was their friend; we were all shocked and sad. Despite my own state of mind, I had to remain focused on what needed to be done. I said, "Okay, guys, we got a job to do here. Let's get to work."

It was like they woke up out of a haze, and they went about doing their jobs.

It was helpful that the state police showed up unsolicited to ask if we wanted them to handle it. "We're veterans here, we know how to do this."

It was extremely difficult, and the next step was to inform Paul's family. So, I then left the scene and headed to Paul and Kathy's house. He was only 40 years old, leaving behind his wife and three children. He was the father of Heather, Paul, and Andrew, who was six weeks old.

When I arrived at the house, I banged on the door and rang the doorbell. Eventually, I saw a light turn on upstairs. I heard footsteps slowly walking down the stairs. I was familiar with the house, and knew the stairs were just on the other side of the door. It was quiet, and it seemed that time stood still forever. Kathy opened the door and I told her what happened. She woke up her young daughter, around 14 years old, and I stood next to Kathy as I shared the news that changed her life in an instant that night. Her son, who was around twelve years old, was sleeping over at a friend's house, so we went over there together, and I told him, too. It was hard. It was really hard.

Paul was a great guy with a terrific family. When I promoted Paul to sergeant, Kathy and I ran into each other, and she said, "Thank you."

I had no idea why she was thanking me, but she explained, "Thank you for promoting my husband to sergeant."

Surprised, I replied, "Well, Kathy, you're the first wife who ever told me that." It was nice to hear.

Once I was assured it was appropriate for me to leave the Cole home, I returned to the sheriff's office. My staff and the chaplains had congregated in our large training room. It was a nightmare none of us ever wanted to experience.

Paul received a hell of a sendoff as the entire community stepped up to take care of the Coles before, during, and after his funeral services. The local Chevrolet dealer provided two large vans to transport the family for the funeral. It was a huge funeral, and people from all over the state attended.

The process of grief is different for everyone, and each of us needs to do what makes sense to us. A day or two after Paul's funeral, Kathy showed up unannounced at the sheriff's office with her family. "I want to see his patrol car."

I tried to convince her not to do that. It was a mess. And the kids, I knew it would be hard for them. "Kathy, this is not pretty."

"I want to see it." she insisted.

I led her out back; they all looked at it, turned around, and left.

"All right. Thanks," she said.

Police department heads are trained in COPS, Concerns of Police Survivors. They taught us that if the surviving family members want to see the car or other tangible objects, let them. Some people want and need to know how their loved one died.

Subsequently, we continued to see Kathy on a regular basis. Months later, I hired her as my secretary. She shared many funny stories about Paul.

When the time felt right, I asked her, "You know, it seemed like there was a long pause before you answered the door that night."

"I looked out the window and saw who it was. I knew the sheriff didn't show up on my doorstep at two in the morning for nothing. And I knew as soon as I opened the door, my life would change forever." she solemnly replied.

KATHY COLE

When Paul died, and when any spouse dies on the job, you can't see yourself or your future. I was in survival mode for a long while just doing what needed to be done. I lost my heart, and there was just so much life we missed together. I had just given birth to our son three months prior, and he was such a special gift for all of us, to have Paul still with us. It was the hardest time of my life, and yet, we made it through. Given all the support we received, we really didn't have any other choice than to make it.

Once some time had passed, I kept myself busy and focused on raising my family. I worked at the sheriff's office as a secretary and eventually became Sheriff Wriggelsworth's administrative assistant. I volunteered as president of the organization MICOPS, the Michigan chapter of Concerns Of Police Survivors. In addition to other initiatives, we raised money for the state memorial near the state capitol. We built it to honor all the Michigan police officers killed in the line of duty. Paul loved golf, and for 20 years, I hosted an annual golf outing in his memory. We raised money to donate to the state memorial.

I was thankful that Gene was the sheriff because he and his family were supportive and did so many good things for us. I would not have been the same person without their generosity and the support we received from the community. Being a family member of someone in law enforcement is extremely special because we all treat each other as family. It was just so humbling to learn about the work people do for the betterment of human beings.

The hardest part of losing your spouse is all the moments they miss, and you miss them, especially when it comes to each of the kids' milestones. Even if the kids didn't share their thoughts or what they missed with me, I know they were missing Paul and wishing he could be at every birthday, holiday, and graduation.

I volunteered to help with police officer training as a panel member of family survivors. The survivors answered questions about line of duty death. We discussed which services helped them the most, what else could have helped, and what needed to be changed. One year, I volunteered my daughter to speak.

Hearing the experiences from a child's point of view is always difficult, but very helpful.

While Heather was on the panel, they asked, "What's the one thing you did for your dad that your mom doesn't know?"

She was about 22 or 23, and she wasn't married yet, so she answered, "Well, my dad always told me that when I turned 21, he was going to take me out to have my first beer. Dad and I laughed about it, and he said, 'We'll sit on the front porch, drink a beer, crush the cans, and throw them in the yard so your younger brother will go pick it up for us.'"

As I listened from the back of the room, my heart sank, and I thought, *I can't even believe she's telling this story. That's so like my husband to say something like that.*

She continued, "So when I turned 21, I took a beer and had a beer at the headstone with my dad."

The next question was tougher, I think, for both of us. "We know losing your dad was terrible. What was the hardest thing?"

Heather stopped. She looked at me, and she said, "My mom was never the same."

Through tears, I nodded "yes."

As I looked into the crowd, I saw all the men wipe away their own tears, and they shouted out, "We're gonna take you out and have a beer!"

Even years later, my family and I are supported in so many beautiful ways.

The memorials were a wonderful tribute to honor Paul's service and memory. After the lockers and memorial statue were built at the sheriff's office, Gene escorted me to see Paul's name and locker. As we stood in front of the statue, you could see how much it meant to him. That meant a lot to me, too.

We have had some really difficult times, but Paul's memory always remains with us. I was lucky to remarry to a man who raised Paul's kids as his own, always with respect to Paul's memory. While the kids are grown, we are a close family and remain filled with love.

Thank you to every single person and organization who generously gave of their hearts to support our family and me. We would not have made it through without knowing and feeling the love from you. You made every difficult moment a little easier. Thank you especially for remembering and honoring Paul for the work he did to protect and serve.

*****

DEPUTY SHERIFF GRANT WILLIAM WHITAKER, INGHAM COUNTY SHERIFF'S OFFICE

Deputy Grant Whitaker worked for me for 18 months, and he was a very young deputy, only 25 years old. He was a former Stockbridge police officer. Local police didn't come across high-speed chases, and he was in pursuit of a suspect in his first high-speed chase.

Very unfortunately, he followed the car down the road about a mile from his parents' house. The road had a huge hump in it, and his car went airborne. When he hit the ground, he lost control, spun sideways, and hit a tree. The impact was so severe that the engine flew out of the car and landed 20 feet away.

I received the call in the middle of the night and headed to the site. They had already taken Grant to the hospital, but he had died on impact. I drove down the road to his parents' house along with the victim advocates who were already there. When we arrived, they had already strung up their Christmas lights even though it was still fall. Their front door was filled with decorations. I walked up, banged on the door, and rang their bell. I didn't realize they don't use their front door, so after the lights turned on, it took them a while to move stuff out of the way to open it.

As I stood inside the house, I said, "I have some bad news. Grant was involved in an accident just down the road here, and it took his life."

The husband understood immediately. The wife, who became a friend of ours, asked, "Sheriff, can you tell me that again. Because I'm just not grasping what you're telling me."

Then we continued to tell Grant's two brothers. It was really sad.

Grant's funeral was in Chelsea, a little town just outside of town, and I was at the service, looking at all the pictures. One picture showed a group of guys with long beards who looked like the guys on the reality show *Duck Dynasty*. I asked the guy standing next to me, "Who are these Duck Dynasty guys?"

He replied, "That's me, Dad, my brother, and Grant."

He had shaved his beard, and there was no way I would have recognized him. They did chuckle about it.

The funeral was an outpouring of many police officers from many police agencies. Grant had a nice sendoff with two miles of police cars in his funeral procession. People on the streets of Chelsea stopped in reverence as the procession drove by. No matter the cause of someone's death, the support extended by our law enforcement families is always a sight to behold. It's really special.

CHAPTER 16 LESSON

A knock on the door in the middle of the night is never good news, unless it's the birth of a baby. Anyone in the field of law enforcement and public safety, as well as first responders and the military, knows this all too well. Spouses and loved ones pray every day for the safety of their hard-working public servants.

Each time I had to knock on the door, no matter if it was for a fellow officer, a friend, or a victim of a crime, I had to present the news that would change their life in a second with stoic, straightforward composure, along with my condolences.

To prepare for these instances, we attend family survivor training. No matter how much training you have or how many times you are called to deliver this news, it never gets easy.

I've learned over the years, in tragedy and grief, there are various ways we come together. It might be bringing a meal, visiting the surviving family members, supporting the children, running errands, planning the services, attending the services, following in the processions, or standing at attention.

Whichever your role or contribution, I promise you, it fills the hearts of those mourning in ways many of us do not understand. Beyond the force of our "professional families," other family members, friends, community members, organizations, and sometimes even the press support the grieving family members.

When I witness the concern, care, support, and condolences offered, I know it is making a difference. This is another fine example of "it takes a village."

PART 5

50 YEARS OF LEGACY, LEARNING, LESSONS, AND LEADERSHIP

1966–2016

CHAPTER 17

LEGACY: IT'S ALL IN THE FAMILY

L EGACY IS AN important component in law enforcement. I don't know the exact percentage, but there is a large percentage of law enforcement professionals who follow a family member's footsteps into their career. That's also true for my family, and it makes me feel good that they found something compelling about my own career that inspired them to follow in my footsteps.

Most people know that families in this field face many challenges because of the long and late hours, the constant worry about their loved ones, and the stress of the job. Even though we deflect the hardships with cop humor, and may get desensitized to difficult and tragic events, we still carry the weight of what we encounter with us. All of these challenges put undue pressure on spouses, parents, children, and even friends.

No one said being married or having a family was meant to be easy. On our wedding day, I told Sandy, "You will be my wife forever," and I meant it. As each one of our sons was born, I was proud to become their dad, and I still am. Our sixtieth wedding anniversary is July 31, 2025, and I remember the day we danced in the Jack Tar Ballroom on our wedding day as if it were yesterday.

Our family and the families of those I've worked with share the same struggles as everyone else. We all have different ways of dealing with it, and hopefully, with the excerpts we share below, you'll find something that is helpful and encouraging to you and your family.

LEGACY: THREE GENERATIONS

As our sons began exploring possible future careers, I told them, "When you all want to do this, I'm not going to hire you. You have to find your own job."

It would be too hard to promote them without people accusing me of nepotism. I also encouraged them to get their undergraduate degree in a field other than criminal justice in case they were injured, or it wasn't what they thought it would be. Each of them completed business degrees, which contributed to each of their respective careers.

SCOTT

Throughout my upbringing, Mom and Dad never steered us toward police work, nor did they steer us away from police work. Growing up in a police family, it was natural to be interested in it, and I was.

All three boys did well in their careers and were promoted within the field. Scott and Mark remain in public safety, and Mike sells communication radios to law enforcement agencies. Scott's first full-time job was with East Lansing Police Department, and he was promoted to lieutenant before he retired to assume his role as sheriff of Ingham County. Mark worked at Eaton County and earned his way to captain. Then he retired and became the Mason City Police Chief. He now works for the juvenile division of Ingham County. They have all made us very proud.

My parents were as far removed from law enforcement careers as any person could be. I find it really interesting that, as of right now, we have three generations of Wrigglesworths in this field. It also makes me very proud that my grandson, Rorie, Mark's step-son, is a deputy for the Ottawa County Sheriff's Office.

Being in law enforcement for five decades has given me the opportunity to see how this profession runs in my family and others, and how these connections from over 40 years ago live on today.

Deputy Bill Bouck worked with the Eaton County Sheriff's Office and worked for me at the Tri-County Metro Narcotic Squad. Now his nephew, Undersheriff Andy Bouck, works for my son, Scott.

Deputy John "Stumpy" Southworth worked for the Jackson County Sheriff's Office when our paths crossed. He and I worked a couple of cases together at Metro Narcotic Squad. His son, Chief Deputy Darin Southworth, also works for Scott.

Corporations might call this nepotism, but in law enforcement, it's called "legacy." It's more common that a new recruit has family in this profession than it is that they don't. I think it's because, at the end of the day, the kids hear the parents talking about their adventures on the force. It creates excitement, and, eventually, it leads them to consider law enforcement as a career.

*Mark Wriggelsworth's swearing-in ceremony as deputy
for Eaton County Sheriff's Office. November 1997.*

*Scott Wriggelsworth's swearing-in ceremony as police officer for the
East Lansing Police Department. January 1994.*

The Wriggelsworth Family in front of the newly named Gene L. Wriggelsworth Training Center,
which was the previous administrative complex and jail.
From left to right: Scott, Sandy, Mike, Gene, Mark, and grandson, Hayden. 2015.

Sandy and Gene with grandson, Rorie, at his swearing-in ceremony
as deputy for the Ottawa County Sheriff's Office. February 8, 2021.

FAITH AND VALUES

SANDY

During my younger years, my mom and I lived across from the Episcopalian church. Going to church helped me through a very difficult time in my life when my dad moved to New York after my parents divorced. Going to church was my rock, and I relied on it a lot.

When we moved to Lansing and Mike was two years old, it was important to me for us to go as a family. Over time, church and faith have become an important part of our everyday life, and we perform many roles at our church.

GENE

Honesty and faith are important to me. If I didn't have a moral compass to do the right thing in my job, my career path would have looked very different. I believe in God, and I go to church. Sometimes you question your faith, especially with the cases I see, but I think that's fairly normal for all of us.

SCOTT

Mom and Dad have belonged to their church forever. They model the pillars of faith with integrity and honesty, and treat people with respect and dignity. We have always followed their lead, and if someone asked me to describe the Wriggelsworths, I would tell them our core values are integrity, honesty, and treating people with respect and dignity. I hope that's what they see in us.

COMMUNICATION

GENE

Each of my roles throughout 50 years had different elements of danger. When I was assigned to the Detroit Riots in 1967, I wanted to keep Sandy from worrying so much about me. I was sure she had seen the news and was already worried. I called her every day and told her everything was fine. She didn't want to hear that the town was burning down, we slept in cars, and bullets flew at us every day. From the news, she assumed life was tough down there. It was tough for all of us, and the only thing that kept me going was knowing she supported me. I couldn't wait to get home to Sandy and Mike.

She never talked about her worries to me. I think she always felt I was fairly safe because I always felt fairly safe, although there were raids when we kicked the door in and a fellow officer standing next to me got shot; and when an officer did a traffic stop the suspect might shoot at us as we approached the car. There were no guarantees, but I think we each managed our worries differently and focused on and prayed for the positives.

Being married to a police officer is not easy. There are always little things that crop up, but you talk about it and work through it.

SANDY

Communication is key. You can't avoid talking about things and you can't avoid sharing your own opinion, even if your spouse's views are different.

When we were first married, it wasn't unusual for us to have a very heated argument. While he was at work, I was home with a new baby and didn't know anybody. When he came home, I was very frustrated because I felt very alone. Who else would I take it out on but him? Then, as I matured, I found out that, you know what? I made wonderful friends by volunteering at church and other organizations. I didn't feel so alone, it fulfilled my social needs, and I felt good that I was doing something to make a difference. That seemed to work for me. Then, when we moved to Lansing, I joined an Episcopalian church and also made a lot of friends through volunteer work.

I don't know how people stay married when they're together 24 hours every single day. Gene and I have always had our own separate interests, and common ones. Our careers were very different, which gave us autonomy to enjoy what we each liked. When I returned to school to finish my coursework and student teaching, and then started working, Gene arranged his schedule to cover the boys for me. Before that, I stayed home for a while and then found different jobs that worked while the boys were at school. Staying busy was key to my own happiness, and it was important for me to be productive while raising a family.

My mother was an extrovert, and I've followed in her footsteps. She was a dance teacher, and I was in dance from three years on up. I loved it. (But I am beginning to think that being in toe shoes is not good for the body in the long run). My dance schedule was full, and as an extrovert, I still like being busy every day.

Our marriage is strong because we found the balance in respecting each other's interests, needs, time, and space as individuals and a couple. We share lifelong friendships with many people. He has his friends, and I have mine, too. Each day, we get up in the morning and we go to the gym to work out together. Then, I go my way and he goes his way for the day when we don't have activities together. At night, we see our family and friends or just relax together.

Now that we are retired, life is very different than when we were living in two different places in our first couple of years. Those were really difficult days, and, as newlyweds, I think adjusting to each other naturally over the first couple of years takes some work. It was very important and helpful to be intentional about what was important to each of us and what we needed. Once we could talk through everything, it all worked.

SUPPORT AND HEALTH

GENE

Sandy's unwavering support of my career and our family is the reason I was able to have what I consider a successful 50-year career. She was one of the more supportive wives around, and she never complained about my shift work and stuff. She could have, because many spouses did. Being married to someone in law enforcement is not easy and it is no wonder this career path has a high divorce rate.

SCOTT

There are a lot of reasons I admire my mom and dad's relationship. The first is their dedication to taking care of their own health. In their eighties now, I can see the difference being healthy and active makes. I believe that by maintaining good health, they have avoided needing to care for each other in illness.

The second aspect of their marriage and parenting I try to model from them is how they seemed to naturally operate, taking a tag team approach in everything they do. To me, that indicates a very healthy relationship because they support each other no matter what each of them need.

CHALLENGES IN THE FIELD AND FAMILY

SCOTT

I was undercover for two years, and it has its own set of challenges relating to family and relationships, but Mom and Dad made it through the long shifts, the stress, and the unknown. Then, on top of those 14 years, Dad entered politics and was elected sheriff for seven four-year terms. That had its own challenges, considering the fact that it is a political position, and part of the sheriff's role is to attend many events at night and on the weekends. Through it all, I've seen their love continue to grow and change, and their cooperation and respect for one another could be why they have been married for 60 years. Their love story continues beyond any hardships, sadness, frustrations, loss, and illness. It's pretty cool to be part of it.

GENE

Unfortunately, the divorce rate in law enforcement is high for a few reasons, in my opinion.

First, it's hard to be apart from one another and you lose that closeness. For instance, when I worked from midnight to eight in the morning, it took about an hour and a half to wind down to sleep. Then, I stayed up because I was due in court at one in the afternoon. After court, I took a nap if I had time, got up, and headed back to work, and did it all over again the next day. That's harder for some people than others, and I can't say I blame them. Marriage needs the connection and closeness of both people to survive. Somehow, Sandy was able to deal with it. I think her community involvement and friendships were paramount to her strength in supporting me. I can't tell you how much I appreciate everything she has done over the years for me, my career, and our family.

Second, they say, "everyone loves a man in a uniform." From my point of view, it's true, because a lot of women throw themselves at us. A lot of guys who were good guys lost themselves in that temptation, and then lost their spouse and family. I just don't know why anyone would risk losing their family and kids over a fling.

I know that temptation is strong, but it was just my belief that when we married, I told her she was going to be my wife forever. And she is. No matter what I experienced, I never let the temptation get to me. Sandy was the only woman I could ever need.

Third, the tragedies and loss that we deal with are very hard for both of us. Some spouses find it too difficult to keep supporting one another through so much loss. It wears on you to hear about the cases, to support their emotions, and to deal with unexpected addictions or behaviors, which are a fourth reason for breakups.

All I can say about avoiding temptation is to remember who you go home to, who loves you, and respect that commitment you made. Ask yourself, *Is it worth losing my family?* Whether you are married or dating or living together, keep your promises, treat each other with respect, and be honest with each other. Talk through the little stuff that creeps up and the big stuff that hits like a Mack truck. Your honesty, open communication, and support of one another are key to maintaining a strong and long-lasting marriage.

WORK-LIFE BALANCE

SCOTT

One of the things my dad always modeled for us was his commitment to my mom and our family. His schedule didn't get any lighter when he became sheriff. You think a dope schedule is complicated? No matter what he was working—state trooper, undercover, or sheriff, he always found a way to be with us and be present. Presence is his gift to us. He wasn't on the phone or distracted with work when he was coaching or watching our games, and that made all the difference.

Health, family, friends, and work are the most important aspects of most people's lives. I think it's important to have a good work-life balance because it allows you to be your best when you're at work, and *for* the people at work. You are also best at home for your family. Your health and fitness are important, too, because if you don't have that, it complicates everything. What I learned from my dad is when any one of those areas is unbalanced, then everything suffers. The more you can keep that in balance, you become the best person for yourself and those who surround you.

Today, Dad and Mom have a full life they enjoy together with their family, friends, and fellow volunteers.

MARK

I learned some helpful tips from a book written by Kevin Gilmartin, *Emotional Survival for Law Enforcement*. It talks about work-life balance with examples of different choices we can make. On our days off, we may want to zone out, sitting on the couch, and maybe drink a few beers. However, those are the times we need to interact with our family. It's a healthier choice. The key is to be sure we are present when we are at work and at home. If we share space with our family but are not engaged or we are distracted, we aren't really there.

If we choose the couch and beer, we get into a vicious cycle or repetitive, unhealthy choices, which is the recipe for divorce.

For me, it helps me to slow down a little bit and not be so wound up about working as much overtime as possible to make my check bigger. Once I learned how to build a work-life balance that worked for my family and me, everything fell into place.

The author stated that it also increases longevity in marriages and closeness within the whole family.

If you are struggling and trying to figure out how to improve areas of your life, I highly recommend this book. It made a big difference for me.

CHAPTER 18

LEARNING IS VITAL TO PROFESSIONAL AND PERSONAL DEVELOPMENT

PROFESSIONAL ORGANIZATION EXPERIENCE/INVOLVEMENT

A LARGE PART of my career was spent participating in and leading several organizations which I found beneficial to my own growth and development, both in my law enforcement career and my personal endeavors.

Each organization is comprised of members and a leadership or executive board. First, I joined as a member to become familiar with the work of the people and organization. Once I wanted to contribute to the leadership team, I applied for various positions on the board and worked my way up, in most organizations, to become president.

Joining organizations in volunteer positions, whether as a member or in a leadership role, offers countless benefits to both your professional and personal growth. At the end of this chapter, there is a lesson with a list to help you determine how to select your own path in making an impact.

BENEFITS OF JOINING ORGANIZATIONS

1. **IMPACT.** Contributing to the greater good of your workplace, family, town, community, country, and world is rewarding and fulfilling.

2. **NETWORKING.** You cannot put a price on meeting new people and developing long-lasting relationships, who later become the people you rely

on for feedback, information, referrals, and who broaden your connections even more.

3. **EXPERIENCE.** The experience, new skills, and knowledge you gain are immeasurable, as are the benefits these will offer you in your career and life. It's the perfect venue to increase self-confidence, learn new perspectives, stay abreast of industry news and community needs, and much more.

4. **FUN WITH PURPOSE.** Joining others to achieve common goals and elicit change is fun and rewarding because it gives you a purpose beyond your own needs. Volunteering and staying active is known to be an important catalyst for improved physical and mental health, too. Our lives are enriched when we wake up and go to sleep with purpose in our lives.

One of the ways Gene spends his Tuesdays–with the Tuesday Toolmen group!
The woman in the red sweater is the recipient of this ramp.

Gene serves patrons at Texas Roadhouse for the Rotary's annual scholarship.
Neighbor Sean Conklin enjoys being served by the retired sheriff. 2025.

Gene celebrates his grandson Jake's last home game on the varsity football team and his last evening of 32 years as a member of the Football Chain Gang program for Holt High School. October 2021.

Roles as Organization President

Michigan Sheriff's Association, President
https://www.misheriff.org/

The Sheriff's Association is an excellent opportunity for sheriffs around the country. As president, we held monthly meetings with the board of directors to bring forward new ideas and needs for the sheriffs.

The Cool Stuff:

- I met a lot of good people.
- The speakers will present, give ideas, and share experiences they have in their own lines of work. Their focus is to offer solutions and perspectives that may aid other sheriffs. For instance, a sheriff from another city will share what worked for them when a prisoner escaped, like how the guy did it and how the jail administrator addressed it.
- Networking is probably as valuable as the meetings and the speakers are, because it gives us the ability to connect with each other. We gain insight from other sheriffs around the country, and it greatly contributes to resolving our

need for resources, camaraderie, and to give and receive support for losses in the line of duty and for family matters.

- As the president, we meet and host out-of-town people. If a sheriff came to town, they usually reached out to meet you. You might also be called to Washington to testify for various reasons.

*****

South Lansing Holt Rotary Club, Two-Term President

https://lansingrotary.org

During my tenure at Rotary, we were the second Rotary in the country and an all-male organization. I didn't see the sense in that, and I brought the first female member into Rotary for the entire state of Michigan. Several people said, "If you bring her in, we are leaving."

I replied, "Help yourself."

And they left. Since then, half of the roles of presidents have been held by women. Progress is good.

The main event for the Rotary Club of South Lansing/Holt is an annual fundraiser to raise money for college scholarships for the high school seniors at Holt and Lansing-Everett. It's held at Texas Roadhouse, who supplies the venue, the menu, and the food. The Rotary members sell the tickets to attend the fundraiser. Each year, we raise around $15,000 for scholarships. It's a fun time, and it is for a good cause. We also have many celebrity waiters, all Rotarians, who have many duties at the event.

To be considered for the scholarship, any student who applies must complete the application process, which requires an interview, essay, and presentation to the Rotary Club. There are several skills they learn in the process of applying alone.

When I was president, I established an interview committee where our members interviewed the applicants. It's a lot of fun to meet the students and learn their plans for their future. We met applicants who were well prepared and those who looked like they rolled out of bed and didn't want to be there.

We ask them, "Do you know what Rotary is?"

"Isn't that where a bunch of guys get together?" some have replied.

Some of them enter into a monologue: "Rotary International is throughout the world, and they do many good things for people."

Polio Plus is a big project that Rotary does where, naturally, we try to eradicate polio.

*****

Michigan State Police Troopers Association, President

When I was elected president of the Troopers Association, I called the director's secretary. I said, "I want to have a meeting with the director, and I'm going to bring our executive director of the Troopers Association to talk about issues."

I wasn't even there a minute and he told me, "There is no trooper going to tell me how to run the state police."

That was the end of the meeting; he walked out. I was stunned, absolutely stunned, that a director of our organization at that level and prestige would treat an employee like that. I was a little bit upset because my intent was to head off grievances.

I then went to the captain's office, who happened to be a friend of mine. Ed Lenon was a great guy, and he should have been the director, but he didn't have the political juice to do it. I told him what happened. He said, "Gene, don't worry about it. I'll take care of it. We'll handle the meetings through my office, and we'll set them up and iron things out. How does that sound?"

I thought to myself, *Oh, here's a guy with some class*, and that's how we handled everything from there on out. This is an example of two different types of leadership, and I preferred to follow Captain Ed Lenon.

*****

Roles as Chairperson

Michigan Sheriff's Coordinated Training Council
https://www.misctc.org/
Licenses all county jail deputies and correctional officers.

Michigan Commission on Law Enforcement Standards
https://www.michigan.gov/mcoles
This is the group that sets law enforcement standards for the whole state. It also licenses all Michigan Police Officers and private security guards. I started out as an appointed member, and then worked my way to become a chairperson.

Lansing Area Safety Council
https://bc.ingham.org

Mid-Michigan Police Academy Advisory Board at Lansing Community College
https://www.lcc.edu/academics/public-service-careers/criminal-justice/
police-academy.html

*****

Roles as Boardmember

Secretary to the Board of Education, Holt Public Schools, 1980–1988
https://www.hpsk12.net/

The media printed a big story about an undercover cop joining the school board. I was on the school board for ten years, and even served as the secretary. Since signing diplomas was the responsibility of the secretary, I signed diplomas for two of my sons!

*****

Roles as Members

Tuesday Toolmen: 2017 to present

After I retired, a woman from the City of Lansing presented at Rotary and spoke about all the programs the city offered and encouraged us to volunteer. She mentioned a Tuesday Toolmen group I found interesting. This group builds ramps each Tuesday for people who aren't able to use stairs and need a ramp to get into their house. I joined them in March and built my first ramp. It was colder than Antarctica, and I thought, *This is kind of crazy to be building in the snow.* But it's kept me useful and it's a good distraction for me. It gives me something to do, and it's fun to work with the other volunteers.

Give-A-Kid-Projects (Holt), Building Maintenance

Sandy belongs to the Give-A-Kid-Projects program in Holt, and I started to do maintenance on their building because it was falling apart. I also help with their many giveaways throughout the year. For Christian Services, we deliver mattresses to those in need. It makes me feel good to see the eyes light up on the little children who see the mattresses come into their home. There's nothing like it. It's hard to believe that some people don't have mattresses. They sleep on the floor or on air mattresses. It tugs at your heart when you see their living situation and realize that giving them a mattress will hopefully help them sleep a little better at night.

The Hundred Club

The Hundred Club is a local community organization that raises money for the surviving family members of public safety people who get killed in the line of duty. Each year, we donate $100 to the fundraising account.

Should someone like a police officer, firefighter, ambulance driver, or other public safety personnel pass away, someone from the group shows up at the family's doorstep the next morning with a $10,000 check for them to use however they need. Sometimes, for those who are injured on the job, we provide a smaller amount to help with medical expenses. Additionally, this group provides scholarship help to all surviving members of the family of the fallen. It is a great organization that has helped a lot of people. It costs $100 per year to become a member.

CHAPTER 18 LESSON

When you consider broadening your experiences, here are the parameters I followed to pick the "right" organizations to meet my goals and objectives:

1. Am I interested in the work, objectives, goals, and impact this organization offers?

2. Do the people operate with integrity, authenticity, transparency, and have genuine desires to make a difference?

3. Will I enjoy getting to know the people and participating in the work?

4. Where do I see my own contributions impacting the group and goals?

5. What will this group contribute to expanding and elevating my own knowledge, experience, and skills so that it will benefit me in my career (or personal life), and guide me to contribute even more to my roles in law enforcement and the people I work with and serve?

6. Are my values, morals, personality, work ethic, and desire to make an impact aligned with the work and the people of this organization?

CHAPTER 19

LESSONS, INSIGHTS, AND WISDOM FOR LAW ENFORCEMENT PROFESSIONALS

BUILD AND NUTURE YOUR FAMILY

THE SUPPORT OF your family is paramount to your success in law enforcement. I've mentioned before I would not have advanced in my career for as long as I did if it wasn't for Sandy's unwavering dedication to me and our sons. Our commitment to our love, our marriage, and the vows we made, our mutual respect and support for each other's careers, and our goal to raise our sons to be productive and contributing members of the world were our priorities in life.

Once we knew our priorities, we knew it required us both to participate and compromise. It's never a 50/50 split, but we didn't look at it that way. Instead, we looked at it as, "this is the life we want, and we will do whatever it requires from both of us." Scott mentioned that he admired our "tag team" approach. While that wasn't intentional, it was a good description.

Oftentimes, for those in careers like mine, the responsibilities in the home and family do weigh heavier on the spouse who isn't in law enforcement. That can't be helped, and we accepted it because we didn't have any control over the long hours and unusual schedules I kept. It helped immensely that Sandy never complained about my hours or my career choices, but for any frustrations she did have, she shared them with close friends. That was helpful because it didn't add that type of stress to our home.

Everyone encounters challenges in their lives, and in this line of work, I believe your faith (if you are religious or spiritual), your family, and your own health, self-development, and advancements will become the foundational pillars for you to be able to do the best job you can in any career.

Improvements in Law Enforcement

SCOTT

I chose law enforcement for the variety of roles and services we offer the community. It was the public safety piece and having the opportunity to serve others that I admired so much from watching my dad. Bringing calm and resolution to other people's chaos or worst day seemed appealing to me.

It's no secret police work was a lot different back in the sixties when my dad became a cop, compared to the early nineties, when I started. Over the past 60 years, I believe we have exponentially improved how law enforcement serves our communities. More compassion, better training, increased services and partnerships, and ever-changing technology are a force multiplier. Simply stated, today we are less focused on arrests and more focused on positive outcomes for the people and communities we serve.

The word "reform" gets used way too often with respect to law enforcement. I like the word "improvement." Our profession has continued to improve and progress. I've dedicated my career to identifying opportunities for improvement, and I work with my team to execute progressive initiatives. When I retire, I want to know that the contributions I made to the sheriff's office improved the processes for the office, employee culture, and public service, just like my dad did for 28 years as sheriff!

FOLLOW YOUR TRAINING AND PAY ATTENTION

It's always important to follow your training. Follow it, and if you do, you'll have a successful career. If you decide to do your own thing, off the training regimen, you'll be in trouble.

Prior to recruit school graduation, we have a chiefs' panel that takes three hours out of a busy schedule to speak with the recruits. The recruits ask them any questions they might have. Questions might include, "What do you expect of me?"

The chief's response would be, "We expect you to learn our regulations."

On your first day, you should go to your department, get the book, and read it. Know what your boss wants from you and then get your training regimen.

One day, there were six of us on the panel. In the middle of the session, one guy put his head on his desk and went to sleep. It angered me, so I stood up and said,

"Hey, (name). We all have busy jobs. We came here to help you all out. Now, I expect you to keep your head off the desk and pay attention."

The academy director sitting in the back smiled. He thanked me afterwards. Follow your training and, most importantly, pay attention.

FIND A MENTOR

Thinking back in my career, I had several people who were mentors to me that I would never, ever worry about asking for advice. My first training officer, Trooper Gordon Smith, was a great guy who was vested in training me the right way, and that's what I wanted. I learned the difference between effective and ineffective training when I went to Flat Rock with another rookie trooper. We were both out of recruit school, but he was a four-year deputy sheriff in Bay County with lots of experience. He could have been my training officer, but I appreciated Trooper Smith's style and patience.

Later, when working for the Tri-County Metro Narcotic Squad, my mentor was Lieutenant Paul Whitford. We were both lieutenants, but he was still my mentor because he had much more experience than I did.

No matter how long you've been in this profession, I would advise you to get a mentor. As you change roles, you may need a new mentor. It helped me to identify who I respected, who did the right thing at all times, and who I looked up to. Find that type of person and form a relationship with them. Learn from them and ask for advice whenever you need it.

KEEP YOUR WITS ABOUT YOU

Be Respectful

Being respectful is always key. Quite frankly, most police officers are respectful, but they have their moments. Remember, bite your tongue if you must, or find a way to cool off.

Right Is Right, Wrong Is Wrong.

Period. And always.

Keep Your Head Down and Mouth Shut

Early on, when I was a sergeant for Metro Squad, I was a little bothered because there wasn't anyone in the unit who I would call a "leader." There were a good number of guys that did their own thing. Some of them, quite frankly, should have been thrown out of the squad. They did some things that were abhorrent to me, and we corrected them.

Letter of the Law vs. Intent of the Law

There are going to be times in your career when you have to decide whether you want to enforce the "intent of the law" or "the letter of the law."

- The "letter of law" is that you write everybody a ticket, no matter what. You don't have any human compassion in doing so.
- The "intent of the law" is creating a safe environment.

When I taught the recruits in the academy, I explained:

> One day, you'll stop a car with a driver who is a mom of three kids with runny noses. The car doesn't have a muffler, the springs are broken, and the shock absorbers were also shot. You pull her over and find out she doesn't have her driver's license with her. You run her in the system and find she has a valid driver's license and no priors. Keep in mind, she has nothing positive in her life. She wouldn't be driving that piece of garbage car if she didn't have to. Your choices are:

> 1. You write the ticket, and she looks at you like the world just ended. She likely won't be able to pay it. You haven't exercised any compassion. That's the *letter of the law.*
> 2. You feel bad for her, and advise her of some safety concerns, and send her on her way. You showed compassion. That's the *intent of the law.*

> If you let her go home, is it necessarily going to be the end of the world? Probably not.

> There will be officers out there who, quite frankly, no matter how much you drill this into their head, they're going to write the ticket. Decide *how you want to serve the public* and make your decisions on that. Often, it's a matter of following your instinct or intuition.

Responding to Crime

When we get a call from dispatch, there are many physical, emotional, and mental reactions we have as we respond. Each situation is unique and calls for different reactions.

- If 911 tells us there is a homicide or domestic situation in progress, we drive very fast with our blood rushing, heavier breathing, and our mind planning our approach: do we run into the house or wait for backup?
- When a car is stolen or there is a robbery or a mugging, and they dispatch the description, we drive cautiously to keep an eye on passing cars or injured persons.
- If we are merely driving or on patrol, we keep an eye on everything to ensure proper order in public situations.

Being on alert is natural for law enforcers because we have to always be ready to intervene. I might be on personal leave or off for the day. If there is an emergency or crime, I must intervene because of my oath.

Remember: Capacity Has Limits

A 911 call comes in with a homicide in progress at 123 Main Street, Johnson City. You're going to go pretty fast, and so is your mind regarding the description of the car and suspects. As you drive fast, you are skimming the roads, looking for similar vehicles. Then, the question of running into the house or waiting for backup runs through your head. All those things and more are racing through your mind and are using a lot of your mental capacity, just like memory in a computer.

Years ago, we lost a very young deputy while he chased a suspect. He'd never been on a high-speed chase before. The rule is to drive about 80% of capacity. If your car has a max speed of 110 mph, the fastest you should go is 88 mph. Instead, he operated at 110% of his capacity, at 121 mph. He was going way too fast and lost control of his car. We lost him that day, and it's a grave reminder that your department puts rules in place for your safety, because the work you do can be life or death on any given day.

Tried by Twelve than Carried by Six

One of my many bosses was a major in the state police, and he was a great guy. They called him "Black Dan" because he was about as mean as he looked. I don't think I ever saw him smile, but I loved him. I'll tell you why. He spoke to us at a recruit school graduation and said, "I'm going to tell you all something right now. When it comes to officer safety, I would rather be tried by twelve than carried by six. Remember that."

Eliminate The Threat

No one in law enforcement wakes up and says, "I'm going to shoot and kill someone today." So, when it comes about on the news that a suspect was shot and injured or killed by an officer, or vice versa, an officer was killed, it's tragic for all parties involved. We are also there to protect the people around us.

Officers are depicted as "the bad guy" in the media when we do shoot someone, but we are trained not to shoot unless we are in a situation where our life, a fellow officer's, or a citizen's life is at risk. The rule is to "eliminate the threat," but the threat needs to be legitimate. There has to be a life-threatening situation to use fatal force.

Let's walk through three examples.

1. If there is a high-speed chase without any gunfire or guns pointed at us, we cannot just shoot the suspect to get them to pull over. Technically, we will not die from pursuing the suspect in a high-speed chase, unless, God forbid, there is an accident. However, if we are in pursuit of a driver in a high-speed chase and his passengers are pointing guns at us or shooting at us from the back seat, we are required to engage. Another instance is if someone tries to run me down with their car. That's felonious assault with a vehicle, and someone could die. For that, fatal force would be justified.

2. Most bank robberies have guns involved, probably all of them do. So, if the suspect has a gun, and he refuses to drop the gun, it is my duty to eliminate the threat to my life and the lives of others. If I'm driving up to the bank with a robbery in progress, and the suspect exits the bank waving a gun in his hand, then I have a right to shoot him to eliminate the threat.

3. I had a friend who worked for me in the Metro Narcotic Squad. Russ is a great guy. He was dispatched to a man with a gun at a house and a woman was inside with him. Russ went to the door; the guy greeted him with the gun and pointed it towards Russ. In self-defense, Russ shot him, and he was killed. It was a clean shot by the rule to eliminate the threat.

Even though it was a good shoot, that is, a justified one, Russ still had to follow protocol. At that point, his life was filled with enormous stress because of the outcome.

Protocol After an Officer Shoots Suspect

1. A supervisor arrives on the scene; depending on the situation, they may read the officer their constitutional rights and ask questions. However, it's always a good idea to call a union rep or an attorney before answering questions. The union rep might recommend not saying anything and to wait a day for questioning. This is good advice, because the officer involved is so revved up, their brain needs to decompress.

2. The officer is required to hand in their gun and badge until they are approved to return to work.

3. If the officer elected to wait a day and have the union rep present, they would go in for questioning.

4. The officer is sent to a psychologist for evaluation of emotional distress and fitness for duty. The psychologist happened to be a friend of ours, Jerry Gallagher, who was our jail psychologist.

5. Russ explained the situation to him, and Jerry said, "Well, how do you feel about it?"

    Russ replied, "Well, I had to do it. I didn't have a choice. I had to do it."

    Jerry stated, "Exactly. You don't have to have any angst over doing your job, so I'm going to clear you."

    Russ was cleared for duty, and he was good to go.

6. Most of the time, the officer is usually cleared.

People and the media do not appreciate this process or the work we do, but that's the job we picked, and shootings are a part of it. The media is also always a part of our job.

We had a case when a suspect was driving under the influence and engaged one of our officers in a high-speed chase. The officer was stressed and fired his gun toward the car even though his life was not threatened. He did not report it, and it only came to light when the suspect was arrested on another charge. The suspect questioned the prosecutor for driving drunk when he had been shot at by a deputy and nothing happened. It was investigated, and sure enough, I learned it was true.

We found bullet damage in the visor of the suspect's car. The officer was fired for numerous felonies, including weapon charges.

Find Your Way Back If You Fall off the Right Path

Some officers can lose their way, focus, and purpose in their position. They may make a mistake or two or do something that wouldn't be appropriate for their role. Find a mentor you can look up to who will help put you back on track. There are plenty out there who understand most, if not all, situations. They tend to be sergeants and lieutenants because they have experience behind them, and they should know how to guide the officer onto the right path.

CONTINUE LEARNING AND SELF-DEVELOPMENT

Rookies receive evaluations after their first six months on the job. When I received mine, I was disappointed that I had so much to improve. Then, after I saw the evaluation my buddy received, I was devastated. He received all "excellent" checkmarks, and I thought that I was working really hard, and possibly even harder than him.

My training officer asked me, "What did you think?"

I was honest with him. "I'm a little disappointed."

"Why is that?"

"Well, my buddy received 'all excellent' marks." I replied.

"You know the difference between you and him?" he asked.

"No."

"You're going to get better, and he's not."

I thought to myself, *Now, this guy is a leader.*

And he was. It felt good to know that he saw I was working hard, and I was moldable. He saw my desire, that I always came in early, and did all I could to succeed. I was eager, I was willing to do the job, and he noticed.

PROGRESS IS GOOD. BE ADAPTABLE TO CHANGE. IT WILL HAPPEN OFTEN.

Changes in Equipment and Tech in My Career

When I started at Flat Rock in 1966, we didn't have the Law Enforcement Information Network (LEIN). Reports came to us through a very slow teletype machine. When we went on patrol, the corporal gave us a sheet of paper with a list of all the stolen cars.

It listed the type of car and license plate number. It might have been a full page long and was pretty useless. I never found a stolen vehicle using that sheet. Additionally, it was usually 48 hours behind the most recent information.

Our car radios were low band frequencies that picked up any state police car or pistol within range.

Under the right weather conditions, we also got "skip," which was when we heard radio traffic from other states. We were a state border post, so if we had a chase that went into Ohio, the post had to call Toledo PD or Ohio Highway Patrol because there wasn't any direct radio contact.

It wasn't long after I started working in Flat Rock that the teletype was replaced with LEIN. That was quite an improvement, especially because we received information so quickly.

Our paychecks were delivered by what was called "pony express," meaning they were relayed to each state post by multiple patrol cars. Often, they were late, which caused us much angst since we weren't paid much. One pay period, Sandy and I were broke, and we had to redeem pop cans to buy toilet paper. It was a very stressful situation considering we had a newborn, and I wondered if I made a mistake changing careers.

VASCAR, Visual Average Speed Computed and Recorded, was the new speed timing computer. It was an interesting system, but short-lived due to operator errors.

Our weapons were updated from .38 caliber revolvers to 9 mm semiautomatic pistols in the seventies, and our long guns were either 12-gauge shotguns or WW2 surplus .30 caliber M1s. Those weapons are long gone, too, as newer weapons have been added.

Breathalyzers are now much improved, with preliminary testing capabilities of use in the patrol vehicles. When breathalyzers first came out, officers had to bring the people they pulled over to the state police posts for testing. It was a problem for MSP, as the breathalyzer operator was required to go to court for non-state police cases. After a few years, most agencies had their own breathalyzers.

When I first started in police work, there was no such thing as DNA testing. You could test body fluids and material basically for blood type to compare with a suspect. It helped to exclude certain suspects, but was not the exact science that DNA provides today.

For fingerprinting, we used to have to take inked fingerprint impressions during arrest processing. Now there is Live Scan Fingerprinting in most police departments, which electronically takes prints and sends them to MSP and the FBI. This greatly speeds up the identification and apprehension of criminals.

Checking suspects and license plates used to be done via radio transmissions. Today, the computer is right in the patrol car and greatly increases the rate of replies, arrests, and stolen car recoveries.

For many years, MSP did not have handheld radios. When you exited your patrol car, you were basically on your own. Today, all officers have handheld radios and cell phones, which increases officer safety.

Many departments also have license plate scanners available right in the patrol car. That helps with identifying stolen cars, improper vehicle registration, and more.

Officers now have pepper spray, as well as *tasers*, which means fewer lethal weapons. This change reduced officer and suspect injuries.

When I started in 1966, these pieces of equipment had not even been invented. If we ran into a confrontation, it usually meant "hands on," which led to fights or wrestling with suspects. This caused so many injuries to officers and suspects. It also led to many lawsuits.

Night vision equipment was a big step in surveillance and for general security concerns. Thank you, US Military!

DON'T EVER FORGET TO SHOW YOUR APPRECIATION

Deputy Stan Granger worked for me twice throughout the course of my 28 years as sheriff. We recently learned that he was in a retirement home. Deputy Granger had never received a retirement badge, and it was important to Scott and me that we changed that. Scott, as the current sheriff, presented it to him at the retirement home. We knew it meant a lot to him because he teared up.

Showing your appreciation throughout your career and even after is crucial. We are in the public service sector, and our work goes mostly unnoticed and unappreciated. I've always tried to make a point to write a note, give a card, award a badge, or verbally acknowledge people's accomplishments, special events, and especially their work. As Maya Angelou said, "I've learned that people will forget what you said, people will forget what you did, but people will never forget how you made them feel."

CHAPTER 20

LEADERSHIP LESSONS FOR EVERYONE

THROUGHOUT MY LIFE, I've had good, bad, and excellent employers and supervisors. I learned I needed to take the bad with the good, and I made mental notes of what I would and would never do as a leader.

Growing up, I likely learned certain leadership skills from my dad because he was very demanding. If we were to bale hay on Tuesday, we baled hay on Tuesday, and it had to be done before I went to football practice. That's how my work ethic was instilled in me, and I demanded the same of my kids, minus the hay baling. We didn't live on a farm.

My mom was a loving person and a hard worker. In a lot of cases, she worked during the day and all night. Yet, she still drove us around and took us to our 4-H ball games and wherever we needed to go. When I started eighth grade, we lived seven miles from town, and the school held dances at the YMCA. After dinner and a long day of work, she drove me to the dance, I stayed there for a couple of hours, and then she returned to pick me up and take me home. As a kid, I didn't realize the work and time that goes into making sure you get where you need to be, but as an adult, I look back and think, *Wow. Mom did all that for me. She was a tough gal and always supportive.* I appreciated her more as I became an adult and had my own kids.

Then there are the leadership skills you learn on the job by observing others or doing the work. Financial acuity is a skill I learned by doing the work. How else could you learn it? Then, I just watched others and took mental note of who I thought of as good role models for the type of person I wanted to become, and those who I did not want to follow.

Growing up in a rural environment on a farm required a lot of attention to detail, which also made me who I am. I don't like unfinished products or projects. If things get started, I expect them to be done in a timely manner.

My people at the sheriff's office figured me out quickly. I had to chuckle at Captain Rick Miller one day. He was a great guy. I had an issue one day and told him what I wanted. As captain, he passed it to the lieutenant and said "Just so you know, the old man wants this done. I'd suggest you get it done. Hurry."

When he mentioned what he told the lieutenant, I asked, "Why is that?"

"Because I figured you out. You tell me you want something, you want it done," he explained.

I chuckled and said, "Exactly."

MY "NEVER DO LIST"

In my rookie years at Flat Rock, there was a trooper who I added to my "Never Do List." I was never going to act like him. He was so sure of himself. On my first day at the Flat Rock State Police Post, I asked a trooper who was sitting at the desk about where to find affordable housing. He replied, "Don't bother. I don't think you're going to make it."

He's the type of guy who made everyone's life complicated because of his position. It's always a power trip for people with his personality type. No matter what you do, it's never good enough. He infuriated me on many occasions. But, with a hierarchical and authoritarian system, I found it best to say nothing, keep my mouth shut, and do what I was told.

Thinking of the following incident still burns me, and it taught me the best lesson on how to treat employees with respect and dignity. I had a robbery case at a restaurant, and paperwork, as most people know, is tedious, time consuming, and a pain—even more so then, because we had the old-fashioned typewriters. For some reason, even though I knew how to spell "restaurant," every time I typed it, I spelled it wrong. We didn't have spell check, backspace, or even Wite-Out back then. The paper we had loaded in the return vessel of the typewriter was five pages thick because it was carbon paper. We had to press the keys super hard to make sure the key hit it hard enough for the carbon copy to show on the fifth page. Feel free to search the internet about carbon paper if you don't know what it is. It was a pain.

I finished my six-page report filled with details and submitted it. He looked at it. "You misspelled 'restaurant,'" and he handed it back to me.

"I guess I did." I handed it back to him.

"Redo it," he said as he ripped it into six thousand pieces.

I couldn't even use the original to type it, so I had to rewrite it all by memory. "Never Do List." Check.

KNOW WHEN TO SAY "NO"

We had a few officers during my career who started with Metro Narcotic Squad and discovered buying drugs undercover was not comfortable for them. It was just too stressful. God bless them for having the courage to see me and tell me, "Hey, Boss, this is it for me. I want out."

Good. Not many people would do that, but they did. When you are not into your role, it's best to find a new one, because you risk putting your life and other lives in danger. It's best to be honest with yourself and do what is best for you.

THINK THROUGH SITUATIONS TO MAKE SURE THEY MAKE SENSE

Lieutenant Paul Whitford was a veteran in drug investigations. We worked together as lieutenants for my entire 14 years. He stayed in it for two more years after I left to become sheriff. One night, one of our undercover officers came into the office and said, "Hey, I stopped down at the local gas station, and these two guys approached me. They wanted to know if I knew where they could get some guns. They'd be willing to trade some dope for some guns."

I thought to myself, *I know I can get some guns out*, and told them, "You can take the guns and arrest these guys."

Paul said, "Okay."

I followed with, "We'll get the guns in the morning from the property room."

Later, Paul said, "I don't like the sound of this. I think it's the feds or something like that. The guy walked up to our undercover and said, 'Want to trade guns for drugs?' It smells like cops to me."

So, we canceled the plans.

The next morning, two ATF agents with long hair and beards marched in, "We picked up some guys who wanted to trade guns for drugs."

I didn't see it coming, and I learned a valuable lesson to be more careful, do a little more research, and make sure it makes sense. How does a deputy, sitting at a gas station, attract two guys out of the clear blue to say "hey?" That just didn't make any sense.

RIGHT IS RIGHT. WRONG IS WRONG.

Anyone that worked with me knew I drew the line at "Right is right. Wrong is wrong." In law enforcement, a lot of situations happen where it might be tempting to tell a "little white lie." When we make a big mistake, we may want to avoid being disciplined or fired. The problem is that those "little white lies" and cover-ups always come to light, and we put ourselves in a worse position with them than if we just tell the truth.

As a leader, when it came to discipline, I made decisions on how to handle discipline and firing. When I knew the truth, I had options on which way to go. However, there were some situations people put themselves in that gave me no choice but to fire them. For instance, the deputy that shot at the person who was pulled over for a DUI. He broke the law. He committed multiple crimes, and I had no choice but to fire and arrest him.

However, the majority of my discipline cases resulted in reprimands because, in this profession and in all professions, as humans, we all make mistakes. There were a couple of instances where someone made a big mistake, and they were petrified they would be fired. They sat in my office in tears, waiting for me to accept their resignation or fire them. In one case, the end result wasn't even that person's fault. In another instance, it was a genuine mistake. The deciding factors for me on how to handle a mistake were:

1. Was it an intentional or genuine mistake?
2. Did it fall under lack of responsibility or human error?
3. Did they blame it on someone else or care about it and own up to their mistake?

Once I assessed these answers, then I knew the direction to take.

In the first case I mentioned, it wasn't the person's fault, but he took it to heart, and accepted responsibility. He felt he should lose his job. "I did this. It was me; it was on me."

Now, being human myself, I know when we own up to a major mistake, we take on that heavy burden. I appreciated that he took his job so seriously. As professionals, when we expect ourselves to do well, succeed, and do our best, no one else can discipline us more than we do ourselves. I knew that to be true with this person. I declined his resignation letter. I put it aside, and as I held a gold envelope, I said, "In this sealed envelope is your discipline. I am going to give it to my undersheriff to keep sealed and in your file for one year. If there aren't any other infractions within that year, we will remove it from your file and give the sealed envelope to you to do with what you wish."

That employee remained with me for more than a decade until his retirement, and I never had him in my office again for discipline. I knew by his commitment to excellent performance that he appreciated my decision, and I was happy because I retained an excellent employee.

SELF-DEVELOPMENT TO BECOME A RESPECTED LEADER

To become a respected and appreciated leader, it takes your own self-resolve and years of learning. I read books, and I surrounded myself with and learned from the excellent leaders I had in my career. I remembered what I admired about them, and then I emulated their approach and style.

When I worked for the Michigan State Police, I worked with some excellent leaders. I was a rookie and knew nothing about police work. My training officer, Trooper Gordon Smith, was a hell of a leader, and he went on to become a post commander in Munising. So were other people down the road, too, like my post commander, Glenn Perry, at Post 11. Both of these men were extraordinary, and used common sense, respect, and compassion to lead others instead of insults, intimidation, and rage.

When I was president of the Trooper's Association, I had a meeting right after my shift at the Civil Service Commission. I left work and went to the meeting still in uniform. The civil service rep took exception to me being in my state police uniform, he called my captain and filed a complaint. Lieutenant Perry, my direct supervisor, called me to discuss the matter. I explained that I had no ill intent and was in a hurry to get to the meeting. I didn't even think about my uniform.

Soon after, I received a note from Commander Perry in my mailbox that said, "Gene, Go ye and sin no more." That's leadership. He didn't think what I did was end-of-the-world kind of stuff, when other leaders would blow their head off yelling at you for these minor mistakes. He knew I didn't go out of my way to make anything difficult or insult other people. It was those types of examples from other leaders that modeled different solutions for me to address issues that came up with my employees.

When I first became sheriff, my first undersheriff, Rick Boyd, was a super guy. His former position was as a lieutenant at the University Police Department. He also worked for me in the Metro Narcotic Squad as an undercover officer. I knew he was a leader.

One day, a deputy wrecked one of our cars doing something stupid. Rick was extremely stressed and upset about it, so much so that I had to intervene. I said, "Rick, Chill out, it's a car wreck. We often wreck cars. It's going to happen a lot in our career."

It did. Finally, I got him off the ledge. Later, I found out that he thought that if he wasn't harder on the staff, he was letting me down. Fortunately, he was a passionate guy, he learned my style, and he no longer subscribed to toxic leadership styles.

In my career, I'm grateful that I saw the best of local law enforcement. It didn't go unnoticed that I was working with excellent people in the field that were also initially state police, too. I am very proud of my affiliation with MSP.

Through those years, I think I learned about leadership by osmosis from hanging around some doggone good leaders. One of those people was an instructor at my recruit school, Trooper Richie Davis. I had the greatest admiration for that man, and I always looked up to him. He worked his way up to be the director of the State Police, which was a big accomplishment. Working with people like him helped me model the leaders I respect and determine who I would emulate as I advanced in my career. I retired as sheriff shortly after he did, and he came to my retirement party along with another director, Colonel Gerald Hough. It meant a lot because they were the kind of leaders I looked up to.

There are examples of good and poor leadership everywhere we look. Watch and learn from other people's failures and successes. You will notice the words people use, the tone they convey, and the nonverbal communication they present. What are they saying or doing that you like or don't like? If you like it, put it in your own "Leadership Do List." If you don't, put it in your "Leadership Never Do List." How will you implement your "Do List?"

Presidents are a perfect example of various types of leadership. As sheriff, one of the perks of the job was meeting US presidents, senators, state representatives, governors, mayors, and the like. Meeting someone with such stature in person is completely different than watching them on a screen. I met former president Barack Obama when he was a US senator campaigning for the presidential election. He campaigned at the Lansing Center, and it fell to the sheriff's office to help with security. At a certain point during his arrival, I welcomed him, shook his hand, and posed with him for a picture.

I met former president Bill Clinton, too, when he was campaigning for president the first time. I wanted to welcome him and shake his hand. He stood behind a rope, and I walked around the rope in full uniform to greet him. The secret service officer stopped me and said I wasn't allowed back there.

"I was invited here," I said. I shook his hand and received a pre-signed photograph of him.

Both exchanges were very quick. Seeing presidents in person is very different from seeing them on a screen. You can feel the energy and the enthusiasm of the crowd. It was fun.

I wasn't a perfect manager. I made mistakes as a trooper, an undercover supervisor, a sheriff, and a leader. I have made my fair share of mishires, and some decisions I would like to redo. It's part of being human. The key is to admit the mistake, learn the lesson, and not repeat it. When you fall, you brush the dust off your pants, stand up again, and put one foot in front of the other.

As you develop your leadership skills and grow into each of your leadership roles, I advise you to pay attention to those who are the most respected, follow your morals, and align with your values. Learn from the appropriate and inappropriate responses and from other people's failures and successes. Remember, right is right; wrong is wrong. Be honest with everyone. Use common sense when making decisions. Learn ways to keep your composure when you need to so you can treat people of all levels with respect and dignity. Remember, there is no "I" in "team;" there is inclusivity. And read some books. Over time, you'll become a leader.

COMMON SITUATIONS WITH EMPLOYEES

"I Don't Want To."

Occasionally, I instructed an employee to perform a task and they said, "I don't want to do that."

I learned to respond in a couple of different ways:

- "Well, I don't care if you want to do it. That's what I'm telling you to do."
- If they didn't like me personally and were being disrespectful, I responded, "I don't care how you feel about Gene Wriggelsworth, but you will respect the sheriff."

Lead by Example

Fortunately, I rarely had to be that stern. It seemed to me that the people who worked for me were motivated to do their best. Anything I asked them to do, they did. As law enforcers, sometimes those instructions came with danger attached, and when we had to do a raid, it was going to be dangerous. They had to run, not walk, and they were the front door person. They did it without question. I like to believe that some of that respect was earned when I offered to be the front door guy when I first started as the supervisor. They were surprised that I was willing to do whatever job they did, and that meant a lot to them. It was always important to me to respect them and treat them as equals. I didn't pull rank on them because I was a lieutenant or sheriff; we were a team and worked together. If I asked someone to risk their life, as their leader, I was willing to risk mine, too.

Each one of us has a different personality, just like there are different types of leadership. Sometimes, people get rowdy or try to do something to see if they get away with it. I had a situation in the sheriff's office where someone was behaving like we were in a fraternity house. I could have walked up and disciplined him in front of the group of people he was entertaining. Instead, I invited him to my office, asked him to close the door, and explained that we were in a professional setting and that behavior was not tolerated. He understood, and it never happened again.

SOLUTIONS FOR LEADER-SPECIFIC ISSUES

The Media

A big part of the sheriff's duty is keeping the public informed, and the media was an important part of those communications. Sheri Jones, an anchor at Channel 6, started reporting about law enforcement matters as soon as she graduated from MSU. She even accompanied us on drug raids to build her career. She was an exceptional reporter, and I enjoyed working with her. She retired from her position at Channel 6 in 2025, and I know she will be missed by the station and the public.

I learned early on in my career that the media would always get their way, or they would always try to, at least. There were cases that were of great interest to the media, and sometimes, they were relentless in their pursuit of answers.

As soon as I started my career, I promised myself that I would always tell the truth to the media. And I did. There were times when I couldn't answer their questions because it was an ongoing situation or because we didn't yet have answers. Regardless, I was always truthful and up front about the issues in question. You can learn a lot by watching how other people handle the media. I learned some of my responses to the media from other law enforcement leaders, and learning from them shaped my approaches and composure.

We had a press conference about a fatal overdose which was an explosive issue. A reporter who I had known for a long time, "Can you tell me why they did it?"

What? I thought. "No. Next question."

I was wondering, *Why would anyone ask that?*

The reporter looked at me like I broke the law. I further explained, "I don't have to answer your question. There's no law that says because you asked me a question, I have to answer it."

When they learned of an officer who shot a suspect, one reporter asked, "Can you tell me why the officer shot the suspect unprovoked? Don't your people have pepper spray or a taser they could use?"

I calmly responded, "Yes, they have all that equipment."

The reporter questioned, "Why don't they use that?"

I explained, "Because he had a gun. If I taser him, and it doesn't faze him, which happens often with some people, he can still shoot the officer."

In another incident, one of the TV stations learned that I fired someone who was negligent in their duty. "How could this happen? Whose fault is this?"

The media is always looking for someone to blame. I said, "Well, that's an easy question. It's my fault. I'm the one that hires people. I'm the one they put in charge to hire people. It's my fault."

They didn't quite seem happy with that answer, so they continued. I could tell they wanted me to tar and feather someone else, and I wasn't going to do it. Once I accepted responsibility, nobody cared. If I had blamed someone else, it would have gone on forever.

That's one of the things I learned in "Leadership 101:" Don't dump your problems on everybody else. We had a lieutenant who was called "Lieutenant Dump Truck" because when something went wrong, he was always dumping it on someone else.

One reporter was insistent about an officer who shot their gun when their own life was not threatened. That is a crime, and they were fired. The media asked, "How could you hire somebody like that?"

I responded as calmly as possible (always stay calm with the media). "That's an easy answer. I hire from the human race. It's a pool of flawed people. We recruit from the human race, and you get some that aren't all that great. But I'll say this, most police officers that I worked with over the years are fine people. They're hard-working, dedicated, want to serve the public, go home at the end of their shift, and live a nice life."

Asked and answered.

LEADERS LEADING LEADERS

One of our responsibilities when it comes to leading others is to get the resources needed for our team to do their jobs. Captain Jim Rapp of the Lansing Police Department was a supervisor of mine. He was one of the greatest leaders I ever worked with. He unexpectedly passed away in 2018, and I'll always remember the teachings he bestowed on me. He knew I wasn't a Lansing cop, but he knew how to take care of my oversized ego, which most of us in law enforcement have. I watched and learned as he taught us to set it aside and do the job. He was excellent in his leadership.

LESSONS IN GOVERNANCE: FILING A GRIEVANCE

In the mid-eighties, the state police went through the ranks and reallocated every drug team commander one level up. The bulletin came out and the paper listed the following reallocations, which meant promotions were effective immediately. All the sergeants were promoted to Lieutenant 1, which meant the next promotion for Paul Whitford and me would be Lieutenant 2. But they didn't promote Paul and me; I thought it was a misprint. We couldn't understand what we thought was a "miss" because we had the largest team, had seized more money, more drugs, and made more arrests than any other team in the state.

I said to Paul, "What's going on here?"

He replied, "I have no idea."

I called the captain. He said, "I knew you were going to call."

I asked him, "What do you think?"

"Here was our thought. You both are assigned to headquarters, and your supervisor is just down the street. We didn't see the need for that extra level of supervision," he explained.

I was located at headquarters, but my office was at the Lansing Police Department, about four or five miles away. I respectfully stated, "Captain, all due respect, my supervisor, John Houchlei has never set foot in my office."

It didn't change his opinion.

With this promotion, I would have received an increase of four to five thousand dollars per year. It's not a lot, but it affected my pension, which is based on your highest salary over the course of a certain number of years. If I didn't get the promotion, it would set me behind $5,000 on my annual calculations for pension payments. It's well known that law enforcement professionals and other public service personnel have lower salaries, which are offset by the benefit of a pension. It's part of our compensation. Considering the effort and successful results Paul and I contributed to in our roles and with our teams, I was disappointed to be passed over for this promotion.

I filed a grievance. It was the only time I filed a grievance in my career because I felt it was worth fighting for.

This was the same year I got elected sheriff. Essentially, I filed a grievance on the way out the door. I was busy with my sheriff role and had forgotten about it.

Two years later, after filing it, I received a letter, finally, that stated, "Your grievance hearing is today at the Civil Service Commission."

Thanks for the same day's notice. I hustled down there by myself without an attorney, and I saw the panel of four or five people who were civil service commissioners and a couple of people with brass on their collars. They asked me to state my case. I explained I headed up teams who brought in more people, more money, and more drugs than any other team in the state. They gave me that same standard "blah, blah." "We will let you know in a few weeks."

About three months later, I received a letter from them. "You lose."

So, I lost.

Fast forward another year or so. I was in a class to finish my degree at Lansing Community College when one of my personnel management instructors, Tom, pulled me aside before class and asked for permission to use my grievance and testimony as an example to the class on how to file a grievance. I agreed. What did I have to lose at that point?

He then said, "Gene, I have to tell you the entire civil service panel was surprised with you. First, you came without an attorney. Second of all, you presented your testimony better than any attorney we've ever had in front of us."

"But I lost," I replied.

"Yes, I know, but you did a good job."

I thought, *That's sad that I lost, but ironic that at least I did a good job.*

From what I heard, Tom continued to use the entire scenario as an example in all of his classes on how to file a grievance and present testimony. Apparently, he ends the lesson with, "Here's what happens. Gene did a good job, fought the good battle, and still lost."

LESSONS IN POLITICS

Learn how to walk the tightrope. As sheriff, the only governing board I had to deal with was the board of commissions. The only aspect of my job was to set the budget, so whenever I needed to purchase guns, equipment, vehicles, or supplies, or hire people, I appealed to the panel of commissioners to set my budget. It's a very thin tightrope to walk because it can be easy, prickly, or difficult to get consensus. Picking your battles, knowing how to walk the tightrope, and how to be strong when needed is important. If they smell weakness or for some reason don't like you, a few of the commissioners can make it difficult and have no problem getting right into your face.

Move personnel when needed. My first budget with the board was stressful because I didn't know what to expect or what to ask. Over 28 years, I was fortunate to generally get almost everything I wanted. For example, my first year, I needed two major positions because we had a big deficiency in management in the jail. We didn't have anyone of any rank to run it, and we had a captain supervising ten guys in the detective bureau. Captains don't usually supervise detectives, but they do supervise 40 staff members for road patrol. Much to the chagrin of the captain and with approval from the board, to make it more efficient, I hired the two majors with proper rank and experience. The change was a great benefit to the sheriff's office.

The agenda. These meetings took a long time to cover agenda items from the sheriff's office and other departments. There could be 40 items on the agenda, and they would approve and clear one or several at a time. For instance, they could say, "Items one through four are on the consent agenda and are approved," then move on to item 5, and so on. I always tried to get my requests on the consent agenda so I didn't have to hang around for the entire meeting.

Learn how to deal with all personalities. I learned quickly that some of the people at budget hearings were not fans of law enforcement professionals, or maybe it was just me. Especially one commissioner. At the first board meeting I attended, I learned this commissioner was not a Wriggelsworth fan. He asked, "Can I have the floor for a moment?"

He then read a poem he read out loud to the remaining board of commissioners that was "anti-Wriggelsworth." He clearly did not like the fact that I received pretty much everything I wanted, and he said so. I was taken aback. First, I've never had a poem written about me, and second, it was filled with venom.

Commissioner Randy Shafer said at a meeting, "If the sheriff asks for it, I think he should get it."

Exactly. I liked this guy. I needed twelve more like him because I didn't ask for frivolous stuff. My requests were based on the need to provide quality law enforcement for our citizens and officers. Unfortunately, sometimes politically, I just couldn't get it to fly.

Build relationships to support you and your needs. I learned little things about how to deal with the different personalities on the board. I learned quickly who I could rely on, and which board members were willing to shepherd my requests through the commission. With their cooperation and support, it wasn't so painful. I also learned to do it "right" by making phone calls right before the meeting. Those requests were added to the "consent agenda," which was covered first. That meant my items would be covered, hopefully approved, cleared off the agenda, and I could leave early.

Commissioners don't educate themselves. The most frustrating part about dealing with the commissioners was when I needed guns, vehicles, or personnel and they fought me on it because they didn't have the knowledge or understanding about the item or the benefit we would receive. They didn't take time to research or learn; they just wanted to state an opinion. Sometimes, they didn't even know anything about it but wanted to deny approval anyway so they could approve something else. The worst was when they wanted to tell me how to run my organization when they had no clue what I did or what I needed.

People count on you. However, I had to be careful sometimes in how to tell them. The other police chiefs watched me because they leaned on me to support their needs. As their sheriff, it was my obligation to get them the resources when needed. It was not so easy. But the thing that worked for me was I made sure I surrounded myself with good people. It made my job easier when I could work with the appointees. Then, I could do battle with the board of commissioners. Learning to deal with people who had different points of view was challenging, but not impossible.

Patience. Patience. Patience. One difficult situation was when I needed to rearm the sheriff's office with 9mm pistols versus the old .38 revolvers. If we used the 9mm, then the officers were on a level playing field with the bad guy (back in those days). There was dissent from one commissioner who said, "Can't you tell me what kind of guns you are buying?"

We did not know at that point, so we had to give them a presentation at the next meeting. The guns were funded after our presentation. It would be extremely helpful and more efficient for the board to educate themselves on the options before they make their decision or discuss it. Another thing that would be helpful would be if the anti-law enforcement board members just trusted that I knew what I was doing.

Knowing your boundaries and your responsibilities is extremely important. The next time they raised havoc was when I was attending the FBI National Academy to advance my leadership skills. I went before the board of commissioners, and as I was closing my presentation, one of the commissioners said to me, in front of all the other commissioners, "Well, who's going to run the sheriff's office when you're gone?"

I replied, "I'm going to run the sheriff's office. I'm not going to the moon. I'm going to Quantico, Virginia. I know I don't have to worry about what is happening at the office for twelve weeks. My team is excellent, and I have every trust in them."

I was able to attend.

Money can run out. Towards the end of my last term as sheriff, the county board of commissioners cut 35 road patrol positions, which also greatly impacted

Scott, the incoming sheriff. It gutted our road patrol, and it was devastating. We went from having about five cars on the road per shift down to one.

The Delhi office contracted with Delhi Township for 20 staff; they had more cars on the road in one township than we did for the whole rest of the county. It bothered me a lot. I didn't get any of those positions back; Scott hasn't, either, but he continues to work on it.

There are two types of townships in Michigan: general law and charter townships. The county board's position and argument, which I can somewhat understand, is that charter townships are required to have police and fire. The general townships can pay for their own police just like Delhi does. How do you argue that?

One of the townships was interested in hiring a community police officer, for which they received a grant for one year. They had a free personnel resource, so we assigned a deputy to their township who was a great asset for them. They loved it. After the year ended, the grant ran out, and the township advised it would no longer fund the position.

That township explained, "We are a 'drive-thru township.' Your cars must drive through our township to get to where they are going all the time. We don't have to pay for anything."

I never thought of that, but they were right. That means that if a deputy was driving through the township and saw a situation, he would take care of it. The timing would have to be perfect, and it didn't always work, but we live and learn. We can't see around all the corners.

However, they didn't want to fund us anymore, even though Deputy Larry Harrison handled several thefts out of a commercial development area. There was a chain of thefts out of one office building. Our deputy was pretty sure he knew who it was. As he went to question the suspect, he took a VCR tape (back when we used VCRs), he labeled it "Robbery at Store" and added the suspect's name on it and went to the interrogation room. As he showed him the labeled tape, he said, "So, what do you know about this larceny that took place here?'

The suspect said, "I don't know what you're talking about."

Deputy Harrison held up the video tape and showed him. It freaked the suspect out, and he confessed. It was a blank videotape, but it worked, and it wasn't illegal. The problem was that there were all types of crimes in that township that would never be resolved with a "drive-thru deputy." The township still didn't want to fund the deputy. It was a huge loss for them because he was an excellent deputy and did great work.

MARK

One trait that I learned from my dad from a very young age is to be early. I'm always early to any commitment. I agree with the saying, "If you are on time, you are late." Dad also had being a hard worker so ingrained in us, as well as following "Right is right. Wrong is wrong."

GREGORY HARLESS, CHIEF DEPUTY (RET.) INGHAM COUNTY SHERIFF'S OFFICE

I started with the sheriff's office in 1985. I credit a lot of where I am today in my career to Gene and the opportunities he gave me.

In 1985, there was a rule that you had to live in the county you served. I didn't live in the county, and when Gene hired me, I had the opportunity to build a house outside the county. I asked the chief deputy at the time, and he said, "It's not a good idea. The sheriff needs to have people that can vote for him. If you live outside the county and you work for him, you can't vote for him." He then followed with, "It doesn't seem to make a lot of sense, but you can ask the sheriff."

I asked Gene and realized that he understood the definition of common sense when he answered, "Greg, if you can do it, do it. I have no problem with where you live."

I've known Gene since the mid-seventies because he was one of my Boy Scout leaders, and he lived two blocks away from where I was raised. When Gene was running the narcotics team, he and his team came to my dad's restaurant for dinner to debrief cases. My younger brothers and I were fascinated, seeing all these scruffy guys wearing long hair and earrings. We knew they were undercover, and they left an impression on eight- and ten-year-old boys.

I've been around him my whole life, and one of the consistent attributes that he models is his loyalty for the people who worked for him. Truly, all of us who worked for him knew that when he gave us his word, he would stand by it. There were hundreds of people he employed to work at the sheriff's office, and we all knew he was committed to doing the right thing.

As chief deputy, for almost eleven years, I worked closely with Gene. We had to make decisions in situations that needed to be handled, like patrol activity, instituting extra enforcement activities or pulling away enforcement, and other situations. My job was to help get it done, carry out the mission, and make sure that we provided services that he and we wanted according to his vision.

Sometimes, there were concerns from the public, the board of commissioners, or people in a department: "You can't do that." "You shouldn't do that." "Why did you do it?" "Why did you have to terminate somebody?" Gene's position was always consistent in how he determined his decisions.

1. Is it the right or wrong thing to do?
2. Is it fair?
3. He always asked what I thought we ought to do, and we talked it through.

Learning how to discuss options and present my ideas gave me opportunities to advance my own leadership skills. I learned that leaders had to make decisions, execute them, and keep steady. The work we did during emergencies could not be treated as a democracy, nor could it be a community decision.

Gene was always true to his word and had our backs no matter what. "Do the right thing; whatever it is, make the call; and let me worry about the politics." He always took the heat for us. Politicians and citizens were sometimes upset, but it's easy to do the right thing because we could always defend what we did.

He did not tolerate liars and often said, "You lie, you pay."

That sounds harsh, but it was true, because the only thing that cops had that people couldn't take away was our integrity. You could call us names. You might think we're the most rotten people in the world. "Do the right thing. Do the right thing all the time. You've still got your integrity in check."

I knew I wanted to maintain my integrity when I retired, and it paved the way for my next career. From my standpoint, I say we did a very good job, better than most law enforcement organizations that I knew when I was working, and it was because we policed ourselves.

We see officers all over the country who use excessive force or are under investigation for misconduct. Gene did not tolerate any misconduct because we never wanted to discredit the sheriff's office or the men and women who wore the badge. Anytime there is misconduct or excessive force from an officer of any kind, it's a smear on the profession. We took it very seriously, and Gene was good about supporting us. He let us clean our house to follow his lead, and we did. Under Gene, a lot of people chose to leave law enforcement for different reasons, and some were given opportunities to walk away instead of being terminated.

We did it with the utmost professionalism, and the proof is that even to this day, I get calls or cards at Christmastime from people that we terminated. That tells me we did something right. Nobody wants to lose their job. Nobody does. But to be respected during the process and be able to leave with your dignity was unforgettable for people. Just because someone made a bad decision doesn't mean they're a bad person. I'm proud of the way we handled this, and I will still talk about it today. Seeing what happens around the country, it's infuriating to see how some departments keep letting things go. Knowing there are officers like ours who are holding up the law, treating people with decency, and always doing the right thing is the bright light for everyone in this profession.

The mark of a good leader, to me, is one who makes a decision and does not waver. If you need to pause to consider the best decision, surround yourself with people who can help you make the right decision. They don't make the decision for you; they provide input, experience, and may help influence you towards the right direction from their point of view. Once that decision is made, we all move forward with it.

Oftentimes, our administrative team had different views, but the sheriff always gave us the opportunity to give input. He instructed, "When I ask you a question, be brave enough and bold enough to tell me what you think. Be confident in defending your decision, comments, or thoughts."

If there was dissent, it was up to us to bring it up. Once he heard all the facts, he said, "I've heard everything everybody has had to say. Based on what I've heard, this is what I want done."

When we knew what we were doing, he said, "Here is our decision: we're going to walk out and be one voice."

He expected that, and I think we operated very well under his leadership. It was clear, concise, and there was no wiggle room in it. We marched forward with the decision when we walked out of that room; it was one voice, the decision was made, we all agreed to do our jobs, and we did it.

It was empowering for me to have a voice, and Gene made that possible. People asked me throughout my career with each promotion, "Why would you want to do that? Why would you want to take on that extra role? Why do you want those calls at night? Why do you want to face the criticisms that will come along with a decision that will be popular or unpopular?"

For me, the choice was easy. I could either apply and test for a promotion or stay stagnant in the same job. I was hopeful that, within my new roles, I could be someone who offered a little bit more of a voice and direction and improved the circumstances. In any profession, we can either sit around and complain about it or put ourselves in a spot where we can try to influence the decision. It worked well when I was put in Gene's administration. Through his command structure and his management style, I had a voice, and he was clear about giving me the opportunity to share it.

When Gene promoted me to sergeant, he again modeled his leadership talent and had genuine care for those who worked for him. Each time he promoted someone, he made a big deal out of it. He invited our families and a bunch of people from the sheriff's office to present our stripes for sergeant stripes, lieutenant bars, captain bars, and major brass. They were all there to witness and celebrate the promotion with us. He took a picture and then said, "Everyone can leave now, because I want to talk to Sergeant Greg Harless."

I can remember what he said 30 years ago like it was yesterday. "Sergeant, as a sergeant, you begin to have more of a voice. A sergeant is very early middle management and is who I consider the 'skin' of the organization. If an 'infection' comes in, it's going to be from a sergeant not doing their job. I don't need to have a bunch of 'yes men' around me. I need somebody that has the courage to tell me if I'm doing something wrong, or if it's not necessarily wrong, but you disagree, or you have another opinion about how things should be going. If any of that happens, I expect you to bring it forward. I don't expect you to just be a 'yes man.'"

He continued, "I can walk down the hallway and get all the 'yes' answers I want, but I want someone who will disagree. I'll tell you why, because you can disagree without being disagreeable."

It was an open invitation, and I didn't have to ask for it. He didn't use his status to give me "permission to speak." He would simply ask me what I thought, and I told him. If I disagreed, I would not be disagreeable.

We literally improved and implemented hundreds of changes and initiatives for the people of our county and personnel. We changed the process for how we did homicide investigations, how inmates would pass through the jail, and I continued leading the Shop With a Hero Program after Matt Myers left the county. I know we made an impact in the county, and I know we made it a better place.

My advice to new law enforcement professionals who want to be in leadership: stick to your values. Don't waver or waffle from them. Don't ride on a political fence. Do the right thing. Always. When you do the right thing, you can always defend it. When you don't do the right thing, you have to lie to defend it, and then you get caught up in all kinds of garbage. Let God figure out the rest.

As I look at Gene and where I'm at today, the opportunities and experiences he gave me allowed me to move on to a new chapter after the sheriff's office. He was my role model for leadership, and he always encouraged self-development which led me to graduate from the FBI National Academy. Since then, so many doors have opened, and I met incredible people. Much of what we did together and what I learned from Gene about leadership is how I lead and work today. Gene has been with me most of my life, he has seen my family grow, and all the big life events. He truly was another father to me. I'm proud of the work we did together because it was right and just.

ALLAN SPYKE, UNDERSHERIFF (RET.), INGHAM COUNTY

Adventure was the reason I joined law enforcement. For nine years, I was deputy patrol from the south end of Lansing to Mason. I served primarily blue-collar folks in lower to middle class neighborhoods, and I enjoyed the adventures that called us to serve. It was a good place to work as a young cop because it was a busy area, and there was never a dull moment.

Then, I received the opportunity to transfer into the specialty unit at the Tri-County Metro Narcotic Squad, and I was in Gene's unit for three years. He was a state police lieutenant in 1987 when I joined, but I knew him well because he lived in my patrol district.

We have a lot of stories about when we worked together at Metro. There was a massive increase in cocaine use, production, sales, and distribution. It was seemingly everywhere. Fortunately, the specialty units are always composed of go-getters from eight different police departments across the state who they know will get the job done. Plus, we had Gene as one of our two lieutenants.

We were a solid team, and his leadership style was admirable because he didn't come off like he was the lieutenant and we were his sergeants. He worked together with us, and we knew he had our backs. There were several impressive qualities about his leadership style that I put in a list:

1. Officers are known for big egos. Now that we were undercover narcotics, we thought we were a big deal. Gene managed all of our egos with the way he led us.

2. Gene had a great sense of humor.

3. He was very direct with his decisions and orders.

4. Gene believed in following the rules: "Right is right. Wrong is wrong."

5. Before each raid, he said, "You were picked for this job for a reason. Use your head, and let's get this job done."

6. He never micromanaged us or tried to hold us back from saying or doing anything we thought was needed. He was very team oriented.

7. He did a good job managing all those personalities, and we did a lot of really good work.

8. Plus, he was a pretty popular guy, too. If you mentioned "Wriggelsworth" to anyone, they knew who you were talking about.

MAJOR JOEL MAATMAN (RET.), INGHAM COUNTY SHERIFF'S OFFICE

My police career started at Lansing Police Department, and I was promoted to sergeant. Then I worked for Gene at Tri-County Metro Narcotic Squad for two years. I had long hair and grew a beard. I returned to Lansing PD after that stint and worked the night shift as a patrol officer. Gene ran for sheriff, and I supported him in his election campaign. Then crack cocaine was popular in the nineties, and I returned undercover at Metro. That was a tough job. Toward the end of my career, I was promoted to lieutenant, and I ran the Lansing Undercover Unit for three years.

In 2006, I worked for Gene in the sheriff's office. What I liked about Gene the most was he was always positive, and he was one of the first supervisors who was willing to mentor me. When I joined the Lansing PD, I worked for great sergeants and lieutenants, but they just didn't seem to know how to develop people. They gave me good information about my career, but I had a lot to learn.

When I worked at Metro with Gene and Paul Whitford, they would tell me what I did right and pat me on the back. When I did something wrong, they told me that, too, and explained why it was wrong. Gene insisted we always be ethical because "right is right and wrong is wrong." That impressed the heck out of me because, in a former position, there were people who might have cut corners to make something happen. For example, if I was questioning someone, and they said they wanted a lawyer, I stopped because it was the law. Others didn't, because they wanted the confession. There was some other stuff, too, that I didn't agree with. Not Gene and Paul; they were "straight-A guys."

Until the day Gene walked out of the sheriff's office, he instilled a high degree of ethics in all of us: "Right is right, and wrong is wrong." That's how my adopted father raised me, too. It was natural for me. I was always impressed that he was politically elected every four years, but it didn't change the way he did business. He lived and worked with great integrity.

Gene was a great boss and leader because he was progressive. What I mean by that is he looked for ways to improve the way we worked. Everything he did made our jobs more efficient and gave us the ability to increase the safety of our citizens and personnel. A lot of people with a similar number of years in the field didn't do anything to make things better.

Before I started working for Gene at the sheriff's office, I was Chief of Security for the Lansing School District. Each year, Gene deputized the officers who worked for me as security guards at the schools. The first day I reported for work, I received a letter from Gene. Each year, he deputized the officers, but his letter stated that he had two instances when the officers went outside of the agreement with the school district, and he was not going to deputize them. It concerned me because it left us without police authority to handle security issues and keep the public schools safe.

Soon after I read the letter, Gene called and said, "Let's go to lunch."

I was convinced he changed his mind and was relieved and excited. As we sat down at the table, I noticed that he had a stack of paperwork. He said, "You know, Joel, PA 330 School District is public."

He proceeded to walk through the paperwork, and after he explained it to me, he said, "If you train your guys, you can have your own police department."

I was blown away. How many bosses and sheriffs are like that? He decided he wasn't going to deputize them, but he investigated how he could help the school district get around the issue with a better option. I trained them and instituted a police department for Lansing PA 330 School District.

Most supervisors and leaders in law enforcement who worked as many years as Gene never wanted to expand or try anything new. They were satisfied with the status quo. Not Gene. He was open-minded and willing to change anything we needed that made a positive difference in how we operated to serve the public.

In the early years, when working at the sheriff's office, there were several school shootings across the country. Unfortunately, they continue today. I recommended to Gene, "We need a plan in place that gives us a process on how to respond. You're the sheriff; you can do this."

I shared my idea. "We can get all the public, private, Catholic, and religious schools to design a process where every police officer in Ingham County knows what to do if they get called to a school shooting. I know the thirteen police departments who will show up to get this training."

Gene replied, "That's a great idea, Joel. Let's do it."

We set up two committees, and it took a whole year to develop the process and hold training sessions for every officer and deputy in Ingham County. It was critical to designate and include respective leaders: an MSU police officer, a Michigan state trooper, an Ingham County deputy, and a Lansing police officer to be first on the scene to find and apprehend the suspect. The "Smart Team" designed the training, and for six years, officers throughout the county attended our three-day school. We also coordinated with the schools to add large numbers to the entrances and exits in an orderly manner to plan which doors to enter during a drill or live call. This initiative was successful and so well-regarded that Eaton County, west of Ingham County, heard about it, observed us, and then adopted it for their own county. Other counties followed suit. We were able to initiate and execute such a program because of Gene's leadership, open mind, and willingness to do the hard work. Without him, it never would have existed.

During the last years of my career, we had an increased number of fatal accidents in our county. There was so much training available at the expert level for accident investigators (AI) to perform their job, but we didn't have anything for the county.

Each month, all the chiefs, assistant chiefs, and staff of all the police departments held a meeting to talk about what's happened and shared new ideas with each other. Different people presented new ideas or new ways to do something that worked for them.

Everyone looked up to Gene as the leader of leaders because of his great leadership skills since he'd been around many years. He was "the man in charge." Gene's leadership style was always to hear and consider everyone's ideas. When it made sense and could be done, he approved it to go forward.

His connections all over the county, state, and country greatly helped when we needed other resources.

In the meeting, he opened it to new ideas and gave each of those with ideas time to share.

"Joel has an idea. Go ahead, Joel," he announced.

I shared my idea of training our own accident investigators, and mentioned a friend of mine, Dan Munford, a Lansing officer who worked at the MSU Police Department, would be a great resource to lead this initiative. Gene approved it, and we coordinated efforts to build the program. When a fatal accident occurs, there is a list of people from different police departments who, if they aren't working, can be called to lead the accident investigation. Ingham County still follows this protocol today.

Again and again, because of Gene, his leadership style, and the programs he put in place, police departments in this county, the state police, and the Ingham County Sheriff's Office all work together, even today. And they care about each other and want to work together. It's not about "us versus them."

It was completely different working for Gene, and it was great to watch him at those meetings. When he said something, people listened.

SAM DAVIS, MAJOR, JAIL ADMINISTRATOR (RET.) INGHAM COUNTY SHERIFF'S OFFICE

The sheriff had a vision and saw how my education and administration experience applied to the role as jail administrator for Ingham County. It took a while before I really realized how running a high school applied to running a county jail.

The sheriff is a very genuine person, very accepting, and very open. I liked the way that he talked to me on a respectful playing field. When he reached out and said, "Hey, Sam, would you like to come work for me?"

I wasn't his underling. It wasn't human resources asking, but the sheriff himself giving me that personal invitation: "I want you on my team." It was a compliment when the sheriff wanted you on his team. From the get-go, I really didn't know him, but the little bit I did know about him made me feel comfortable.

On my first day, he welcomed me into his office and talked about his open-door policy which was genuine. He always said, "Come on in." He was never too busy to meet with anyone. He was willing to train and teach.

Early on, I was sitting in my office trying to figure out what I was going to do, and here came the sheriff, waltzing in to check and see if I needed anything. I said, "I don't know what I need."

He replied, "You got this. You can do this, Sam."

He repeatedly gave me that sense of confidence that I could do the job, and that he was confident in me. He expressed his belief in me through what he said, his everyday connection, and nonverbal communication. He walked the talk, "I'm no better than you all are. I just have these extra stars on my collar, but I'm just one of the guys."

I knew I could work for him.

*****

As principal and superintendent of high schools, I managed some real troubling times and some very challenging folks. I learned that the skills I had and the expertise I honed benefited both environments because managing human behavior is managing human behavior, regardless of the venue.

All people have the same needs, whether you are disciplined, suspended, or expelled from school, or whether you are in jail overnight or for the rest of your life; the human response is the same. The basic needs people have are to be respected, have people listen to them, know that people are concerned about them, and trust those people are looking out for their best interests.

Gene was just down-to-earth. Growing up, I didn't have the most positive impressions of cops, especially as a Black man. This is why I had some trepidation about taking the job. There wasn't a love in my community for law enforcement and, for me, wearing that uniform was not going to be the best received in my neighborhood. I knew the sheriff and I were aligned in morals and values once he iterated how he trained his deputies at the jail. "We are not here to punish these people. The court gave them their punishment. We are their caretakers, and we are to treat them with respect."

The more I explored the role, the more I came to know the sheriff and learn how we would work together. I began to recognize how my career in teaching and administration was relevant. I worked with kids and their angry parents, teachers who were frustrated with their jobs and losing interest in teaching, athletes who felt entitled and privileged, and their parents, who felt the same.

There were kids whose parents were substance abusers, kids who did the same, and kids who were suicidal. It was a lot of hard and complicated work.

Violence, crime, and chaos were not new to me. One of the nation's first school shootings took place in 1978 at Lansing Everett High School, on my floor, outside my door. I grew up on the west side of Lansing, and it was tumultuous times in the sixties and the seventies, I knew that. I saw some strange things when I was growing up, but I never thought that school was not a safe place. It had been safe for me all the time when I was growing up. I never thought about kids carrying weapons. I never thought about being so mentally unbalanced, unstable, and angry to the point that you would be completely confused enough to go out and take someone else's life.

For the kids in middle school and high school, I was responsible for their daily safety and their mental well-being from dealing with bullies, drugs, and sexual activities while at school. I wasn't responsible for their lives 24/7/365. Converting to a place where I was responsible for the lives of about 700 inmates and about 100 deputies felt much larger. Fortunately, it didn't take long for me to recognize that my experience in schools had been a precursor or natural segue to what I was about to experience.

Even with that experience, I did need some training for this new role.

Licensing. I had to attend the State Corrections Academy and pass the exam within one year of starting the job. It required a lot of reading about policy and procedures. There was a group of us who were all new to the sheriff's office and attended the academy together. We learned about policy, procedure, and correctional law altogether. I was their boss; at the same time, I was their equal, but I was their boss. Since we were all learning the same stuff at the same time, we built a special bond together, allowing us to support each other as we grew into our new positions. We learned from each other how to better understand the rules and regulations about what you can do, what you can't do, what you can say, and what you cannot say.

Acclimation Period. Without that, the academy and the people who became my colleagues and team members, I would not have acclimated as well; it was nice to have ten or so folks who were in the same boat as me at the academy who worked for me at the jail. Getting acclimated was the most difficult part, at the beginning. I had never been in a jail before or visited the county jail. Here I was, walking through all areas of the facility beyond the locked doors, the sally port, and into the housing units.

Weapons. When they asked me about my weapons experience, I said, "When I was in seventh grade at the YMCA camp, I had the opportunity to shoot a .22 at a target."

That was the beginning and the end of it. As a corrections officer, the sheriff had the ability to and did make me a special deputy, which allowed me to carry a sidearm, but I had to go through the training with our firing range down. I learned how to handle a weapon.

Police Academy. The sheriff is self-effacing. During my third or fourth year, the sheriff asked, "I'd like you to attend the police academy."

I replied, "No thank you. I'm not interested in doing that but thank you for offering."

He seemed okay with it and didn't have a problem with my decline. I never felt forced to say "yes." A couple months later, "Sam, have you given any thought to maybe going to the police academy?"

I answered, "No, boss, not really."

He said, "Okay, well, if you want it, the opportunity is there."

By the third time he asked, I thought, *My grandma didn't raise a dummy. The sheriff wants me to go to the police academy.* He asked in the same way, as it wasn't forced, but was I interested? Since I wasn't raised to be oblivious, we had a little bit more serious conversation about it.

After I heard more, I said, "Okay, you want me to go? I'll go to the police academy."

Mind you, I'm 58 years old at that time.

The Police Academy Program was 18 weeks long, and we were up at six in the morning. I didn't think to ask, and no one mentioned, whether I needed to do both my job and the Academy. I did the Academy in the day and went to the Jail at night to keep my foot in law enforcement and corrections.

I was still learning my role at the jail, and my next responsibility to learn was how to release inmates. I wanted to know how to process the people in holding, look at the jail roster, review the files, make the decisions and calculations needed to release them. I didn't realize those long days and having my feet in both jobs, so to speak, would impact me so much. And I learned yet again the type of good person and boss the sheriff is.

While doing the releases, I made a mistake with about fifteen or so folks when I released them early. Nobody caught it until a judge called for one of our inmates. She couldn't find him and learned he had been released. "Who released him? How can he be released? He's still committed to jail."

I was at the police academy when I received a call from Kathy Winslow, who said, "You need to go back to the sheriff's office."

I knew that couldn't be good. When I arrived, I learned what happened. I was devastated. I released people early in the community. If one of them gets hurt or if they hurt someone else or commit a new crime or whatever, that's all on me. I've let the community down. I let the sheriff down.

As a grown man at 58 years old, I sat in the sheriff's office very upset and anxious. I was so distraught. I handed a letter to the sheriff and resigned.

"I'm not taking that," he refused.

"I did it," I confessed again.

The sheriff said, "I owe you an apology. I should have told you and made it very clear that when you're in the law enforcement academy, that's all you do. That's your job. You're getting paid to do that. We had other people take care of the jail while you were gone. You should have been made very clear on that. I failed as your boss because you didn't know that."

I was stunned.

Then he began to tell me some stories. "We all make mistakes, Sam. This was an honest mistake. I bet you one thing. I bet you'll never do it again."

I said, "You're right."

Then, he said something that shocked me even more. "I won't accept your resignation. Now, you'll have to meet with the undersheriff, because there is going to be some discipline."

I replied, "Okay."

"Because I cannot set a precedent for this, but you're not going to lose your job. I'm not accepting your resignation," he explained.

When I met the undersheriff, I knew he talked with the sheriff. He said, "Sam, I'm going to give you some discipline. I don't know what it is. The sheriff gave it to me in a sealed envelope. I'm going to put it in the file drawer here. I'm not putting it in your personnel file. It's right here. You've been disciplined."

This was how the sheriff's office team worked.

When I retired from the sheriff's office, he gave it to me. It's still sealed today. I told my deputies about that. When I taught at Michigan State, I told my students, and I tell the folks who work for me right now, "If you are truly remorseful for what you've done, no one can do that any more to you than what you've done to yourself."

I don't know if it was a reprimand. I don't think it was. I think it was counseling. It didn't matter. I had a paper on me because I made an error in judgment, but it didn't define me. And I know that the undersheriff didn't get to just put that in his folder in his office without having Gene Wriggelsworth say, "This is how we want to handle this." To me, that is a perfect example of him being an extraordinary leader.

During that experience, he talked about his own mistakes that he had made. It just endeared him to me even more and is part of why I think he's such a super guy. Today, I train folks for the American Jail Association on a national level, which Gene encouraged me to get involved in. When people talk about their leaders and sheriffs, I always talk about my sheriff, Gene, and give them examples of his leadership and his personality. They often say, "That's the kind of sheriff we wish we worked for."

I always reply, "I had the privilege of working with him for a decade."

What I like most about Sheriff is that he is so easy to talk with, and I could discuss any topic with him. He is genuine, and I know the word is overused, but transparency is how he always operated. If I talked to a commissioner, I could talk with them about jail operations, but if I talked about a budget item, they would say, "Stay in your lane."

The sheriff never operated that way; he built us as a team to work together and support each other. He introduced us to everyone, and he even introduced me to judges who were very comfortable working with the sheriff. For someone to be elected for seven consecutive terms, totaling 28 years, people obviously knew he was doing something right. He was never about busting heads or writing traffic tickets; rather, he actually cared about folks. He accepted everyone and trusted everyone who worked with or for him. You can always tell that he enjoys people and his generosity is limitless.

He didn't just support me in my career, but also in my personal life. If I needed a referral for anything or any advice, he openly shared what or who he knew. Like the police academy, he recommended I get involved in the American Jails Association for professional development and networking, and even after retirement, I'm still involved.

For so many reasons, Sheriff is a true leader.

DARWIN SHAVER, MAJOR (deceased 2025), INGHAM COUNTY SHERIFF'S OFFICE

Gene took over a sheriff's office that was in disarray and turned it into one of the finest sheriff's offices in the State of Michigan. He is a fantastic sheriff, police officer, servant to the community, volunteer, family member, and person because he does everything with his heart. He loves his wife, Precious, and his family more than anything else.

Even though Gene was intimidating, I had great respect for him. Right is right. Wrong is wrong. He was decisive in every decision. Even people who were close to him were not given any leeway. Everything he did and everything he asked us to do was always good for the sheriff's office or the community.

Gene didn't stop his work at the office; he was a community leader, too. During election year, a lot of politicians ask for donations, and soon after you contribute, they ask for more. Gene held a golf outing every year to raise money, and he used that time to get contributors' viewpoints on what they felt was needed. For seven terms, he raised enough money at the golf outings for each election. He was clear with his directions to us about supporting him. Any politicking I wanted to do was on my own time. No patrol cars or county time could be used. You knew beyond a shadow of a doubt he was ethical in all areas of his life.

Gene has a natural ability to lead; respect is earned, not demanded, and he earned the respect of everyone that worked for him or with him. Gene was very fortunate to have a fantastic undersheriff, Rick Boyd. Together, they made a great team because leadership starts at the top.

Since this line of work is stressful, there are a lot of heavy drinkers, divorces, infidelity, and other challenges. Gene did not put up with it; it was black and white with no in between. He did not put up with officers being crazy and wild, and it didn't take long for them to get themselves in line.

He was fair. In this line of work, the way people treat one another is very bothersome. One year on Christmas Eve, a husband was drunk; he threw the Christmas tree in the front yard and smashed the presents. The accidents when children were injured or when we had to pry the children out of their parents' hands because of a court order for protective custody was super hard. It was all that emotional stuff that was hard to deal with.

With Gene, we knew we had to work hard and do the best possible job we could do. When we made a mistake, he had our back; if we were wrong, we paid the price, and he said, "Learn from your mistakes. First and foremost, do not do anything to embarrass the sheriff and office while on and off the job."

He brought the community together for several initiatives so people would understand why he needed more guns or more cars to do our police work. He worked with car dealers for his fleet and involved as many people on the board of commissioners as possible. That was never an easy feat. If there was a shooting, he brought the news media together and brought in the different facets of the community to see how he could support the neighborhoods. Other reasons he was successful were that he always looked for ways to make the sheriff's office better and kept the community educated and informed.

Gene is a family man first, and it was a pleasure to watch how he talked with people to defuse situations. He respected them and showed compassion. I really believe this was a calling for Gene. He couldn't have done everything he did without the support of his family, and they contributed to his success. Sandy sacrificed so much and supported Gene so willingly. They supported him because they loved him and knew he was doing a good job.

Not many people spend 50 years in law enforcement. Gene was called, and he did it for the community and did the best he could with his officers. Officers were proud to work for and with Gene; you didn't just work for him, you worked with him, and he, with you. All his dedication and work were never "about Gene;" It was truly about how and what he could do to make the world a better place.

Since he retired, he hasn't slowed down, and he still volunteers, still cares, and is genuinely a good person. He is a good police officer and sheriff, and a damned good family man.

He and Sandy have been involved in more things than most families are involved in. They didn't do *one* great thing; they still do a lot of great things, like being involved with Give-A-Kid-A-BACKPACK for back-to-school and Christmas donations, building ramps for people with disabilities, delivering mattresses for Christian Services, and so much more.

All leadership starts from the top. He was the top cop, and he changed Ingham County and the State of Michigan for the better.

CHAPTER 20 RECAP

1. Right is right. Wrong is wrong. Honesty is always the best policy.

2. Be professional at all times, especially while in uniform and in public.

3. Check your ego, because we need to operate as one team and have each other's backs.

4. Treat everyone as an equal within the team and in external departments and offices.

5. Keep your temper in check and learn how to control your emotions.

6. Be decisive.

7. Be consistent: treating people equally and fairly, with expectations.

8. Understand that people are human, have flaws and weaknesses, and will make mistakes.

9. Own up to your mistakes; take responsibility.

10. Always look for opportunities to collaborate with colleagues and contribute to the overall mission of the organization.

CHAPTER 21

A 50-YEAR LAW ENFORCEMENT CAREER, TIME TO RETIRE

Sheriff Gene Wriggelsworth. Seventh term as Sheriff of Ingham County Michigan, 2012–2016.

Gene's large collection of badges throughout his 50-year career.

Gene and Sandy celebrate their 58th wedding anniversary
at Dusty's English Inn, Eaton Rapids, Michigan. 2023.

*****

In 2016, I hit my fiftieth year of a robust career in law enforcement. As I reflected on the previous five decades, it was a long and short blink all tied in one. It was the fastest 50 years of my life! Time is funny that way. As I looked at the past and looked ahead at what my future with Sandy might be, I was feeling that it was time to consider retirement.

50 years is a long time in one career, but my roles were varied, working for Michigan State Police as a state trooper, being undercover police for the Tri-County Metro Narcotic Squad, and serving as a sheriff for Ingham County. I was grateful to not have spent 50 years assembling widgets on a factory line. Instead, I entered recruit school and my future began. I hope my father isn't worried anymore that I walked away from all that money in manufacturing.

I knew it was time when my natural persona to remain calm, cool, and collected unraveled a bit at a commissioner meeting earlier that year. The secrets to success in politics are being respectful, knowing your role, and avoiding the use of any negative comments or tones. As sheriff, the commissioners could not tell me what to do in terms of my role and responsibilities, but they did have control over my budget. During the meeting, a particular commissioner who didn't find much favor with me for some reason brought up a deputy that did something that was none of his business. Completely unlike me, I lost my temper and blew up at him.

When I left the meeting, I thought to myself, *This is a mistake. This guy votes on my budget.* I analyzed it all the way home. I walked in the door and said, "Sandy, I'm going to retire. I'm not going to run again. This incident tonight tells me I've had enough."

That was the deciding factor. It was time. I never should have let loose like that.

It happened to be early in the election year, too. My son, Scott, was a lieutenant at the East Lansing Police Department and had mentioned to me that he may be interested in running for sheriff. After Sandy I discussed it, I shared with Scott that I was not running and that I would gladly endorse Scott in his run for the next sheriff. He filed as a candidate, ran his campaign, and won the election by a large margin. It was a terrific victory party. He would agree with me that it may have been likely that voters thought they were still voting for me, so having the same last name was in his favor. He's been reelected two more terms, and that was based on earning his wins with his own name. His next term ends December 31, 2028.

Gene passes the torch to his son Scott Wriggelsworth as he becomes the newly-elected Ingham County Sheriff. Election night, November 8, 2016.

Swearing-in ceremony for Scott Wriggelsworth, the new sheriff of Ingham County, presented by Gene Wriggelsworth. 2016.

So I retired, and I thought it would be easy sailing. After working as long as I did every day, it's not easy to retire. I busied myself with projects around the house. I worked in my tool shop in the basement, where I make wall clocks in different shapes and lacquer them. They make really nice gifts. Sandy and I went on a couple of long-weekend trips, and I spent time with my three sons and their families.

About a month or two into retirement, there was a rash that grew on the back of my hand. I couldn't get it to go away, so I went to my dermatologist, Dr. Gregory Messenger. He looked at it and said, "You have stress-induced psoriasis."

Shocked, I replied, "What? This is stress? I'm retired!"

He replied, "That's your new stress. You haven't adjusted to it yet."

I couldn't believe it. I was playing around in my shop, spending time with my wife and family, and that was stressful! That was when I realized that my career was focused on serving people and making the world a better place. I missed it, and fortunately, I remembered I heard about the Tuesday Toolmen group who built ramps for people who couldn't use stairs. I looked into it and signed up. I also joined Give-A-Kid-Projects and remained in The Hundred Club, among many other organizations.

While I was retired, Scott was the sheriff, and he continued to advocate for a new jail and administrative complex for the first two years of his first term. After many months of discussion, the board of commissioners agreed to place the issue on the August 2018 ballot to let the voters decide. Prior to the vote, Scott rolled out a massive campaign to educate the public on why it was needed. It was voted on and the $80 million budget was overwhelmingly approved by the public. It took four years to construct, and the new jail and administrative complex opened on February 16, 2023. Occasionally, I popped in to see how it progressed. It was a big project, and it was fun to watch.

On my 78th birthday, Scott came to our home and said he had something to show Sandy and me. As we drove by the sheriff's office, there was a large, illuminated sign, "Gene L. Wrigglesworth Training Center." Scott swore it was pure happenstance that the name was installed on my birthday, but what a present!

*The new Ingham County Justice Complex with the naming of the
Gene Wriggelsworth Training Center. November 7, 2022.*

SANDY

It's been a good ride. That's what I say, and I don't regret a minute of it. The first two years in Flat Rock were difficult, but I think that's usually true of anybody starting out. We kept going and did whatever we needed to work. Family was very important to me. Scott mentioned that the closeness of our family is rare, and it's special. That makes me feel like Gene and I did do our best, and it had a positive effect on our three boys. I hope we have set a good example for them, their families, and our future generations. After getting married, we wanted to raise our children to be good people and good citizens. I joined some wonderful organizations and met some wonderful people who are now a big part of our lives. Now, in retirement, we do whatever it is we want to do with our family and friends, and we give back to our wonderful community as much as we can. I just love it.

If I had to do it all over again, I would. I think every step in my career, including the challenging ones, made me better at my career. The only thing I would change was taking Sandy down to Flat Rock, because it was so difficult for her to be away from everyone she knew. She still stuck by me; I don't know why, but she did. And she's still with me today, too! Once she started building her own path to her own success, life really smoothed out. Other than living in Flat Rock, I wouldn't change anything. And for that, I know I'm blessed, and I am extremely grateful.

Chapter 21 Lesson

There are so many clichés about knowing when to quit something and when to start something new. They say to "hire slowly, fire quickly," and that "one bad apple spoils the bunch." What I know is that when you know it's time to go, whether it is to retire, change jobs, or get promoted, listen to the cliché: "Follow your gut. You'll never go wrong when you follow your gut." Intuition is one of the greatest internal guides we have. Listen carefully to it and use it in all areas of your life! Even if it is a cliché.

Thank you for your generosity.

Here is a small collection of many special gifts you have given me along with your kindness and support through the years. Thank you.

Retirement photo gift from Kirk MacKellar, my son Mark's father-in-law.

Cherry Oppenlander gifted Gene this quilt of some of the golf outing T-shirts.
It is with deep sorrow that we share that Cherry Oppenlander passed away on August 7, 2025.
Her friendship and generosity will always be remembered.
https://www.dignitymemorial.com/obituaries/mason-mi/cherry-oppenlander-12479969

*The MSP plaque holds the actual letters from the building of the Michigan State Police
Headquarters at 714 South Harrison Road, East Lansing. The building was demolished in 2012.*

*The ICJ plaque holds the actual letters from the building of the previous Ingham County Jail
that was replaced with the new Ingham County Justice Complex in 2023.*

"A good friend is like a four-leaf clover: hard to find and lucky to have."

Class of 1993 Reunion

Party crashers. Gene and Sandy crash their son's, Mark's, Holt High School class reunion with long-time Holt teacher Dan Ernst, a.k.a. "Dirt," and his wife, Jan. 1993.

Dinner with dear friends. Gene and Sandy on the left, Wendie and Bill Pike on the right. 2025.

Sandy and her friends sporting custom T-shirts specially made for the golf outing. Each election year, people from the community attended the fundraiser to support Gene's election as Ingham County Sheriff.

*Gene at his 80ʰ birthday party with Sheri Jones, Channel 6 media anchor, who started
her media career as an MSU grad and bravely joined Gene and his teams on drug raids.
Sherry recently retired from Channel 6 and is enjoying her own retirement.
Thank you, Sherry, for your objective and accurate reporting over these years. 2025.*

*Gene's book team for his first book, 50 Years of Duty.
From left to right: Traci Ruiz, Connector; Sandy, Co-Author; Gene,
Author; Cindy Tschosik, Co-Writer; Scott, Advisor; and Mary Jo, Photographer.
At Gene's 80ʰ birthday. November 2024.*

"The love of a family is life's greatest blessing."
— Eva Burrows

Gene and Sandy on the beach in Frankfort, Michigan.

Gene and Sandy's son Mike's 40th birthday. 2006.

Gene and his three sons on Father's Day in Frankfort, Michigan.
From left to right: Mark, Mike, Gene, and Scott. 2025.

Gene and Sandy's 60th Wedding Anniversary
July 31, 1965 – July 31, 2025

Gene and Sandy join Reverend Tim Flynn, rector of St. Michael's Episcopalian Church, in Lansing, Michigan as he bestows a blessing upon them for their 60th wedding anniversary on July 31, 2025.

Gene and Sandy in Mackinac, Michigan for their 60th anniversary. 2025.

Gene and Sandy celebrate their 60ᵗʰ anniversary at the Grand Hotel on
Mackinac Island, Michigan on July 31, 2025.
From left to right: Scott, Mary Jo, Mark, Kelly, Sandy, Gene, Kelli, and Mike.

The Wrigglesworth Family
Four Generations

Seated in front row center: Gene and Sandy Wrigglesworth.
Standing in back row, left to right: Hannah, Jacob, Kelli, Hayden, Andrew, Mary Jo, Scott, Mike,
Mark, Rorie holding Kai, Ryan, Kaili, Kelly, and Jake.

Hannah   *Charlotte, Makenna, Hailey*   *Reece*

"I can no other answer make,
But, thanks, and thanks,
And ever thanks."
– William Shakespeare

Appendix

Recap of Chapter Lessons

PART 1 LESSONS – THE BEGINNING

CHAPTER 1 LESSON – I DIDN'T KNOW WHAT I DIDN'T KNOW

1. **Open Yourself to Possibilities.** Oftentimes, other people see more in us than we do. Listen carefully and stay open to the seeds they plant in your brain and heart.
2. **Never Stop Learning.** Study, pay attention, and don't take education for granted, especially the meaning of exams. Those "silly questions" on the entrance exam were critical to my work for all 50 years and even today. And yes, I learned the importance of "inflammable" and "flammable."

CHAPTER 2 LESSON – FAMILY IS EVERYTHING

1. **Family Is Everything.** Stress, lack of sleep, and night shifts are just three factors that contribute to the disruption of families. The key to avoiding or reducing stress is to spend as much free time as you have with each other to balance the bad and the good.
2. **Be Flexible in Your Journey.** Life is not always linear for a lot of us.
3. **Identify Your Individual and Family Values.** Hold strong to them, for they are your foundation in how to live, learn, and grow as one and together. Here are the ones we covered in this chapter:

   Sandy

   - Communication
   - Church/Faith

Gene

- Work Ethic
- Honesty
- Faith

Mike

- Work/Life Balance
- Unconditional Support
- Encouragement

Scott

- Collaboration
- Integrity
- Respect/Dignity

Mark

- Strong Marriage and Family
- Work Hard
- Arrive Early

CHAPTER 3 LESSON – LIFE IS NOT LINEAR

Each one of our lives is unique, and this extends to both our personal and professional paths. No matter where you start, it does not define where you must stay. If you desire to do one thing and change your mind later, do what it is that makes you happy. In law enforcement, the opportunities are limitless when you work hard, operate with integrity, and treat others with respect.

CHAPTER 4 LESSON – IT TAKES A VILLAGE

1. **It Takes a Village.** Who are the people you consider members of your "village?"
2. **Write a List.** To determine the members of your "village," write a list of people in your life who fill the following roles:
   - Personal Life
     - Family

- Friends
- Neighbors
- Vendors
- Townspeople (first responders, village officials, teachers, doctors, etc.)

- Professional Life
  - Co-workers
  - Employers/Executives
  - Bosses/Supervisors/Team Leads
  - Coaches/Mentors/Sponsors
  - Vendors

- **Give Thanks.** Have you ever considered saying, "Thanks for being a part of my village. This is how you have helped shape me into the person I am today."

*****

PART 2 LESSONS – 22 YEARS AS A MICHIGAN STATE TROOPER YEARS 1–8

CHAPTER 5 LESSON – THE FIRST EIGHT YEARS FROM FLAT ROCK AND BEYOND

1. When starting a new job or getting a promotion in your career, I learned it was best to listen more than talk, observe more than act, and respect everyone. You never know who your next supervisor will be or who will work for you some day.

2. There are a lot of troubled people in our society, and in most cases, they didn't arrive where they are on purpose. It helps you to seek to understand their plight first, see yourself in their shoes, and find out what you can do to serve them. There are some who have no interest in improving their life, and some are looking for a hand up. Be aware of those who need and want a hand up. You will change more lives that way and make the world a better place.

CHAPTER 6 LESSON – A DAY IN THE LIFE OF A MICHIGAN STATE TROOPER

You are going to meet people you like, dislike, love, and hate. Hate is a strong word. Learn to control yourself when you have to work with or for someone you don't like or get along with. If you must. . . bite your tongue, count to ten, take a walk, do it. It's not worth the risk of getting written up or tarnishing your own reputation.

CHAPTER 7 LESSON – UNFORGETTABLE AS A MICHIGAN STATE TROOPER

The hardest part of your job will be the losses you endure. Each one of us deals with grief differently. There are books to help you process grief, there are therapists to help you deal with grief, and so many other resources. No matter which paths you choose, just be sure that you are keeping yourself from stuffing it all down and ignoring it.

CHAPTER 8 LESSON – IN MEMORIAM, THE ULTIMATE SACRIFICE, 1966–1974

We often say, "Life is too short," and it is. In law enforcement, I can't stress the devastation we endure when our coworker wakes up one day and doesn't make it home the same night. The lives of their loved ones will never be the same. And it happens in other fields, too. That's why I firmly believe it's worth making the effort to never go to bed angry, never end an argument without an apology, share your love and feelings with everyone you care about, and always kiss and/or hug goodbye. Be grateful every morning you are gifted another day, and every evening that you make it home.

*****

PART 3 LESSONS – 22 YEARS AS A MICHIGAN STATE TROOPER, UNDERCOVER YEARS 9–22 AT TRI-COUNTY METRO NARCOTIC SQUAD

CHAPTER 9 LESSON – DAD AND HUSBAND BY DAY/DRUG BUSTER BY NIGHT

I recommend honing your skills to build relationships from your first day on the job with every level of any organization in your career. At first, I was very hesitant about being in the same building with all the state trooper supervisors and directors because I just wanted to be left alone to do my job. I assumed I would be "hounded" or micromanaged.

However, it ended up being quite the opposite. Instead, I found shaking hands and passing by people at all levels put a face to my name, and they remembered who I was. It also carved the way for me to take opportunities to share the cases I had and build my reputation. I believe being amongst the leaders also commanded me to stand a little taller, kept me on my toes, and raised my level of professionalism around the office.

When my supervisors and even the Director of the Michigan State Troopers observed or heard about an accomplishment, they kept it in mind and later referred me for special assignments, like training in New Mexico, placement in the Tri-County Metro Narcotic Squad, and promotions.

Look for opportunities in your job that put you in front of others and that will get you recognized for your achievements. It greatly improves chances for later opportunities.

CHAPTER 10 LESSON – THE DRUGS, THE RAIDS, AND THE ODDITIES

Don't do drugs!

CHAPTER 11 LESSON – UNFORGETTABLE AS UNDERCOVER LIEUTANANT

Sometimes, when in a difficult or long-time role, it will feel as if it's time for a change or new opportunity. I loved being undercover for Metro. I did it for 14 years and had the pleasure of working with the best of local law enforcement. The time had come when I told Sandy I was getting tired. It was a very demanding and rewarding position with a lot of responsibility. Plus, as you get older, you do get tired, no matter how much you don't want to admit it. The shifts could be 12-18 hours long or more, and I felt it was time for something new.

At any stage of your career, be sure to check in with yourself, because you may be faced with circumstances, such as your age, life balance, finances, health, or family, that make it so you desire to advance or change your career. Don't hold yourself back from exploring that next step and do what is best for you in your life.

CHAPTER 12 LESSON – IN MEMORIAM, THE ULTIMATE SACRIFICE, 1974–1988

Every day, the media reports on tragic and fatal events. Most of us are desensitized to the tragedy of it and move about our day. Next time you hear about someone injured or killed, just pause without judgement or negative thoughts. Think about the victim and those who survive them. Remember that anyone who is injured or dies is loved by someone and deserves respect, and their loved ones deserve empathy. If you are a praying person, send them all a little prayer.

*****

PART 4 LESSONS – 28 YEARS AS THE SHERIFF OF INGHAM COUNTY, MICHIGAN

CHAPTER 13 LESSON – A DAY IN THE LIFE AS THE SHERIFF OF INGHAM COUNTY

Whenever you start a new leadership role in your career, these are the most important steps in the first weeks:

1. Build relationships with:
   a. Core leadership team
   b. Direct reports
   c. Remaining staff
   d. Peers in other divisions, offices, or departments

2. Set the example you want employees to follow, such as:
   a. Communications styles, tones, behavior
   b. Dress, style
   c. Decorum in behaviors and interpersonal skills
   d. Timeliness, schedules, benefits
   e. Influence between internal and external interfaces

3. Establish and explain:
   a. Expectations
   b. Acceptable and unacceptable behaviors

  c. Individual and team responsibilities

  d. Divisions of duty

  e. Expected routines, processes, and procedures

  f. Technology use and abuse

4. Prepare your own:

  a. Expectations

  b. Operations, plans, processes, and procedures

  c. Schedule

  d. Timeline of opportunities for self-development and career advancement

CHAPTER 14 LESSON – ADVANCEMENTS FOR THE INGHAM COUNTY SHERIFF'S OFFICE

For many of us, it's important that we leave the place we live or work better than when we found it. Initiating these advancements for the sheriff's office and Ingham County citizens was an absolute honor. However, the reason they were successful and impacted our communities so much was because of all the people involved who also made a difference in their career, life, family, and community. It certainly takes a village, and these initiatives sure did take a village.

 Where in your life, family, or community can you improve the lives of others? I believe part of the reason we are here is to do exactly that. You don't have to create your own initiative or reinvent the wheel. There are plenty of community events within your town, county, church, school, and social organizations. Sandy and I have found that it is very helpful to pick the activities you enjoy and to prioritize the types of contributions you want to see make a difference.

CHAPTER 15 – UNFORGETTABLE AS THE SHERIFF

Special Safety Tips

I do believe any upstanding and law-abiding citizen would be stunned at the number of crimes and types of crimes that are committed daily. Often, "staying safe" seems like it would be so simple. In reality, many people don't know how to report crimes or suspicious acts they see, or how to keep themselves safe. Here are some tips which I hope you find helpful to keep yourself, your family, and your community safe.

How to Report or Respond to a Crime or Suspicious Acts

When we get a call from dispatch, there are many physical, emotional, and mental reactions we have as we respond. Each situation is unique and calls for different reactions. If 911 tells us there is a homicide or domestic situation in progress, we drive very fast, with our blood rushing and mind planning our approach: do we run into the house or wait for backup?

When a car is stolen or there is a robbery or a mugging, and they dispatch the description, we drive cautiously to keep an eye on passing cars or injured persons.

If we are merely driving or on patrol, we keep an eye on everything to ensure proper order in public situations. Being on alert is natural for law enforcers because we have to always be ready to intervene. I might be on personal leave or off for the day. If there is an emergency or crime, I must intervene as a part of my oath.

How Can You Help Us Fight Crime?

When you are suspicious of behavior or witness a crime, try to gather as much information as possible. When you write down information, type it into your phone or take pictures; it is the best way to help us and reduce the stress from having to remember it.

- For vehicles: With as much detail as possible, describe any people, vehicles, directions headed, and location. On vehicles, it's best to get a license plate and/or the make/model/color of a vehicle. For instance, black Chevy SUV and license plate number. If you notice anything unusual like tinted windows, a dent, or a smashed light, that will be helpful, too.

- For people: Document anything you see or remember, including gender, height, age, colors of hair, beard, mustache, eyes, and skin color. All are important. Any clothing, masks, or unique shoes that stand out and are easy to remember—a gray hoodie, black jeans, red tennis shoes. Don't forget to mention any tattoos, scars, or odors, like perfume, bad breath, cigarettes, or drugs. If they are with other people or children or pets, that is also important information.

- Lastly, the location and direction the vehicle or person was seen and where they went next helps us zero in on finding the perpetrator. We had one brave victim who shared a bunch of information she remembered with us, and the guy passed by the scene as we interviewed her. When she pointed him out, we grabbed him immediately.

CHAPTER 16 LESSON – IN MEMORIAM, THE ULTIMATE SACRIFICE, 1988–2016

A knock on the door in the middle of the night is never good news, unless it's the birth of a baby. Anyone in the field of law enforcement and public safety, as well as first responders and military, knows this all too well. Spouses and loved ones pray every day for the safety of their hard-working public servants.

Each time I had to knock on the door, no matter if it was for a fellow officer, a friend, or a victim of a crime, I had to present the news that would change their life in a second with stoic, straightforward composure, along with my condolences.

To prepare for these instances, we attend family survivor training. No matter how much training you have or how many times you are called to deliver this news, it never gets easy.

I've learned over the years, in tragedy and grief, there are various ways we come together. It might be bringing a meal, visiting the surviving family members, supporting the children, running errands, planning the services, attending the services, following in the processions, or standing at attention.

Whichever your role or contribution, I promise you, it fills the hearts of those mourning in ways many of us do not understand. Beyond the force of our "professional families," other family members, friends, community members, organizations, and sometimes even the press support the grieving family members.

When I witness the concern, care, support, and condolences offered, I know it is making a difference. This is another fine example of "it takes a village."

PART 5 – 50 YEARS OF LEGACY, LEARNING, LESSONS, AND LEADERSHIP

NOTE: CHAPTER 17 HAS THE LESSONS

CHAPTER 18 LESSON – LEARNING IS VITAL TO PROFESSIONAL AND PERSONAL DEVELOPMENT

When you consider broadening your experiences, here are the parameters I followed to pick the "right" organizations to meet my goals and objectives:

1. Am I interested in the work, objectives, goals, and impact this organization offers?

2. Do the people operate with integrity, authenticity, transparency, and have genuine desires to make a difference?

3. Will I enjoy getting to know the people and participate in the work?

4. Where do I see my own contributions impacting the group and goals?

5. What will this group contribute to expand and elevate my own knowledge, experience, and skills so that it will benefit me in my career (or personal life) and guide me to contribute even more to my roles in law enforcement and the people I work with and serve?

6. Are my values, morals, personality, work ethic, and desire to make an impact aligned in the work and the people of this organization?

CHAPTER 19: LESSONS, INSIGHTS, AND WISDOM FOR LAW ENFORCEMENT PROFESSIONALS

NOTE: CHAPTER 19 HAS THE LESSONS

CHAPTER 20 RECAP – PROFESSIONAL ATTRIBUTES FOR LAW ENFORCEMENT PROFESSIONALS

1. Right is right. Wrong is wrong. Honesty is always the best policy.

2. Be professional at all times, especially while in uniform and in public.

3. Check your ego, because we need to operate as one team and have each other's backs.

4. Treat everyone as an equal within the team and in external departments and offices.

5. Keep your temper in check and learn how to control your emotions.

6. Be decisive.

7. Be consistent: treating people equally and fairly, with expectations.

8. Understand that people are human, have flaws and weaknesses, and will make mistakes.

9. Own up to your mistakes; take responsibility.

10. Always look for opportunities to collaborate with colleagues and contribute to the overall mission of the organization.

CHAPTER 21 LESSON – A 50-YEAR LAW ENFORCEMENT CAREER, TIME TO RETIRE

There are so many clichés about knowing when to quit something to when to start something new. They say to "hire slowly, fire quickly," and that "one bad apple spoils the bunch." What I know is that when you know it's time to go, whether it is to retire, change jobs, or get promoted, listen to the cliché, "Follow your gut. You'll never go wrong when you follow your gut." Intuition is one of the greatest internal guides we have. Listen carefully to it and use it in all areas of your life! Even if it is a cliché.

Endnotes

1. "Honoring Officers Killed in 2024." The Officer Down Memorial Page (ODMP), 2025, https://www.odmp.org/search/year/2024. Accessed March 9, 2025.

2. "Sergeant Paul Lawrence Cole." The Officer Down Memorial Page (ODMP), 2025, https://www.odmp.org/officer/14814-sergeant-paul-lawrence-cole. Accessed March 9, 2025.

3. "Trooper James R. DeLoach." The Officer Down Memorial Page (ODMP), 2025, https://www.odmp.org/officer/301-trooper-james-r-deloach. Accessed March 9, 2025.

4. "Trooper Steven J. Niewiek." The Officer Down Memorial Page (ODMP), 2025, https://www.odmp.org/officer/302-trooper-steven-j-niewiek. Accessed March 9, 2025.

5. "Police Officer Julie A. Engelhardt." The Officer Down Memorial Page (ODMP), 2025, https://www.odmp.org/officer/4592-police-officer-julie-a-engelhardt. Accessd March 9, 2025.

6. "Trooper Larry Forreider." The Officer Down Memorial Page (ODMP), 2025, https://www.odmp.org/officer/5011-trooper-larry-lee-forreider. Accessed March 9, 2025.

7. "Patrolman James Spencer Johnson." The Officer Down Memorial Page (ODMP), 2025, https://www.odmp.org/officer/7175-patrolman-james-spencer-johnson. Accessed March 9, 2025.

8. "Sergeant Todd Lawrence Leveille." The Officer Down Memorial Page (ODMP), 2025, https://www.odmp.org/officer/26191-sergeant-todd-lawrence-leveille. Accessed March 9, 2025.

9. "ODMP's COVID-19 Law Enforcement Memorial." The Officer Down Memorial Page (ODMP), 2025, https://www.odmp.org/search/incident/covid-19. Accessed March 9, 2025.

10. "Police Officer Mac J. Donnelly, Jr." The Officer Down Memorial Page (ODMP), 2025, https://www.odmp.org/officer/4186-police-officer-mac-j-donnelly-jr. Accessed March 9, 2025.

11. "Trooper Gary T. Rampy." The Officer Down Memorial Page (ODMP), 2025, https://www.odmp.org/officer/10988-trooper-gary-t-rampy. Accessed March 9, 2025.

12. "Trooper Charles B. Stark." The Officer Down Memorial Page (ODMP), 2025, https://www.odmp.org/officer/12712-trooper-charles-b-stark. Accessed March 9, 2025.

13. "Police Officer Dean A. Whitehead." The Officer Down Memorial Page (ODMP), 2025, https://www.odmp.org/officer/14105-police-officer-dean-a-whitehead. Accessed March 9, 2025.

14. "Deputy Sheriff Grant William Whitaker." The Officer Down Memorial Page (ODMP), 2025, https://www.odmp.org/officer/22290-deputy-sheriff-grant-william-whitaker. Accessed March 9, 2025.

15. "Darwin Shaver." Estes-Leadley Funeral Homes, July 2, 2025, https://estesleadley.com/obituaries/darwin-l-sy-shaver/. Accessed July 22, 2025.

16. "History." Flat Rock, MI, 2020, https://www.flatrockmi.org/community/history.php. Accessed March 31, 2025.

17. "Flat Rock." *Wikipedia, The Free Encyclopedia*, 2024, https://en.wikipedia.org/wiki/Flat_Rock,_Michigan. Accessed March 31, 2025.

18. "Flat Rock." *Wikipedia, The Free Encyclopedia*, 2024, https://en.wikipedia.org/wiki/Flat_Rock,_Michigan. Accessed August 1, 2025.

19. Lavery, Kevin. 2017. "Black, White and Blue: Two Police Officers Remember 1967 Uprising." WKAR Public Media, July 26, 2017, https://www.wkar.org/special-coverage/2017-07-26/black-white-and-blue-two-police-officers-remember-1967-uprising. Accessed 3/31/2025. Note: Permission granted to reprint on 4/15/2025.

20. "Steven Bruce DeVries | Berrien County, MI." Sheriff's Office, Berrien County, MI, 2025, https://www.berriencounty.org/408/Steven-Bruce-DeVries. Accessed April 2, 2025.

21. "Steven Bruce DeVries | Berrien County, MI." Sheriff's Office, Berrien County, MI, 2025, https://www.berriencounty.org/408/Steven-Bruce-DeVries. Accessed April 2, 2025.

22. "Trooper Steven B. DeVries." The Officer Down Memorial Page (ODMP), 2025, https://www.odmp.org/officer/4056-trooper-steven-b-devries. Accessed April 2, 2025.

23. Fosmoe, Margaret. "U.S. 12 Section to Be Named after Fallen Michigan Trooper." *South Bend Tribune*, May 19, 2016, https://www.southbendtribune.com/story/news/crime/2016/05/19/us-12-section-to-be-named-after-fallen-michigan-trooper/117265926/. Accessed April 2, 2025.

24. "Trooper Larry Lee Forreider." The Officer Down Memorial Page (ODMP), 2025, https://www.odmp.org/officer/5011-trooper-larry-lee-forreider. Accessed April 9, 2025.

25. "DRUG SLANG Warning Signs." BHDDH, 2015, Drug-Slang---guide-FINAL.pdf. Accessed April 20, 2025.

26. "DRUG SLANG Warning Signs." BHDDH, 2015, Drug-Slang---guide-FINAL.pdf. Accessed April 20, 2025.

27. "Darwin L. 'Sy' Shaver." *Lansing State Journal*, 2025, https://www.lansingstatejournal.com/obituaries/ppet1219402. Accessed July 8, 2025.

About the Author

Gene Leroy Wriggelsworth grew up on a small dairy farm near Henderson, Michigan with his parents, two sisters, Fay and Lois, and one brother, Wayne. He hunted and fished with his wonderful neighbor and friend, Jack Crambell, for many years, and they are still friends to this day. Gene attended a one-room school in Henderson until eighth grade, when he was then bussed to Owosso schools. In high school, he played football on a league championship team and wrestled during his senior year, winning the 165 lb. State Championship Title in wrestling. Gene and his friend, Bill Pike, have terrific memories about working on the farm, playing football,

and their families remain close today. After high school, Gene had a few manufacturing jobs and married his high school sweetheart, Sandy Gramse, the prettiest woman at Owosso High School. Together, they proudly raised three great, wonderful sons, Michael, Scott, and Mark, who married Kelli, Mary Jo, and Kelly, respectively, and who brought their 11 grandchildren and one great-grandchild into the world.

After getting married, Sandy became pregnant with Michael and Gene applied for the Michigan State Trooper School, from which he graduated in 1966. He began his career as a Michigan State Trooper and spent eight years in uniform before being promoted to sergeant, and then lieutenant as an undercover officer with the Tri-County Metro Narcotic Squad, where he served 14 years. In 1988, he was elected sheriff of Ingham County, serving seven consecutive four-year terms for a total of 28 years, making him the longest-serving sheriff in the county's history.

Gene is a firm believer in advancing his professional and personal life through continued education, giving back to his community, and leaving his positions in a better state than when he began. During his 28 years as sheriff, Gene graduated from the FBI National Academy and completed his bachelor's degree, as well as many other career advancement courses. He held positions of authority as president, chairperson, secretary, and board member while volunteering for many nonprofit organizations. In the sheriff's office, he implemented several initiatives and programs to advance the services the office provided, and to advance the support for the deputies and staff.

Gene is a respected leader among law enforcement professionals, known for his effective collaborations with state, municipal, local, university, and federal agencies. His legacy of service, protection, and respect continues to influence and inspire today's law enforcement leaders.

In retirement, he volunteers and enjoys time with his wife of 60 years, Sandy, their three sons, three daughters-in-law, 11 grandchildren, and one great-grandchild. In addition to writing this book, he also builds ramps with the Tuesday Toolmen for people with disabilities, is the longest-serving member of the South Lansing/Holt Rotary, participates in other advocacy projects, fishes, and connects with friends.